"This brilliant and absorbing collection of rigorous research articles, thoughtful political interventions, and innovative artworks is immensely important to the work of committed scholars, activists and organizers. There is much that teaches, fortifies, motivates, and mobilizes here."

—**Laleh Khalili**, author of *Sinews of War and Trade: Shipping and Capitalism in the Arabian Peninsula* and *Time in the Shadows: Confinement in Counterinsurgencies*

"*Making Abolitionist Worlds* is an urgent reminder that theorizing and practicing abolition must take place across prison walls and the boundaries imposed by the colonial state, heteropatriarchy, settler colonialism, white supremacy, and capitalism. Finally, here is a journal providing a platform capacious enough to embrace the insurgent knowledge of activists, the analytical rigor of scholars, and the visionary power of artists."

—**Jackie Wang**, author of *Carceral Capitalism*

"As the world we know is shattering more rapidly than we might have ever imagined, comes *Making Abolitionist Worlds*, an urgent call to build anew. These pieces movingly remind us that liberation will not transpire solely through opposition; it demands radical inquiry, imagination, creation. This collection brilliantly illustrates a core truth: we don't need 'alternatives to incarceration,' we need a wildly recreated society in which incarceration is unthinkable. *Making Abolitionist Words* will nourish and fuel struggles for transformation."

—**Maya Schenwar**, author of *Locked Down, Locked Out: Why Prison Doesn't Work and How We Can Do Better* and coauthor with Victoria Law of *Prison by Any Other Name: The Harmful Consequences of Popular Reforms*

"*Making Abolitionist Worlds* is a rich and compelling mixed-genre collection of radical perspectives that makes an urgent contribution to abolitionist world-making. Inspiring and incisive, these political interventions advance collective and transformative revolutionary praxis—what we need, now more than ever. On fire, indeed!"

—**J. Kēhaulani Kauanui**, author of *Hawaiian Blood* and *Paradoxes of Hawaiian Sovereignty* and editor of *Speaking of Indigenous Politics*

"The Abolition Journal project offers a unique, revolutionary lens through which to view, analyze, and fight against capitalism and patriarchy on the terrain of the prison-industrial complex. It aims to combine an abolitionist message with a democratic production process that prioritizes the participation of those directly affected by incarceration. What a welcome and needed approach! I am confident the project will help intellectuals build ties of solidarity across race, class, gender, nationality, and other borders that block liberation. In its finest moments, this project will help teach us, as Mumia says, to 'fight with light in our eyes.'"

—**James Kilgore**, author of *Understanding Mass Incarceration: A People's Guide to the Key Civil Rights Struggle of Our Time*

PROPOSALS FOR A WORLD ON FIRE

Amanda Priebe

MAKING ABOLITIONIST WORLDS:
PROPOSALS FOR A WORLD ON FIRE

ABOLITION: A JOURNAL OF INSURGENT POLITICS
ISSUE 2

Abolition Collective, editors

Making Abolitionist Worlds: Proposals for a World on Fire
Abolition: A Journal of Insurgent Politics

Edited by Abolition Collective
This edition © 2020 Common Notions

ISBN: 9781942173175
LCCN: 2020941305

Common Notions
c/o Interference Archive   c/o Making Worlds
314 7th Street   210 S 45th Street
Brooklyn, NY 11215   Philadelphia, PA 19104

www.commonnotions.org
info@commonnotions.org

Design and typesetting by Morgan Buck and Josh MacPhee
Antumbra Design | www.antumbradesign.org

Printed in Canada by union labor on acid-free, recycled paper.

"Abolition requires that we change one thing, which is everything. When one says prison abolition, one cannot be talking about only prison . . . . It's building the future from the present in all the ways we can. "

—Ruth Wilson Gilmore

Abolition: A Journal of Insurgent Politics is a collectively-run project supporting radical scholarly and activist ideas, poetry, and art, publishing and disseminating work that encourages us to make the impossible possible, to seek transformation well beyond policy changes and toward revolutionary abolitionism.

We are developing our capacity to work across carceral walls, and we encourage currently incarcerated people to send us their writings, submissions, and thoughts about this publication. Contact Abolition at:

abolitionjournal@gmail.com
Abolition: A Journal of Insurgent Politics
1321 N. Milwaukee Avenue PMB 460
Chicago, IL 60622

ACKNOWLEDGEMENTS

The publication working group for issue two included: Kevin Bruyneel, Jaskiran Dhillon, Andrew Dilts, Erin Hoekstra, Paula Ioanide, Brooke Lober, Brian Lovato, Naveed Mansoori, Eli Meyerhoff, Amanda Priebe, and Dylan Rodríguez. Reviewers from within and beyond Abolition's editorial review board gave invaluable feedback on articles in the issue and provided vision, inspiration, and guidance for the working group. We thank Michele Beckett and Erika Biddle for their copyediting expertise. Our comrades at Common Notions—Malav Kanuga, Ash Goh, Alexander Dwinell, Andy Battle, Morgan Buck, and Josh MacPhee—continue to be amazing, supportive, and patient. Most importantly, the collective is deeply thankful to our contributors and for their patience in seeing their work arrive in print.

CONTENTS

Introduction   I

Manifesto of the Abolition Journal   7

Intervention: Meeting Mumia Abu-Jamal:
The Most Well-Known Political Prisoner in the US
Robyn C. Spencer   10

Intervention: Dis-Organizing Prisons
and Building Together, Inside/Outside
Stevie Wilson   23

Intervention: A Family Like Mine
Shana L. Redmond   27

Intervention: Abuse Thrives on Silence:
The #VaughnRebellion in Context
Kim Wilson   29

Intervention: From the Vaughn Uprising:
'For a Safer, More Secure, and More Humane Prison'
On Behalf of the Prisoners at James T.
Vaughn Correctional Center   33

Article: Moving Through Flames:
Toward an Insurgent Indecency
Katherine Kelly Abraham   42

Intervention: Is Marxism Relevant?
Some Uses and Misuses
David Gilbert   64

Art: Out of the Shadows of Caste and
Into Our Consciousness
Priti Gulati Cox   90

Article: Democracy Against Representation:
A Radical Realist View
Paul Raekstad   92

Intervention: Abolitionist Democracy:
Fear, Loathing, and Violence in the 2016 Campaign,
with Notes for 2020 and Beyond
Joy James   115

Intervention: The Pitfalls of White Liberal Panic
Dylan Rodríguez 122

Art: Tear Down White Supremacy
Jesus Barraza and Melanie Cervantes 127

Intervention: As the US Oligarchy Expands Its War,
Middle-Class White People Must Take a Side
Robert Nichols 128

Article: Aggrieved Whiteness: White Identity Politics
and Modern American Racial Formation
Mike King 131

Art: In this Place 206
Nilda Brooklyn and Adrien Leavitt 157

Article: Already Something More: Heteropatriarchy and
the Limitations of Rights, Inclusion, and the Universal
J Sebastian 159

Intervention: "We Can Be Here Another Five Hundred Years":
A Critical Reflection on Shiri Pasternak's *Grounded Authority*
Nick Estes 183

Intervention: 'How Does State Sovereignty Matter?'
Shiri Pasternak 194

Art: O wind, take me to my country /
O love, take me to my country
Jess X. Snow 198

Intervention: Zionism and Native American Studies
Steven Salaita 199

Intervention: Embodied Refusals: On the Collective
Possibilities of Hunger Striking
Michelle Velasquez-Potts 212

Intervention: Notes on Photography, Power,
and Insurgent Looks
Stefanie Fock 230

Art: We Are Not in the Least Afraid of Ruins
Amanda Priebe 237

Intervention: It Has to Burn Before It Can Grow
An Interview with Amanda Priebe by Brooke Lober 238

About the Contributors 254

Index 258

INTRODUCTION

As we complete this issue of *Abolition: A Journal of Insurgent Politics*, the planet is literally on fire. Across Greece, Lebanon, South Korea, China, Siberia, Australia, California, and Brazil, linked processes of climate change, land exploitation, and profiteering instigate environmental degradation, and produce the conditions for devastating blazes that burn with no end in sight. With the world already on fire, 2020 also saw the emergence of a global pandemic that laid bare the oppressive structures of racial and colonial capitalism in which "group-differentiated vulnerability to premature death" strikes even more brutally.[1] For a moment, at least in parts of the United States, it was as if an emergency brake was pulled and seemingly "impossible" things were suddenly very possible: moratoriums on evictions, spending on public health, canceling rent, the release of incarcerated people. But as soon as the race and class disparities of the pandemic became starkly clear—disparities driven by the ongoing violence of white supremacy, settler colonialism, and capitalism—demands to "reopen" and return to "normal" have threatened to overtake these possibilities. Once again, the state of emergency ruthlessly exposes Black, Brown, and Indigenous people to sickness, poverty, abandonment, and death. Yet within this inferno—stoked by the racial-capitalist state—there is a *counter-conflagration*. There are fires being set against the state.

Mutual-aid societies—drawing expressly on the long history and practices of African American mutual benefit societies, the

---

1. Ruth Wilson Gilmore, *Golden Gulag: Prisons, Surplus, Crisis, and Opposition in Globalizing California* (Berkeley: University of California Press, 2007), 28.

Black Panther Party, anarchist collectives, the often unrecognized reproductive labor of women, and queer and trans survival—sprang up across the US, like seeds released from a lodgepole pine (*pinus contorta*).[2] And on the third day of the uprising sparked by the murder of George Floyd, the Minneapolis Police Department's Third Precinct station was set ablaze. Within a week, major news outlets in the US were reporting that a majority of those polled thought that the destruction of the precinct house was fully or at least partially justified.[3] Images of the precinct station on fire travelled the globe, with masses of people cheering it as a righteous response to the hideous violence that the video of Floyd's murder exposed: not only the murder caught on tape, but the overwhelming police violence that has been delivered upon Black people in the US for generations.

As protests spread around the world, demands to defund, dismantle, and disband police departments have moved decisively into the mainstream, with school districts and cities across the US mounting and winning defunding and disbanding campaigns. As of this writing, "abolition" is suddenly having a bit of a popular moment, at least when focused on the police, if not also on prisons. And as students of abolition, we know that we are being called to do this and more: dismantle the present world and build it anew. This has always been the abolitionist project. Now, more than ever, we must guard against cooptation, reformist takeovers, and the rehabilitation or redemption of institutions and practices that are intolerable. Now, more than ever, we must refuse to be demobilized and captured by electoral politics. Now, more than ever, we must *clarify the abolitionist struggle as the struggle against patriarchy, capitalism, heteronormativity, ableism, colonialism, the state, and white supremacy.* And now, more than ever, we must insist that these institutions and practices operate together and must be abolished together.

---

2. This is, of course, a settler name for the species of tree in question. It is known as wazí čháŋ by Lakota peoples or qalámqalam by the Nimiipuu/Nez Perce peoples. What is more important than finding the correct term, however, is to notice the ways that the very language and metaphors that we turn too are always already overtaken by settler memory and settler epistemology. As we invoke the regenerative forces of the seeds of this particular tree, we do so acknowledging that our own understanding of it has been shaped by the material and linguistic violence of settler colonialism. Any abolitionist project that does not attempt to grapple with this reality is sure to reproduce, knowingly or not, that foundational violence.

3. See https://www.monmouth.edu/polling-institute/documents/monmouthpoll_us_060220.pdf.

The pieces in this issue were written, reviewed, and revised for final submission prior to the pandemic's emergence, the recent uprisings against the police, and our increasingly abolitionist moment. And yet, while the authors here could not have addressed this moment itself, they and the abolitionist critique and visions they offer and represent are as apt and urgent as ever—if not more so. Abolitionist critique and abolitionist world-building were already the visionary response that we need, and they suddenly have currency and agency. The overlapping and interrelated crises of the moment remind us to hold the line and not depart from our convictions. The processes that will guide us on a path for collective survival were already there, continue to be there, and must continue to be fought for. As the Zapatistas famously said: we must demand "a world where many worlds fit."

We also recognize the energetic increases of a radical climate justice movement and Indigenous resurgences that fight to maintain possibilities for life on this planet, alongside uprisings from Chile to Bolivia to Lebanon, from Hong Kong to France to Iran, and many more sites of mass rebellion, themselves manifesting as a vibrant and creative "world on fire." As Abolition collective member and artist Amanda Priebe writes, "Abolition is a concept of both creative growth and creative destruction, and the duality and tension inherent in the creation of something new." This issue, *Making Abolitionist Worlds: Proposals for a World on Fire*, takes inspiration from Amanda Priebe's work of the same name. It consists of articles, art, memoirs, reports, and interventions elaborating abolition's full meaning: as we creatively destroy the oppressive structures and conditions of racial-colonial capitalism, we renew our reality, making other worlds through the painstaking creation of collective frameworks for justice, freedom, self-determination, and interdependence. We offer *Making Abolitionist Worlds: Proposals for a World on Fire* as a meeting ground for people living, surviving, and working in and across the realms of art, activism, advocacy, education, and anti-incarceration.

As with our first issue, *Abolishing Carceral Society*, there is no singular perspective or position represented across the range of works in this issue. What unites them is an unapologetic commitment to an abolitionist project that is antiracist, decolonial, anticapitalist, feminist, and radically queer. The contributions to *Making Abolitionist Worlds* offer readers and viewers a range of points of intervention for engaging with the meaning and urgency of an abolitionist politics of critique, analysis, and direct action. We expect and hope readers will see how abolitionist critique, imaginaries and world-rebuilding imperatives are even more vital as our global crises escalate and proliferate. To this end, the authors and artists published here demand a radical reimagining of the meaning and practice of democracy, among other things, given the perils of inclusionary politics in a cis-heteropatriarchal, colonialist system.

This demand requires greater attention to the dynamics of insurgent political practice with a reparative component, enjoining us to "envision a continuum of alternatives to imprisonment—demilitarization of schools, revitalization of education at all levels, a health system that provides free physical and mental care to all, and a justice system based on reparation and reconciliation rather than retribution and vengeance," as Angela Davis writes.[4] While we are compelled by this vision of a society replete with abundant resources available to all, perhaps the language of "alternatives to imprisonment" is, in itself, a dead end. As Mariame Kaba, in her effort to "transform harm," argues that transformative justice conceived capaciously is:

> not the alternative to incarceration/alternative to prison. That's so limiting, it's not enough. It's completely dependent on the current view of how we contain and address harm. And what we need is the ability for having our imaginations unleashed, for the ceiling on our imaginations to be removed. And as long as the PIC [prison-industrial complex] exists as the center of our work, that can't happen. Because the PIC's job is to make us completely unable to imagine anything else.[5]

Rather than setting the limit of our radical imaginary at opposition to the conditions of genocidal warfare that make up the prison system, in camaraderie with the queer world-making of José Muñoz,

---

4. Angela Davis, *Are Prisons Obsolete?* (Seven Stories Press, 2003), 107.

5. Mariame Kaba, interview with adrienne maree brown and Autum Brown, *How to Survive the End of the World* "The Practices We Need: #metoo and Transformative Justice Part Two" podcast audio, November 7, 2018, https://soundcloud.com/endofthe worldshow/the-practices-we-need-metoo-and-transformative-justice-part-2

we might figure abolition as a perpetual horizon, a "utopian herme-
neutics." Horizons guide and direct our work, but as they perpetually recede ahead of us, they also refuse to let us become complacent
with half-measures, finished solutions, or reformist reforms. Such
an open-ended project of liberation inspires us to build, to create,
and, with Frantz Fanon, remain always those who question.

Leftist abolitionist movements grapple with the complex challenges of simultaneously *opposing* oppressive institutions while
proposing new ways of making the world. Building on the concept
of "abolition democracy" that W.E.B. Du Bois used to describe
the unrealized radical potential of the Reconstruction era, Angela
Davis reinterprets this concept for the prison abolitionist movement to describe "the creation of an array of social institutions
that would begin to solve the social problems that set people on
the track to prison, thereby helping to render prison obsolete."[6]
Likewise, Stefano Harney and Fred Moten call for an abolitionism
as: "Not so much the abolition of prisons but the abolition of a
society that could have prisons, that could have slavery, that could
have the wage, and therefore not abolition as the elimination of
anything but abolition as the founding of a new society."[7] To expand and deepen the concept of abolition democracy, we envision
Abolition: A Journal of Insurgent Politics as part of a broader movement to create an "abolition university"—space-times for studying
and organizing collaborations, resistances, and decolonizing subversions aimed toward dismantling racial-colonial capitalism—a
movement that some of our collective members and other comrades have been theorizing and enacting through "abolitionist
university studies."[8] Indeed, the project of Abolition Collective is
an experiment in such world-making, and this journal is a project that contributes to a larger, undefined but nonetheless active
method for the creation of a vivacious, unruly, always-in-process
abolitionist practice of collective study. To complement our first

---

6. W. E. B. Du Bois, *Black Reconstruction in America, 1860–1880* (New York: Free Press,
1998); Angela Davis, *Abolition Democracy* (Seven Stories Press, 2005), 96.

7. Fred Moten and Stefano Harney, *The Undercommons: Fugitive Planning and Black
Study* (Wivenhoe/New York/Port Watson: Minor Compositions, 2013), 42.

8. Abigail Boggs, Eli Meyerhoff, Nick Mitchell, and Zach Schwartz-Weinstein,
"Abolitionist University Studies: An Invitation," *Abolition Journal Blog*, August 28, 2019,
https://abolitionjournal.org/abolitionist-university-studies-an-invitation/.

issue's relative emphasis on the destructive, world-dismantling qualities of abolitionist theory and practice aspects, this second issue's title, *Making Abolitionist Worlds: Proposals for a World on Fire*, encapsulates our throughline on how abolitionists' creativity emerges in, through, and with destruction, to recall Mikhail Bakunin's germinal phrase, *in a world on fire*.

It is worth reaffirming our commitment set out in our inaugural issue that *Abolition: A Journal of Insurgent Politics* is open access, available both online and in print, and strives to be as accessible as possible. As "access" is a politically and socially produced object, we recognize that we will fail in this goal more often than we succeed. We are thus committed to an open-ended and ongoing practice of reflection, and welcome critiques and suggestions about how to make this work more available across the barriers established by capitalism, colonialism, racism, sexism, ableism, and heteropatriarchy.

In particular, and in keeping with our desire to build and support abolitionist study, this issue has been produced collaboratively, and we have organized our editorial review without official support from universities or other neoliberal institutions of higher education. Our notion of peer review understands our peers to be in the streets, comrades in arms, and movement actors for whom the questions and issues pursued are anything but just "academic." Submissions for *Abolition* are evaluated and critiqued by experts from a wide range of fields, including nonacademic social movement participants. We eagerly invite readers to join us in this work, as contributors, collective members, editorial members, or with proposals to guest edit a special issue. In this spirit, the Abolition Collective is excited that the journal's upcoming issues will be on Spirituality and Abolition (edited by Ashon Crawley and Roberto Sirvent) and Abolitionist Feminisms (edited by Alisa Bierria, Jakeya Caruthers, and Brooke Lober).

MANIFESTO OF
THE ABOLITION JOURNAL

Abolitionist politics is not about what is possible, but about making the impossible a reality. Ending slavery appeared to be an impossible challenge for Sojourner Truth, Denmark Vesey, Nat Turner, John Brown, Harriet Tubman, and others, and yet they struggled for it anyway. Today we seek to abolish a number of seemingly immortal institutions, drawing inspiration from those who have sought the abolition of all systems of domination, exploitation, and oppression—from Jim Crow laws and prisons to patriarchy and capitalism. The shockingly unfinished character of these struggles can be seen from some basic facts about our present. The eighty-five richest people in the world have as much wealth as the poorest half; more African American men are in prison, jail, or parole than were enslaved in 1850; we have altered the chemical composition of our atmosphere threatening all life on this planet; Women, gender nonconforming, and trans people are significantly more likely than cisgender men to be victims of sexual and domestic violence; rich nations support military interventions into "developing" countries as cover for neocolonial resource exploitation. Recognizing that the institutions we fight against are both interconnected and unique, we refuse to take an easy path of reveling in abstract ideals while accepting mere reforms in practice. Instead, we seek to understand the specific power dynamics within and between these systems so we can make the impossible possible; so we can bring the entire monstrosity down.

We must ask questions that are intimately connected with abolitionist movements if we are to understand these dynamics in ways that are strategically useful. How do those in power use differences of race, gender, sexuality, nationality, and class to divide and exploit us? How do we build bridges across these divides through our organizing? Activists on the ground ask such questions often, but rarely do those within universities become involved. Instead, academia has more often been an opponent to abolitionist movements, going back to the coconstitution of early universities with colonialism and slavery, and the development of racial science and capitalist ideologies. Academic journals have functioned to maintain a culture of conformity, legitimated with myths of "political neutrality" and "meritocracy." At the same time, colleges and universities have always been terrains of struggle, as radical organizers have found ways to expropriate their resources: from W.E.B. DuBois's abolitionist science at Fisk University to the Black Campus Movement of the sixties. Inspired by them, we refuse to abandon the resources of academia to those who perpetuate the status quo.

Instead, we are creating a new project, centered around *Abolition: A Journal of Insurgent Politics*—for research, publishing, and study that encourage us to make the impossible possible, to seek transformation well beyond policy changes and toward revolutionary abolitionism.

Our journal's title has multiple reference points in a tense relation with one another. "Abolition" refers partly to the historical and contemporary movements that have identified themselves as "abolitionist": those against slavery, prisons, the wage system, animal and earth exploitation, racialized, gendered, and sexualized violence, and the death penalty, among others. But we also refer to *all* revolutionary movements, insofar as they have abolitionist elements—whether the abolition of patriarchy, capitalism, heteronormativity, ableism, colonialism, the state, or white supremacy. Rather than just seeking to abolish a list of oppressive institutions, we aim to support studies of the entanglement of different systems of oppression, not to erase the tensions between different movements, but to create spaces for collective experimentation with those tensions. Instead of assuming one homogenous subject as our audience (e.g., "abolitionists of the world unite!"), we write for multiple, contingent, ambivalent subjectivities—for people coming from different places, living and struggling in different circumstances, and in the process of figuring out who we are and untangling these knots to fight for a more just and liberated world. With Fanon, we are "endlessly creating" ourselves.

Abolition takes cues from the abolition-democracy espoused by figures like W.E.B. Du Bois, Angela Davis, and Joel Olson. Our orientation toward academic insurgency builds upon the struggles of the Black campus movement against the White University, the American Indian movement against the Colonial University, feminist and queer movements against the Hetero-Patriarchal University, and anarchist and communist movements against the Capitalist University. As efforts to revolutionize academia originated and drew their lifeblood from movements outside and across the boundaries of academic institutions, today we recognize that our journal's radical aspirations must be similarly grounded. We must therefore facilitate collaborations of radical academics *with and in support of* movements that are struggling against oppressive regimes and for the creation of alternative futures. Recognizing that the best movement-relevant intellectual work is happening both in the movements themselves and in the communities with whom they organize (e.g., in dispossessed neighborhoods and prisons), the journal aims to support scholars whose research amplifies such grassroots intellectual activity.

All of our publications will be accessible, free, and open access, refusing the paywalls of the publishing industry. We will also produce hard-copy versions for circulation to communities lacking internet access. Yet, we are not abandoning peer review—sharing writing with respected comrades and giving each other feedback before wider circulation—which can be useful for movements to strengthen and amplify their intellectual activities. As peer review is ultimately based on relationships of trust, we ask why academics on the opposite side of our struggles are our "peers." Instead, we commit to building relationships with activist-intellectuals for whom a new kind of peer review can serve as an insurgent tool to expropriate academia's resources for knowledge production.

"Abolition" as a concept, process, and reality becomes the common ground upon which we meet, struggle, and join together in solidarity.

MEETING MUMIA ABU-JAMAL

THE MOST WELL-KNOWN
POLITICAL PRISONER IN THE US

Robyn C. Spencer

He glided towards us, Samuel L. Jackson cool. Unexpectedly, we were confronted by his physicality. With each stride, disembodied voice became flesh and icon became man. The room, full of men huddled with their loved ones in a tender web of public privacy, faded into the background. He was in front of us, taller than I envisioned and smiling. Uncertain at first, I gave his outstretched hand a firm shake, paused, then leaned in for an embrace. Our familial grins belied this awkward dance. We had never met in person before, but we were far from strangers.

He was Mumia Abu-Jamal, an award-winning journalist, a former member of the Black Panther Party, and the most well known political prisoner in the United States. We were two Black women who were members of the Campaign to Bring Mumia Home (CBMH), a grassroots organization formed by scholar-activist Johanna Fernandez in 2012 to bridge Mumia's long-standing support base in the movement to free political prisoners with a new generation of young people fighting to end mass incarceration. CBMH members had been placed on Mumia's list of authorized visitors and serendipitously, me and Sophia's names had been the first two to be cleared. For years we had occasionally written to Mumia and spoken to him on the phone when he called into conference calls, meetings or events. The opportunity to meet him in the flesh had pushed us out of our beds at 5 a.m. that chilly fall

morning and jump-started an unforgettable journey.

After the first set of greetings, Mumia immediately gave us the rundown: Visitation 101. We took photos right away. Us: shorn of money, phones, underwire, and full of purpose. Him: clad in a burgundy jumpsuit, bearded, bespectacled, easing into an unguarded pose. Next stop: snatching the salad, the one with spinach, from the vending machine. Among the chips, reheatable nachos and candy bars, anything green was gold. We picked a spot in the rows of side-by-side seating and he sat between us. We could have been anywhere: a living room, a doctor's waiting room, the departure gate of an airport, or a park bench. But our surroundings were not so benign. Over a dozen cameras clocked our every move and a guard walked around periodically to ensure food was shorn of wrappers and to disentangle lingering embraces. Violence sat cocked in the background.

We were in SCI Mahanoy, a 2,300 bed, medium-security prison carved out of the harsh Pennsylvania landscape where coal once ruled and industrial development has faltered ever since.

Prisons like SCI Mahanoy have filled an economic void, serving as an important employer for local residents and a magnet for visitors who purchase goods and services from struggling businesses. Frackville, the official prison zip code, is 96 percent white, with a 6.6 percent unemployment rate, and 21 percent of its residents living beneath the poverty line.[1] Such areas have been fertile ground for the anti-immigrant, white supremacist message of the Trump administration and 70 percent of Schuylkill County turned out for Trump in 2016.[2]

MUMIA'S STORY

Mumia's history of incarceration began long before SCI Mahanoy—its sinews connect activist generations and movement genealogies in ways that point to the dismantling of America's carceral state.

In 1981, Mumia was convicted of killing police officer Daniel Faulkner in a late-night incident in Philadelphia and sentenced to death.[3] Mumia has maintained his innocence and his legal team has pointed to witness manipulation, a biased judge, and other

1. TownCharts, "Frackville, Pennsylvania Economy Data," http://www.towncharts.com/Pennsylvania/Economy/Frackville-borough-PA-Economy-data.html.
2. "2016 Presidential Election Results," NY Times https://www.nytimes.com/elections/2016/results/pennsylvania.
3. Johanna Fernandez, "10 Facts About the Mumia Abu-Jamal Case," The Feminist Wire, January 21, 2014, https://www.thefeministwire.com/2014/01/10-facts-about-the-mumia-abu-jamal-case/.

irregularities and bias in his trial.[4] At the time, he was a popular investigative radio journalist who had been targeted for his exposé of police corruption, his Panther affiliation and his positive reporting of MOVE, a Black radical organization whose natural living and anti-authoritarian politics had run afoul of the Philadelphia police and whose compound would be bombed by a military-grade bomb a few years after Mumia's arrest.[5] His supporters consider him a political prisoner; that is, a person targeted for their dissident politics. He is not alone.

There are several dozen political prisoners in the US, most of whom are veterans of the most radical wings of the movements of the 1960s and 1970s. Political prisoners are an intrinsic part of the larger system of mass incarceration, which imprisons 2.3 million people, a rate that is more than five times higher than any other country in the world.[6] Political prisoners, according to carceral studies scholar Dan Berger, are "canaries in the coal mine." He has argued that "some of the most distinguishing features of the American prison state—aggressive policing, hefty charges, preventive detention, lengthy sentences, parole denial and prolonged solitary confinement—were first deployed as a means to stop radical social movements beginning in the 1960s."[7]

These movements faced repression from COINTELPRO, the FBI's counterintelligence program which launched a multi-pronged campaign of infiltration, harassment, spurious arrests, surveillance, and disruption against Black radicals, the New Left, and others in the 1960s. Members were targeted for surveillance, arrest, and conviction because of their convictions and aspirations to dismantle racial capitalism, US imperialism and often, their support of the use of political violence and armed self-defense.

---

4. Kouross Esmaeli (dir.), Justice on Trial: The Case of Mumia Abu-Jamal (2009), Big Noise Films, 65 mins. Available at https://vimeo.com/173713381.

5. Gene Demby, "Why Have So Many People Never Heard of the MOVE Bombing?" Codeswitch, NPR.org, May 18, 2015, https://www.npr.org/sections/codeswitch/2015/05/18/407665820/why-did-we-forget-the-move-bombing.

6. Wendy Sawyer and Peter Wagner, "Mass Incarceration: The Whole Pie 2020," Prison Policy Initiative, March 24, 2020, https://www.prisonpolicy.org/reports/pie2017.html.

7. Dan Berger, "Beyond Innocence: US Political Prisoners and the Fight Against Mass Incarceration," Truthout, July 24, 2015, https://truthout.org/articles/beyond-innocence-america-s-political-prisoners-and-the-fight-against-mass-incarceration/.

Their trials were shaped by irregularities and illegalities, they received harsh sentences and often faced punitive periods of solitary confinement and other human rights violations in prison.[8]

Mumia has condemned the criminal justice system and the prison-industrial complex in his dozens of radio commentaries and nine books,[9] advocating instead for collective resistance and societal transformation. The injustice of his imprisonment, the clarity of his analysis, and the urgency of his writing attracted support from veterans of the Civil Rights, Black Power, and New Left movements; students, labor union activists, and well-respected human rights champions like Nelson Mandela, Desmond Tutu, Noam Chomsky, and Angela Davis.

MELDING MOVEMENTS

In 1971, Angela Davis wrote: "In the course of developing mass movements around political prisoners, a great deal of attention has inevitably been focused on the institutions in which they are imprisoned."[10] She argued, "the political receptivity of prisoners—especially Black and Brown captives—has been increased and sharpened by the surge of aggressive political activity rising out of Black, Chicano, and other oppressed communities." These conditions were evident in the early 1990s. During this period, the mobilization around Mumia's case dovetailed with a mass movement born in the face of skyrocketing incarceration rates, the war on drugs, and rising police brutality and violence epitomized by the Rodney King beating. This movement condemned the carceral state, traced the history of racial criminalization back to enslavement and its aftermath, rallied against state violence and raised the question of prison abolition. It was led by local grassroots groups, like NYC's Campaign to Free Black Political Prisoners and Prisoners of War, and national organizations such

---

8. Joy James (ed.), *Imprisoned Intellectuals: America's Imprisoned Intellectuals Write on Life, Liberation, and Rebellion* (Lanham, Maryland: Rowman and Littlefield, 2003).

9. See, for example, Mumia's recorded radio essays on Prison Radio, www.prisonradio.org.

10. Angela Davis, "Political Prisoners, Prisons, and Black Liberation (1971)," *Viewpoint Magazine*, September 15, 2017, https://www.viewpointmag.com/2017/09/15/political-prisoners-prisons-black-liberation-1971/.

as the Malcolm X Grassroots Organization,[11] Critical Resistance,[12] the Jericho Movement,[13] and INCITE![14] Books like Michelle Alexander's *The New Jim Crow: Mass Incarceration in the Era of Colorblindness* (2000), Angela Davis's *Are Prisons Obsolete?* (2003), and Ruth Wilson Gilmore's *Golden Gulag: Prisons, Surplus, Crisis, and Opposition in Globalizing California* (2007) provided the intellectual foundations of the movement while blogs like US Prison Culture[15] and research initiatives like Prison Policy[16] amplified strong structural critiques of prisons. Incarcerated men and women using everything from their pens to hunger strikes[17] to challenge their conditions have also played a decisive role.

After decades of appeal, Mumia's death penalty was commuted to a life sentence by the Supreme Court of Pennsylvania in 2011.[18] In 2012, he was transferred to general population in SCI Mahanoy. This partial victory reinvigorated his traditional base of support and brought his case to the attention of a new generation of activists who flooded the streets in the wake of the killing of Trayvon Martin that same year. The cry of Black Lives Matter[19] and Say Her Name in the face of police killings[20] in Ferguson, Baltimore, and other US cities flowered into the Movement for Black Lives (M4BL), a network of fifty organizations representing thousands of activists. In 2016, the M4BL created a wide-ranging

---

11. Malcolm X Grassroots Organization, https://freethelandmxgm.org/

12. Rose Braz et al., "The History of Critical Resistance," Social Justice, special issue edited by Critical Resistance Publications Collective, Critical Resistance to the Prison-Industrial Complex, Vol. 27, No. 3 (81), Fall 2000: 6–10. Available at https://www.jstor.org/stable/i29767220.

13. National Jericho Movement, https://www.thejerichomovement.com/about.

14. INCITE! Women of Color Against Violence, https://incite-national.org/history/.

15. US Prison Culture Blog, http://www.usprisonculture.com/blog/.

16. Prison Policy Initiative, https://www.prisonpolicy.org/.

17. Josh Harkinson and Maggie Caldwell, "50 Days Without Food: The California Prison Hunger Strike Explained," Mother Jones, August 27, 2013, https://www.motherjones.com/politics/2013/08/50-days-california-prisons-hunger-strike-explainer/.

18. Ed Pilkington, "Former Black Panther Spared Death Chamber as Prosecutors Admit Defeat," *The Guardian*, December 7, 2011, https://www.theguardian.com/world/2011/dec/07/abu-jamal-death-penalty-pennsylvania-black-panthers.

19. Black Lives Matter, https://blacklivesmatter.com/about/.

20. Madison Park, "Police Shootings: Trials, Convictions are Rare for Officers," CNN.com, October 13, 2018, https://www.cnn.com/2017/05/18/us/police-involved-shooting-cases/index.html.

policy platform which included restorative justice[21] and the abolition of prison, declaring that "until we achieve a world where cages are no longer used against our people we demand an immediate change in conditions and an end to all jails, detention centers, youth facilities and prisons as we know them."[22]

Mumia's case, rooted in repression, surveillance, and the dismantling of 1960s liberation movements, is one key to the carceral apparatus this new generation of activists seeks to replace. These young people have supported him as he fought back against attempts to silence his voice through the Revictimization Relief Act in 2015,[23] and through his battle for Hepatitis C treatment after suffering illness and almost going into a diabetic shock in 2015.[24] These cases have shed light on prison conditions and *Abu-Jamal v. Wetzel* (the Hep C case) has been used by incarcerated men in Missouri and promises to continue to provide critical legal precedent for the fight for a humane standard of prison health care. Much like the cries to "Free Huey" and "Free Angela" in the 1960s, Mumia's name has become shorthand for the injustices of the criminal justice system. His case bridges the distance between people who are ensnared in a politicized carceral apparatus through mass incarceration and those who are considered political prisoners.

Sophia and I literally embody this history. Born in the 1970s, I had been politicized in the 1990s activist upsurge and had learned about Mumia when the death penalty loomed over him. I joined the Free Mumia Coalition, helmed by former Black Panther Safiya Bukhari in New York, and over the years I remained connected with his case. I joined the CBMH in 2014. Sophia was born in

---

21. Restorative Justice Initiative. http://www.restorativejustice.nyc/.

22. The Movement for Black Lives, "End the War on Black People," https://m4bl.org/policy-platforms/end-the-war-on-black-people/.

23. Eugene Volokh, "Court Strikes Down Law Aimed at Mumia Abu-Jamal and Similar Criminals who Speak Publicly After Being Convicted," Washington Post, April 28, 2015, https://www.washingtonpost.com/news/volokh-conspiracy/wp/2015/04/28/court-strikes-down-law-aimed-at-mumia-abu-jamal-and-similar-criminals-who-speak-publicly-after-being-convicted/.

24. Sameer Rao, "Pennsylvania Department of Corrections Ordered to Treat Mumia Abu-Jamal's Hepatitis C," *Colorlines*, January 4, 2017, https://www.colorlines.com/articles/pennsylvania-department-corrections-ordered-treat-mumia-abu-jamals-hepatitis-c.

TEACH-IN AND MARCH IN PHILADELPHIA ORGANIZED BY THE CONCERNED FRIENDS AND FAMILY OF MUMIA ABU-JAMAL, WHERE A SUPPORTER DRAWS PARALLELS BETWEEN MEEK MILLS AND MUMIA, ON DECEMBER 9, 2017. PHOTO CREDIT: JOE PIETTE. ALL RIGHTS RESERVED.

1989 and learned about Mumia in a class at college. She had been a part of the CBMH from its inception. Together, we reflect the intergenerational nature of the movement to free Mumia, its many waves, its connection to state violence and its regeneration in the crucible of Black Lives Matter. Our gender is not incidental. Just like vocal women of color and femmes have been at the helm of the M4BL, the Bring Mumia Home Campaign, is led by women like Pam Africa, Ramona Africa, the late Safiya Bukhari, and Johanna Fernandez.

SITTING WITH MUMIA

What does one say to the most well-known political prisoner in America? Sophia and I had prepared appropriately political topics to stuff into any holes that might appear in the conversation, had memorized greetings and messages from other CBMH members, and had questions ready for the book party we were planning for his latest release, *Have Black Lives Ever Mattered?* But it turned out that we didn't need the scaffolding. The three of us fell into an easy rapport. Mumia immediately dubbed Sophia "Wisdom" and asked me both about my child and my recently published book, referring to both of them as my babies. He seemed eager not just to talk but also to ask questions and listen.

Our conversation unfolded languorously. Mumia turned the "Italian Sicilian" dressing on the salad into a dissertation on Hannibal, general of the Carthaginian army. We moved from the Mediterranean to the Caribbean. Junot Diaz's brilliance in *The Brief Wondrous Life of Oscar Wao* led us deep into the battlefields of French defeat in the Haitian revolution, which then led to Algeria, Frantz Fanon, and neocolonialism. We moved from there to 1960s New York and Panther Afeni Shakur's role in the defense of the Panther 21 in the late 1960s and early 1970s. Here, our voices became a chorus, upholding the brilliance of Tupac Shakur's "Dear Mama," the powerful 1995 tribute song to Afeni. We moved to the importance of women's activism, then and now. From Maxine Waters's latest clap back to Trumpism, to the cancellation of WPN's "Underground" and the power of seeing Harriet Tubman portrayed on television. From the cultural impact of Nichelle Nichols as Uhura on Star Trek, to Safiya Bukhari and Afeni Shakur's role in the NY Panthers, to Black Lives Matter activist Ash Williams[25] confronting Hillary Clinton on her famous quote that "we have to bring them to heel" and the role of the Clintons in accelerating mass incarceration. It was clear that he had remained a sharp analyst of mainstream news, popular culture, and grassroots activism.

Like Malcolm, Mumia had a ready smile and a quick wit. Although cut off from social media, he was as aware of Trump's tweets and eccentric mannerisms as he was about his disastrous policies for people of color. He was a skilled impersonator who replayed dramatic scenes from his life complete with critical and often comedic commentary. He told us that he was deeply inspired by the young activists in M4BL and enjoyed hip hop, citing TI, Lupe Fiasco, and Jay Z as favorites. Like the discovery that he was a Trekkie, these revelations were profoundly humanizing.

We shifted through comfortable pauses; mini lectures; intense dialogue and blackity black nonverbals. It seemed like

---

25. Alex Lubben, "We Spoke to Ashley Williams, the Black Queer Organizer Who Interrupted Hillary Clinton," *The Nation*, February 26, 2016, https://www.thenation.com/article/we-spoke-to-ashely-williams-the-black-queer-organizer-who-interrupted-hillary-clinton/.

every topic was a morsel to be savored; every shared opinion was a revelation; every divergence was an invitation to drill deeper; and every new bit of information needed to be tucked away for future research. We talked with deep political purpose and with light-hearted abandon. We forecasted him traveling, teaching, and getting back into the studio after he was released. We were *liming* (the art of doing nothing, hanging around, gathering, socializing; Trinidad), *gyaffin'* (informal, meandering talk; Guyana), *skinning our teeth* (grinning; Jamaica and Guyana), and shooting the shit in diasporic defiance of the ways we were governed by the clock, patrolled by watchful eyes, and disciplined by the institution. We turned those three chairs into a classroom, a church, a kitchen—a place where our words melded like gumbo.

Somehow it was easier to talk about everything but where we were. But soon enough we dared to ask him about life behind the walls. Mumia has been locked up since he was twenty-seven years old. He is now sixty-three. He spent thirty years on death row, 28.5 of them in solitary confinement in a room the size of your average parking space. He'd been in general population since 2012 and was facing life. In our conversations, he'd often used the term "when I was in the world," to describe the time before his arrest. Yet, prison was also his world. What could he—would he—tell us about being inside?

Mumia spoke in broad strokes. He had successes as a jailhouse lawyer helping himself and advising others despite the 1996 Prison Litigation Reform Act which made it harder for incarcerated people to file lawsuits against prisons in federal court. He had developed a respectful relationship with some of the other incarcerated men, some of whom nodded, shook his hand, and introduced him to their family in the waiting room. From commissary to contraband, from inflated prices to exploited labor, from the employees to the contractors, his words illuminated the bowels of the prison-industrial complex[26]—the economies within. He talked about the quotidian survival strategies he had snatched out of the jowls of death row and about the last six years in general

---

26. Prison Culture, "What is the PIC?," October 12, 2010, http://www.usprisonculture.com/blog/what-is-the-pic/.

MUMIA WITH SON, CIRCA 1980

population. His tone was dispassionate, and he was open about the realities of outmoded technology, lousy food, hypersurveillance, endlessly shifting rules and regulations, and constant roadblocks. Gallows humor and books armored him.

Yet, heartbreaking details spilled out from the crevices of his matter-of-fact storytelling. That moment when he felt wind unfettered by walls for the first time and thought it was going to "turn him around." The flowers that caught his eye, whose delicate, fragrant petals he had not wanted to disturb with a touch. The baths, a hard-won medical prescription for the chronic skin condition left behind in the wake of Hep-C, doled out only on Mondays. Our visits featured the muted soundtrack of his insistent scratching. The exposed skin on his neck, shin, and forearm was darkened and discolored by shades of red and pink. Damn, I thought. Water and wind on hungry skin, flowers that lingered in the full bloom of eyes grown accustomed to shades of gray—it was a sensorial reminder of all that prison takes from us. Of course, what it takes most of all is time.

The inhumanity of 36 years—more than 13,100 days in prison, over 10,400 of which were spent in solitary confinement—lay

between us like a rancid odor no one wanted to claim or acknowledge. My mind thought: but how do you survive this? My lips said
nothing. Instead, I thought of my own life. I was eleven years old
the year Mumia was incarcerated. I was all elbows and knees, lived
for "Fame" on TV, and rode my bike in endless loops around my
Brooklyn neighborhood. Thirty-six years was the yawning gulf between the much-coveted beeper of my tween years and the apps on
my phone calibrating my middle-aged life. While he was incarcerated, Mumia's children had grown up and he'd lost both parents,
a sibling, and a child. In single file, in that grim room, I silently
mourned for Mumia's yesterdays and all that could have been.

It was love—of friends and family, of the worldwide movement determined to secure his release—that provided his oxygen.
He told us that more than once, looking deep into our eyes almost
willing us to understand that it was not a platitude. Supporting
court appeals, organizing street actions and grassroots political
education are crucial parts of what the political prisoner movement describes as "the work." But the movement's lifeblood are
the many unseen acts of humanity that nurture the spirit of political prisoners: writing letters and sending birthday cards, amplifying their writings, raising money for their commissary, visiting
them, sending books, accepting phone calls, and emotionally supporting their families. In that moment, Mumia radiated gratitude.

We ended the visit by asking him for our marching orders. He
advised us to pivot from the spectacle of the daily headlines to the
news unfolding under the radar, especially the stories of successful
acts of resistance and victories. He reminded us to keep an eye on
judicial appointments at the federal and state level, and keep the
pressure up through direct action in the streets. In January 2018,
Mumia's contention of judicial bias in his case was given new life
as newly sworn in District Attorney Larry Krasner's office has be-
gun to review the role Ronald Castile, former DA and PA Supreme
Court Justice, played in Mumia's case. One scenario could be that
Mumia's legal appeals could be reinstated, potentially resulting in
a new trial. The outcome of this investigation remains uncertain
but it represents a major breakthrough. Activists and supporters
packed the courtrooms in February and March 2018, even as they
challenged the legitimacy of the larger criminal justice system.

At the end of the visit, Mumia walked us back to the processing desk and made a joke about us getting our freedom papers, the documentation that was our ticket to the outside. Under the guard's watchful eyes, we leaned into the second allowable embrace. We had spent a total of 8.5 hours together on our two visits, and likely, we would not meet again inside those walls. We locked eyes and instinctively, I started nodding over the tightness in my throat. "Good-bye" was not an option. Instead, our movement salutations tumbled over each other. "Stay strong." "Ona move." "Long live John Africa." "All power to the people." To this, we added our "I love yous."

INTERVENTION

DIS-ORGANIZING PRISONS AND BUILDING TOGETHER, INSIDE/OUTSIDE [1]

Stevie Wilson

DIS-ORGANIZING PRISONS

When I was asked to define prison organizing, I was stuck for a moment. I realized that I had never defined what I do as a prison organizer. First, my concerns have always been about more than the prison itself. Second, my work extends beyond prisons and jails. Third, and most importantly, my goal has always been to disorganize the prison, to make it less effective, to deny it what it needs to continue: people, money, and an uninformed and misinformed public. I therefore feel I'm more capable of discussing and defining prison disorganizing than prison organizing. My work has focused on three areas: political education, cooperation, and solidarity. It is diametrically opposed to what prison administrations are working to establish among imprisoned folks: ignorance, isolation/alienation, and enmity. Malcolm X said, "The greatest mistake of the [civil rights] movement has been trying to organize a sleeping people around specific goals. You have to wake people up first, then you get action."[2] Political education is the starting point.

---

1. The following intervention was initially published by incarcerated abolitionist Stevie Wilson, as a two-part essay on the blog "Dreaming Freedom | Practicing Abolition." [See Stevie Wilson, "Dis-Organizing Prisons" and "Building Together, Inside/Outside," *Dreaming Freedom | Practicing Abolition*, December 5, 2019, https://abolitioniststudy. wordpress.com/2019/12/05/dis-organizing-prisons-by-stevie-wilson/ and https://abolitioniststudy.wordpress.com/2019/12/05/building-together-inside-outside/.]
2. Malcolm X, quoted in Marlene Nadle, "Malcolm X: The Complexity of a Man in the

I know that studying penal abolition gave me the vocabulary, the language, to express what happened to me, my friends, and my communities. I knew that something terrible had happened and that we had been traumatized. But I had no words for it. I couldn't explain it. Prison teaches us that all our problems are in our heads. That all we need is cognitive behavioral therapy and our lives will be better. Racism, sexism, homophobia, transphobia, xenophobia, and classism have nothing to do with how our lives turned out. Studying opened my eyes and healed my spirit. Through study, I acquired the language to name my pain and frustration. Naming the pain was the first step toward healing. I wasn't crazy. It wasn't all in my head. When I read *Policing the Planet* and learned about broken windows policing, I acquired the language to tell others what happened to me and my communities and why.[3] When I learned about neoliberalism, I learned to connect the dots between what was happening in my neighborhood, school district, and the prison.

Political education helped me see who the real enemy was and who was responsible for my pain. When you're hurting and you don't know who is responsible, you tend to lash out against those closest to you. Many of us are behind the walls because of long-suffering pain and misdirected anger. Through study, I gained awareness and knew that other prisoners are not the cause of my pain. I began to see others with new eyes. My education made me more compassionate towards others.

I didn't want to keep this good thing, this knowledge of what was really going on, to myself. I started to share materials with others. I started holding rap sessions about the prison-industrial complex (PIC) in the yard. I found that others were just as hungry for an answer to what was going on as I had been. We started to meet regularly. This is where cooperation became critical. You see, the Pennsylvania Department of Corrections (PA DOC) has rules against borrowing and lending reading materials as well as unsupervised prisoner gatherings, so we had to get creative and

Jungle," *Village Voice*, Vol. X, No. 19, March 2, 1965. Available at https://www.villagevoice.com/2020/02/05/malcolm-x-the-complexity-of-a-man-in-the-jungle/.

3. Jordan T. Camp and Christina Heatherton (eds.), *Policing the Planet: Why the Policing Crisis Led to Black Lives Matter* (New York: Verso Books, 2016).

be vigilant. Together, we found ways to create study groups, trade books and zines, and make copies of materials. We made groups with agendas we knew the administration would approve, like "Life Changes: A Grief Support Group," and turned it into a transformative justice-healing circle called "Circle Up."

In total, we created and maintained four study groups. We put what we learned into action. When one of our members was brutally assaulted by two officers and placed in solitary confinement, we practiced solidarity. We contacted our outside allies and created a phone zap campaign to make sure our comrade was safe and would not be charged with assault. Within two weeks, he was transferred to a prison closer to his family and back in general population.

The cycle doesn't end. We study, we care for each other, we practice solidarity. This is how you disorganize a prison. This is how you disrupt the prison-industrial complex.

BUILDING TOGETHER, INSIDE/OUTSIDE

I have a simple analogy I use to describe our movement—it's a bird. Abolitionist principles and ethics are the head of the bird that guide us and direct the work. Without these principles, we are dead. It is important that we keep our head clear. It is important that we remember that it is not groups or personalities that guide us; it's principles and ethics. An abolitionist principle like not remedying harm with harm reminds me that caging and exiling people who do harm is not the answer. An abolitionist ethic like radical compassion reminds me that the time to love someone is not when they've done well or pleased me, but when they've messed up or angered me. Principles and ethics must guide us.

The wings of the bird are inside and outside activists. In order for the bird to fly well, to fly straight, it needs two equally strong wings. If one of the wings is weaker than the other, the bird will fly crooked. If one of the wings is broken, the bird won't be able to fly at all. It becomes easy prey. Each wing is critical to the bird's ability to fly well. Inside and outside activists need each other. One without the other leads to failure. Inside activists need outside activists to listen, provide material support, be study partners, sponsors, and accomplices in actions. Inside activists need outside activists to remember that we are not one type: many of us are not able-bodied, neurotypical, cisgender, heterosexual males. Our different social positions affect our experiences of incarceration. Inside activists need outside activists to make room for us at the table. Invite us to participate in workshops and conferences. Formerly incarcerated is not a substitute for the experience of those who are currently incarcerated. We are tired of not being participants in conversations that are about us.

Together, with strong principles and strong wings, we can effect great changes in this world.

A FAMILY LIKE MINE

Shana L. Redmond

One hug at the beginning of the visit and one at the end. With the exception of holding hands on the way to the vending machine for his favorite snack, this was the extent of the physical contact that we were allowed. Two hugs. This is how I learned to show love to my father; a repetitive sequence of events that transpired for almost nine years, though never often enough—at best six or seven times a year. There was never enough contact, never enough time to believe that this was anything other than it really was: the cold and calculated violence of capture.

I was twelve when my father was arrested and by the time of his release just prior to my twenty-first birthday, I had come to notice and appreciate the tiny victories as they came. Originally, he was housed in the county jail. While there I could not touch him. He was behind glass and although he was always smiling, it was hard to imagine him as anything other than part of a curated scene. Rather than being fully animate in real time, he appeared— like all of the other men who walked the line ahead of him—to be on display, posed, being made to do what some unknown person told him to do.

In spite of this, I relished these weekly visits and worked hard to make my few minutes on the telephone count. With three children and a partner to speak to, time was precious. When he was sent to one of the half dozen prisons that he would know over the time of his sentence, I was scared and sad. We would no longer be in the same city. Little did I know, however, that now there would be no dirty glass, no telephone static to manage. I

27

would be able to touch him. This was a win and I cherished it, no matter the circumstances.

With hundreds of letters written between us, and many more miles driven, those were an unforgiving nine years. We both missed a lot. Yet no matter how difficult, the visits took away a bit of the sting and loneliness of our distance. During them I could see his smile for what it was—older and complicated but genuine and necessary. So too was mine. He was as much my lifeline as I was his.

I am fortunate to now have my father home. He is healthy and moving through the world with an integrity that no one can take from him. But those nine years are never far from either of our minds, especially as I continue to watch in horror as the prison-industrial complex lurches forward. To read the news, on the verge of the holidays no less, that hundreds of US jails and prisons have terminated in-person visits and replaced them with virtual sessions by phone or computer is stunning, even if the rationale is not. Incarcerated women and men continue to be treated as carrion for vulturous telecommunications companies (via prison brokers and administrators) who justify their actions by trotting out the familiar ruse of security. Exposed here is the cruelty required to sustain the economic logics of carceral crisis and the pervasive damage wrought by such demands.

The active retention of ties between those inside and those outside is not simply a matter of preservation for families like mine. It is fundamentally about the rights of incarcerated people to continue living, even in the shadows of so much death. The deprivation of proximity and touch is an attempt to impose slow death, which is continually resisted by incarcerated people and their communities through gestures both grand and modest. These moments of love and affirmation are the signals and struggles that we share across the wall and the resolve that announces a collective promise to be present for as long as it takes.

INTERVENTION

ABUSE THRIVES ON SILENCE
THE #VAUGHNREBELLION IN CONTEXT

Kim Wilson

My two sons are incarcerated at the James T. Vaughn Correctional Center (JTVCC) in Smyrna, Delaware. On February 1, 2017, inmates at Vaughn took a stand against the dehumanizing and abusive conditions of the prison and the beginning of Donald Trump's presidency. Building C became the site of national media focus with images of heavily armed response teams surrounding the entrance and awaiting orders. It looked like a scene from a movie, but this wasn't a movie.

This was life.

News reports offered little insight on what was unfolding at this Level Five prison (i.e., maximum security) less than twenty miles from Wilmington, Delaware. Written reports pathetically relied on the facility's Wikipedia page, and then only for the purposes of citing a few statistics and highlighting an incident from more than a decade ago. The hot takes would soon follow.

I found out about the situation while scrolling through my Twitter feed. The Associated Press tweeted that prison guards had been taken hostage and that all state prisons were on lockdown.

My heart sank.

Having someone you love in prison is hard enough, but having two people you love in prison is devastating. It requires that you shield yourself in ways that it's hard for other people to imagine because you are always expecting bad news.

29

At 1:06 p.m. on February 1, 2017, *DelawareOnline* released an audio recording in which the caller said the men at Vaughn acted because they wanted better treatment, access to education, and transparency in the system.[1] The caller was unable to give his name because he was one of the hostages. However, this did not stop the reporter from asking him multiple times for his name. The caller sounded scared (he described having something on his head, and he told the reporter that he was just doing what he was told). When the call was over I knew that was likely the last time that the public would hear from those inside.

A prison lockdown creates an information black hole. Only bits and pieces of information are allowed to trickle out during moments of crisis, and these are usually staged events with officials standing around delivering statements and not taking questions. The control of information is designed to limit what the public knows, but it's also designed to isolate those inside from those outside. The control of information also serves law enforcement interests by making it easier to track people that post things online that can't or wouldn't be known if one does not have access.

Building C houses 150 men. Anyone that has been to Vaughn knows that each building is isolated from the others with a series of razor-wire topped fences, electronic gates, and locked doors. There's no mistaking that you've entered a maximum-security facility when you enter Vaughn. Even the reception room is inaccessible to visitors until a guard buzzes you in and out.

By 1:42 p.m., I had already called the prison to request information on my sons. I was told that the prison was not releasing any information at that time and then I was instructed to call back later that night around 8:00 or 9:00 p.m.

What took place at Vaughn is connected to the broader political situation in the United States. The caller said as much. While we currently don't know the identities of those involved in what

1. Like most jurisdictions in the US, Delaware DOC assigns individuals to sex-segregated facilities on their basis of their birth-assigned sex. At this time of writing, this is currently under review, based on an ACLU lawsuit and DOJ ruling from March of 2016. Margie Fishman, "Transgender inmate sues, claims civil rights violations," The News Journal, August 8, 2016, https://www.delawareonline.com/story/news/2016/08/05/trangender-inmate-sues-delaware-prison-leaders-civil-rights-violations/88076320/.

has become known as the #VaughnRebellion, what we do know is that these men were willing to risk their lives to illuminate the abuses inside Vaughn, and they did so by deliberately pointing to the president and his policies. This is an important moment that is being overlooked because national politics are rightfully the concern of the moment.

It is also the case that mass incarceration reform movements often highlight well-known facilities like Rikers, Pelican Bay, Angola, and Attica. At less notorious prisons, abuses tend to thrive unchecked because these facilities are not on people's radar.

The #VaughnRebellion is already being described as a single event that ended on February 2, 2017, when law enforcement stormed Building C in the early hours of the morning. However, if we take what the men in Vaughn said seriously, then we should look at the #VaughnRebellion in the context of other movements for social justice that have mobilized in recent years and that show no signs of waning.

The #VaughnRebellion cannot be disconnected from the broader struggle against extrajudicial police killings of Black people in the United States. Freedom from abuse from corrections officers and other prison staff is part of the same struggle to end police violence.

Read thusly, the #VaughnRebellion is also a direct response to unjust federal policies that are likely to influence the conditions within state prisons in Delaware and around the country. At a time when the federal government has targeted vulnerable groups of people in this country, the #VaughnRebellion should be seen as a signal that solidarity includes solidarity with incarcerated people.

The men of Vaughn are demanding better treatment, education, correct status sheets, and effective rehabilitation. They are telling society that they will not be disappeared and forgotten. They are saying, unequivocally, that they matter, and that they will not be denied their humanity even if it risks them more time or their lives.

In the coming weeks and months we are likely to hear from self-appointed "experts," taskforces, committees, and other groups that will be charged with analyzing what led up to the #VaughnRebellion so that it doesn't happen again. The concerns of the incarcerated people at Vaughn will not be centered in those investigations. The central focus will be on "safety" (as defined by the institution).

In my experience, as both a scholar of mass incarceration and a mother of two incarcerated men at Vaughn, Delaware officials are masters of illusion. They will make it appear as if they have taken the demands for better treatment, education, rehabilitation, and etc. seriously, while they double down and intensify their use of harsh punishment, and increase surveillance of anyone they perceive to be a threat to the smooth operation of the prison. This includes not just the incarcerated people at Vaughn, but also the people on the outside who they see as rabble-rousers. Much of the public will likely have lost interest in what happens at Vaughn because that's how these things go. But for those of us with loved ones on the inside we need to stay vigilant, engaged, focused, and determined in our efforts.

Abuse thrives on silence. I don't believe that we can afford to ignore the #VaughnRebellion as some outlier event in an otherwise model prison (though prison officials and politicians will try to push this line—hard). We don't know who was involved in the #VaughnRebellion, but I stand in support with them and with everyone else at Vaughn that is subject to abuse. There are many inside that are legitimately afraid to speak up. There are also those outside who feel as though they can't speak up because they worry that they will be banned from the prison. This is a legitimate concern, and I worry that I'll be banned from seeing my sons for writing about the #VaughnRebellion.

This is how power and control work. This is how abuse works. In the struggle for justice, I can't allow fear to stop me.

INTERVENTION

FROM THE VAUGHN UPRISING: 'FOR A SAFER, MORE SECURE, AND MORE HUMANE PRISON'

On Behalf of the Prisoners at
James T. Vaughn Correctional Center

To: Warden Parker, James T. Vaughn Correction Center
From: Thomas Gordon #455684

Re: Human Rights

> *"It is imperative upon those of us who fight monsters to do everything in our power to not become one in the process."*
> ~Anon

> *"To those of you who deny us our human rights in order to feel secure, you deserve neither humanity nor security."*
> ~Anon

What happened in C-Building was both tragic and inevitable. Only those who were blind or naïve can claim that they did not see that incident coming. It was not sparked by any one event, but by a series of events, that with time began to slowly boil over.

Due to the conditions of this prison and the treatment of those held within it, it was only a matter of time before we (as I stand in solidarity with them) were forced to take actions into our own hands. Our attempts at diplomacy were ignored, our pleas for help fell on deaf ears. There was no other way for you to know our struggle, for you to acknowledge our plight. What had to be done was done.

No one wants for this type of incident to happen again. No one wanted this to happen in the first place. We all have a duty and a moral obligation to ensure that what occurred never occurs again. To do that we must first realistically address the issues that brought us to this point.

We, as inmates, know that when we are incarcerated, we lose certain "civil" rights. What we do not lose and what should not be taken away from us are our "human" rights. Under no circumstances should we be treated as less than human beings, nor shall we be expected to settle for such treatment.

We do not want the keys to the prison. What we want is fairness, impartiality, transparency, and humane treatment. Below you will find a list of our fair requests that will help you all in your goal of making this a safer, more secure, and more humane prison. I hope that you consider all of these points sincerely.

We respectfully request:

1. **Human Rights.** Everything on this list can be placed under this one category. We want human rights, decent treatment, respect as men, and to be treated fairly.

2. **Food.** We would like to be properly fed and to receive bigger portions at all meals. We would like an end to the "heart healthy diet"[1] and for all foods to be removed from the menu when it is clear that the majority of prisoners do not eat it. The Delaware Department of Corrections throws away a ton of food on a daily basis. There is no reason that not only could our portions be bigger but that the prison could pass out seconds and thirds as well. We therefore request: 1) larger portions; 2) an end to the "heart healthy diet"; 3) "seconds and thirds call" at the chow hall until any food that would be thrown away is eaten, with each tier rotating on days to eat last; and 4) an end to using food as punishment by attempting to starve people into submission, especially in the Solitary Housing Unit (SHU).

---

1. While a "heart healthy diet" may sound desirable to the larger public located outside of the prison walls, individuals incarcerated in Delaware, Pennsylvania, and beyond consistently report that the proportions associated with this "diet" as administered by the Department of Corrections leaves people underfed and hungry.

3. **Access to Programs.** There are extremely limited program options for the inmates in this prison, to the point that if you are not a drug addict or a sex offender there is really nothing for you. We want better programming opportunities for all prisoners. We also want an end to the sham practice of handing out "program packets" to the individuals housed in the SHU and Maximum Security (MAX). All prisoners should be afforded the opportunity to receive adequate programming. An area shall be set aside (such as the visiting room and Bldg. 20 holding cells for the inmates in MAX/SHU) for them to receive such programming from a counselor or other party approved to run such programs or groups.

4. **Education.** Education should be afforded to all inmates no matter what their classification status. Even if it is provided through "In House Mail" courses for those inmates housed in the SHU/MAX. The Department of Corrections should hire the teachers needed to ensure that this gets done. Education, just like programming, should not be a privilege to be stripped away. It should be our right.

5. **Visits.** The Delaware DOC should afford inmates with more opportunities to have visits with their families and loved ones and should eliminate hurdles placed in the way of our support groups who come to show us their love by visiting us. To do this, James T. Vaughn Correctional Center (JTVCC) should: 1) offer visiting schedules equal to or greater than those offered at Sussex Correctional Institute (SCI); 2) Tear down the wall in the visiting room, which is there to cause not only a physical separation, but a psychological separation as well; and 3) allow inmates to hold the hands of their visitors above tables and to give longer hugs. Our family and loved ones are our greatest deterrent against both prison re-entry and prison misconduct, so why would you hinder us from having ample contact with them? JTVCC should follow SCI's example in this department as they do a better job at running visits fairly and humanely.

6. **Better Pay.** All inmates employed by JTVCC should be given a pay increase of at least five dollars a month. It is still slave

labor, but this will at least allow even the lowest paying job to get more than twenty-four soups, two bars of soap, and a writing tablet a month. Inmate workers should also be paid "overtime" equal to that in the real world, which is "time and a half."

7. **Fair and Impartial Disciplinary Hearings.** The entire disciplinary process at JTVCC is old and outdated. Furthermore, it is widely known that Lt. Savage is incapable of conducting fair and impartial hearings. Not only should Lt. Savage be removed from this position, but the way hearings are conducted should be changed completely. We believe that disciplinary hearings should be conducted by a "board" of three-to-five DOC staff of the rank of Lieutenant or higher along, with one mental health clinician and one DOC Counselor. All parties should hear all of the evidence for and against the inmate and then make a joint decision with any dissenting opinions written down along with the majority's ruling for the inmate. Appeals should also be run in the same manner, except that the board of DOC staff should have at least a rank of Staff Lieutenant, along with one Captain and the Warden or his/her designee.

8. **A Fair and Impartial Grievance Process.** JTVCC has a hidden policy to hinder inmates from receiving remedies for issues and incidents that should be grievable, by deeming such grievances as "non-grievable" when filed or returning them "unprocessed." This practice has to stop! Our grievance process is our only inhouse recourse for a lot of issues and it should work smoothly. In order to do this:

   • "Requests" should be allowed to be processed by the grievance office and should not be returned as "unprocessed." Currently, any grievance that staff doesn't want to go through is thrown out as a "request." Deeming grievances "non-grievable" or "unprocessed" due to them being "requests" is the most abused process in the JTVCC's grievance policy. It actually even goes against the written language of the grievance since for remedies you are clearly asked "Action requested by grievant." Your grievance should not be deemed non-grievable nor returned unprocessed simply because you make a "request." This has to stop.

- "Staff issues" should be grievable issues as well. The current policy of having inmates write the Staff Lt. or the Warden is a flawed policy since neither the Warden nor the Staff Lt. ever respond to such writings. Staff issues should be allowed to be grieved and any grievances against staff alleging "misuse of force" or "prisoner abuse" should be investigated by an Internal Affairs Officer. The DOC should hire the appropriate officers to ensure that this is done.

- All grievances alleging misuse of force or prisoner abuse should be deemed an "Emergency Grievance" and should be treated as such. You cannot expect safety and security for yourselves when we are being denied the same.

- Internal Affairs should keep officer files detailing allegations of misuse of force or prisoner abuse against inmates when alleged against said officer. These files shall include all such grievances against an officer, no matter the outcome of the grievance investigation. This is needed in order to show a pattern of abuse and excessive force. There are several officers who are widely known by both inmates and staff to regularly use excessive force and abuse inmates. These officers should be disciplined by the DOC when it is readily apparent that they have a pattern for such behavior.

9. **Transparency.** Once a year, the DOC should publish a "pie-chart" in the prisoner newspaper detailing how the money allocated to the prison is being spent. It should also include a separate chart detailing how the money earned in commissary is being spent. We believe that we have a right to know these things. This issue is highly important to us.

10. **Mental Health.** The abuse, mistreatment and punishment of individuals seeking mental health treatment needs to stop, along with the Mental Health Director Lezley Sexton's allowance and support of such actions. Lezley Sexton and DOC's policy of using medication as a punishment also needs to stop.

The treatment of mental health prisoners and prisoners seeking mental health treatment in this prison has been nothing less than cruel and appalling! This has to stop.

11. **New Appointment of Personnel.** We are calling for the appointment of a new Commissioner, Warden and Deputy Warden. A lot of us watched this prison take a turn for the worse under the authority of the now acting Commissioner Perry Phelps. We believe that a lot of our inhouse grievances began with his appointment as Warden. He is therefore unfit to change a system that he destroyed. To allow him to continue carrying on would be the equivalent of allowing a wolf to herd the sheep. Deputy Warden Scarborough should also be replaced. He is also a part of the problem, and indeed one of the main reasons, that inmates seeking mental health support are mistreated and punished. It is widely known that those are his personal policies. We also call for the ouster of the acting warden if he is unwilling to institute the fair changes listed herein, as such an unwillingness can only lead to more problems.

12. **Regular Rotation of Staff.** We are asking that staff be rotated to new buildings and new duties every three-to-six months. This allows us all a chance to have a break from each other and to give any possible tensions a chance to cool down before they boil over. This will also allow the DOC the opportunity to "follow the paper trail" of certain Correctional Officers who have a pattern of mistreatment and abuse towards inmates and therefore will give the DOC the chance to place such staff on duties away from any prisoners before things get messy.

13. **"Stingers."** Stingers should be sold on commissary as they are in most other jails or boiling water should be provided to all inmates, including those housed in MAX/SHU, by increasing the temperature of the hot water in our cell/building sinks so that it is adequate enough to cook food and heat coffee. If "stingers" are not sold on commissary, then they should be reduced to a Class 2 Infraction.

14. **Access to Shaving Supplies.** Inmates in all housing areas should be afforded razors twice a week in order to shave. There are many inmates in this prison who shave or need to shave regularly for religious and sanitary purposes. Those of us who choose to shave should be allowed to do so. This is a policy that was once allowed but was then stopped by then Warden Phelps. We should be allowed state-issued razors two times a week and better shaving razors should once again be sold on commissary. The DOC doesn't stop double/ triple celling inmates because the practice leads to fights, so they should not stop selling and providing razors because they lead to one or two people getting cut. Instead, those incidents should be dealt with on a case by case basis, not by acts of mass punishment. We want razors back for all inmates no matter their classification.

15. **Vendor Packages.** At least two vendors should be allowed into the prison for the purpose of allowing inmates to purchase one sixty-pound package a year ranging from food, electronics, sneakers, hygiene, etc. Inmates should also be allowed one 30-pound package consisting of only foodstuffs for the months of November and December. The DOC can approve different weights and allowable items for different classification levels. By allowing two vendors it will ensure that no one vendor can monopolize the market and hike the prices for inmates and their families.

16. **Cleaning Supplies.** Inmates should not be denied cleaning supplies. There is no reason that DOC should not want first, a clean prison, and second, for the inmates to practice cleanliness. However, DOC staff frequently deny inmates the material to properly clean the tier, the showers, and our cells. This needs to stop! Right now, 18C tier is completely filthy. No one can remember the last time the showers have been cleaned. The tiers and cells are covered in filth and scum. Back on January 2, 2009, a nonviolent protest was staged on this issue alone. Since then nothing has changed. The showers on this tier should be deep cleaned no less than three times per week and inmates should be given full cleaning supplies at

least three times per week consisting of: 1) a dust broom; 2) a toilet brush; 3) a sponge; 4) a cleaning rag; 5) a bucket; 6) soap balls; 7) Comet; 8) a mop; and 9) a mop bucket. These supplies should be readily available on all tiers.

17. **Goodtime.** We would like an increase of earned goodtime credits from five days a month to ten days a month. Additionally, all inmates should receive "goodtime" credits for participating in work, school, or programming no matter what their classification status.

18. **Recreation.** We would like the "rec" schedule to go back to the "pre-riot" schedule for all buildings.

19. **Library.** All inmates should be afforded access to the Library no matter their classification status.

20. **Indigent Supplies.** All indigent supplies should also include lotion and deodorant.

21. **Investigation into Postriot Actions on the Part of Staff.** There should be a full investigation into the actions of DOC staff after the riot. This must include all of the alleged mistreatments and abuse/assaults of inmates during the mass shakedowns in buildings 23, W, etc. This investigation should be conducted by an independent organization outside of the DOC.

22. **Reassignments / Transfers of Staff.** We request the transfer of or reassignment of duties for all the DOC staff listed below, who have an extensive history of abusing and mistreating prisoners.*

*Captain Wiley, Lt. Drace, Sgt. Payton, Sgt. Gill, Sgt. Beckles, Sgt. May, Sgt. Forkum, CO Arabia, Lt. Ratcliffe, Lt. Savage, Lt. Wallace, Sgt. Fredrick, Cpl. Jensen, CO Green (on the 8am–4pm shift), CO Linsey, Sgt. Barromia (assigned to Bldg 18, on the 12am–8am shift), Sgt. Chalice, Sgt. Dejesus, Lt. Tyson, Staff Lt. Reynolds

This list is not all encompassing. We picked the worst of the worst Correctional Officers (COs), some of whose actions cannot and will not be forgiven. These staff have stars next to their names. If they cannot be disciplined by the DOC, then we will be forced to once again take actions into our own hands. We will no longer settle for being kicked while we are down. This is your opportunity to prove to both your staff and to us inmates that you will not settle for the blatant abuse and mistreatment of any prisoner. Our lives matter as well.

We hope that you give a lot of thought to these twenty-two requests. These issues are all very important to us. Please feel free to take your time. We have patience, a lot of time, and most importantly nothing to lose.

On behalf of my brothers in the struggle,

Thomas Gordon
SBI #455684

MOVING THROUGH FLAMES

TOWARD AN INSURGENT INDECENCY

KatherineKellyAbraham[1]

Let us burn this motherfucking system to the ground and build something better.

—Claire Vaye Watkins[2]

INTRODUCTION:
THE CONTEMPORARY STATE AND THE "DECENT FELLOW"

The call for abolition asserts that contemporary sociopolitical and economic institutions are inherently unfixable and beyond reform or rescue. The fantasy of radically changing political structures from within is simply not a viable option for those concerned with destroying the mechanisms of carnage that shape modern life and its attendant regimes of governance, such as: the global war machine, the prison-industrial complex, transnational resource extraction and its manifestation in national sacrifice areas.[3] Rather than drawing from these regimes of death for social and legal

---

1. The authors wish to be cited as KatherineKellyAbraham. This listing of their names does not reflect a hierarchical order of any sort. In fact, their names can be shifted around as suits the needs, purposes, and whims of a given author, piece or citation.

2. Claire Vaye Watkins, "On Pandering," *Tin House* 17 (2): Winter 2015.

3. As we advance in the following section, we use the term "national sacrifice area" as developed by Simon Ortiz. In *Woven Stone*, Ortiz defines national sacrifice areas as the delineation of specific geopolitical areas that can be destroyed with impunity in order to consolidate Euro-American power—vis-à-vis resource extraction, for example. [Simon Ortiz, *Woven Stone* (Tucson, AZ: The University of Arizona Press, 1992), 337.]

recognition, power, and welfare—what we broadly refer to as the "state"—we consider what it would mean to the modern ordering of life to utterly destroy the state, to refuse its seductions and ruses of power, and to incinerate it until nothing remains but ash.

That cities across the United States are currently burning in response to the murder of George Floyd, among countless other Black people at the hands of the police, feels intimately connected to the argument we seek to stage. We are witnessing the inflammation of racialized, gendered, and classed imaginaries bursting once more into social consciousness and public life. Reverberating through the flames are several centuries of extraction, execution, and extinction that drive the so-called "American Dream." To advance such a call means to take seriously the rich tradition of scholarship that positions the state as a technique, practice, and effect of modern governance; to fight the optimization, rationalization, and normalization of this state; and to refute the embodied and moralizing claims that call upon this state to arbitrarily distinguish between violence and nonviolence.

The calculation and quantification of bodies and daily life cuts up the population through a network of biological and political realities. In this way, people are differentially valued, making possible larger, more nuanced, systems of death, capitalism, and colonialism: systems we argue are ultimately ordered and maximized by the state. As Michel Foucault contends, the state functions as "a schema of intelligibility for a whole set of already established institutions, a whole set of given realities."[4] Understanding the state as diffuse, yet coherent, allows for critical reflection about how its function exceeds its form. As a schematic and reality, we perceive the state as providing a legible matrix for the parameters of self-management and self-conduct: for social and political order. Attendant to Frantz Fanon's critiques that calls for decency and order are colonial projects, we argue that this process remains shaped by Euro-American geocultural power at the "objective as well as subjective level" of experience and perception.[5]

We understand state power as generative of inherently colonial

4. Michel Foucault, Security, Territory, Population: Lectures at the Collège de France, 1977–1978, trans. Graham Burchell (New York: Picador, 2007), 286.

5. Frantz Fanon, Black Skin, White Masks (New York: Grove Press, 2008), xv.

relations of rule: relations that produce sociopolitical, juridical, and affective orientations, sensibilities, and subjectivities.[6] As Glen Sean Coulthard argues, "colonial relations of power are no longer reproduced primarily through overtly coercive means, but rather through the asymmetrical exchange of mediated forms of state recognition and accommodation."[7] The violence of the state is accompanied by incremental efforts at rights and inclusion to sustain its legitimacy. We add that the state accomplishes this mediation via the internalized politics of decency.

The project of this piece is not to think about how to make life more livable under current regimes of power through incremental shifts or legal changes. Rather, we seek routes to alternative worlds based in the total abolition of these regimes because of their astonishingly responsive capabilities, which render profound social transformation impossible. By design, the state successfully incorporates its margins and continually extends its representation in order to further its grasp on the body politic: for instance, the inclusion of women in combat roles or the Supreme Court ruling on same sex marriage.

Simultaneously, and without coincidence, the state manipulates its boundaries through violent forms of capital accumulation and proxy wars, marks borders with fences and deportations, and uses its streets as a costly theater for punishing subjects that deviate from its aims. The fundamentally lethal interests of state power have not changed since the European invasion of the Americas. Instead, global technologies of communication and visibility have forced the state to create the illusion of a more transparent, democratic, and equal society. The state relies on fantasies of "individual" participation (civil rights, voting, recognition, and protest) as much as it relies on its authoritarian power to revoke those fantasies without notice or recourse.

As the violence executed by the state continues to shape everyday life in this country, we believe that it is by no means extreme to posit that one solution is to destroy—to burn down—contemporary

---

6. When we use the term "colonial state," it is to reference these troubling interconnections within the geopolitical context of the Americas, as we elaborate in the next section.

7. Glen Sean Coulthard, *Red Skin White Masks: Rejecting the Colonial Politics of Recognition* (Minnesota: University of Minnesota Press, 2014), 15.

institutions of governance, policing, comfort, and to cooperatively dismantle the workings of the state. For us, a radical project of abolition and insurgent political praxis refuses to negotiate with the state or seek recognition from any of its bureaucratic apparatuses. Political projects that compromise with the state—in order to secure small-scale concessions—have proven insufficient. Everyday violence, such as police brutality, continues to erupt unchecked. Ultimately, mainstream social justice organizing and activism treats the state as a central means of stopping the very political violence that insures its core function, operation, and maintenance.

State tactics shift, but are nonetheless continually productive of social protocols for acceptable, legible citizens and aberrant, disposable subjects: a division and existential deviation that we argue is rooted in Euro-American colonial power, white supremacy, and heteropatriarchy.[8] This power, which continues to inform the tangible parameters of the modern state, must remain the strategic target of abolition as a practice and vision if new worlds or alternative spaces of sociopolitical organization are to exist and thrive. One of the central challenges that insurgents face is the fact that colonial state power remains occluded by the representational moorings of the civilizing mission, such as the political conceptions of respectability, civility, and decency that remain the ideological cornerstones of nonviolent democratic participation.[9] These notions legitimize certain forms of organizing and comportment over others, ensuring that state power is distributed, unchanged, into the hands of those that best serve its interests.

The terms "decency" and "civility" are used interchangeably in this article to describe a particular form of exclusionary, homicidal, and suicidal politics. This politics demands inclusion within

---

8. Fanon, Black Skin, White Masks, xvii.

9. We loosely define insurgents as those political subjects who adamantly and violently refuse the seductions of the state, including its comforts and promises of safety. Consequently, these subjects are rendered disposable by the state, or are the focus of violent forms of state control, such as imprisonment, torture, and execution. To say that insurgents put their lives on the line for their politics is not an understatement. However, we do not make distinctions in this article between "good" insurgents and "bad" insurgents precisely because of the way Euro-American power is recuperated vis-à-vis these categorizations. We consider this struggle to be the necessary and ongoing work of insurgent political organizing and strategizing.

the colonial state—at the expense of dismantling white supremacy, heteropatriarchy, and capitalism on a global level. Here, Aimé
Césaire describes decency's relation to barbarism:

> I make no secret of my opinion that at the present time the bar-
> barism of Western Europe has reached an incredibly high level,
> being surpassed—far surpassed, it is true—by the barbarism of
> the United States. And I am not talking about Hitler, or the pris-
> on guard, or the adventurer, but about the *'decent fellow'* across
> the way . . . the *respectable bourgeois.*[10]

For Césaire, the problem of colonial domination did not rest solely with its acts of death dealing expressed "openly . . . in broad
daylight."[11] Rather, Césaire held that this problem of domination
also resided in: its "decent" homes, families, schools and churches, its "respectable" citizen-subjects who turned a blind eye to the
genocide shaping everyday life in colonized locations long before
Hitler and World War II.

The continued advancement and adoption of decency as the
only legitimate form of politics fortifies colonial statecraft and
power. These politics legitimize the passive participation of the
"decent fellow" and the "respectable bourgeois." The danger of
this passivity is that it perpetuates an outside, *indecent* constituency. This indecent constituency figures as the biopolitical break in
the population that threatens to overrun state interests, whereby
Muslims are always-already terrorists, Blacks are always-already
looting, and whiteness remains the standard by which diversity
is measured and extracted.[12] When everyday violence is deployed
in the name of this ideology of decency, the state's judgment continues to be divided by race, class, gender, and sexuality. This

---

10. Aimé Césaire, *Discourse on Colonialism* (New York: Monthly Review Press: 2000),
47. [Emphasis added.]

11. Césaire, *Discourse on Colonialism*, 49.

12. For Foucault, the term "biopolitics" describes the contemporary techniques and
technologies of governance used to maximize the productive and classificatory ordering of known political and biologic "life" as an expression of sovereign or state power.
Rather than the state wielding power through its ability to end life, power expresses
itself through the right to know, maximize, and shape the conditions of life. Examples
of this include public health infrastructures, institutions such as prisons or schools,
conditions of labor, the bureaucracy of state management expressed in statistics, etc.

violence is perceived as the natural expression of civilization and key to its maintenance and safety. When those who decry these judgments deploy violence, they do so outside of the Euro-American parameters of the "decent," and are thus marked for rationalized, legitimized, "civilized" annihilation. Legalized violence takes many forms under state rule including unprosecuted police killings, military operations, and the restricted access to forms of care via poverty or other mechanisms of disenfranchisement.

As the state is intent on maintaining interpretive and legal control over violence via decency, we see a counter-politics of *indecency* as entirely necessary to dismantle its power. Our call to *burn it down* is thus a promotion of indecency as a necessary practice, in order to refuse colonial state structures and seductions. The next section outlines the role of decency in channeling political responses to environmental genocide in the US Southwest. We draw from what has been dubbed the "EPA Spill," which occurred during the summer of 2015 and had devastating impact on occupied Indigenous lands in the Four Corners region (Northwestern New Mexico, Northeastern Arizona, Southwestern Colorado, and Southeastern Utah. In the following section, we outline the mechanisms of embodiment that fortify colonial state power vis-à-vis decency and as articulated by the 2016 presidential election. To answer *Abolition*'s call "to make the impossible possible," in the final section, we conclude by addressing some of the challenges of our "indecent politics" and position.

DECENCY, COLONIAL RECOGNITION, AND ENVIRONMENTAL GENOCIDE IN THE US SOUTHWEST

An important step towards formulating a viable politics of indecency is to rebuke what Fanon called "colonial recognition": the desire to acquire, adopt, or wield colonial power in its currently known, felt, embodied, and codified registers.[13] We contend that this desire must be violently negated in order to stop the dangerous reproduction of colonial power as an ongoing feature of life,

---

13. Fanon, *Black Skin, White Masks*, 192–193.

governance, and capital accumulation.[14] To understand why colonial recognition remains a contemporary problem, we turn to the work of Egla Martínez Salazar. Martínez Salazar insists that the replication of modern power depends upon the fleshed, symbolic, and psychological categories of governance implemented by settler colonial regimes in the Americas (i.e., the Invasion).[15] Despite the supposed independence of the Americas from former imperialist centers (e.g., Spain, Portugal, England or France), she argues that the fundamental norms of colonial power, such as cisheteropatriarchy, capitalism, and white supremacy, were *never* dismantled or destroyed. Instead, what Martínez Salazar calls the "colonizer's heirs"— what Césaire termed the decent fellow or the respectable bourgeois—sought, acquired, and consolidated this power in its Eurocentric form, thereby gaining hegemonic control over so-called "post-colonial" social fields.[16]

Thus, Martínez Salazar insists that colonial statecraft and recognition are not obsolete phenomena. Instead, these phenomena continue as remastered, relational dynamics of rule, legitimizing "economic, racial, and gender gaps" between and within nations: nations that remain organized around Euro-American geocultural norms. She terms these relations the *global coloniality of power.*[17] In

---

14. As outlined in the introduction, when we use the term "colonial power" in relation to contemporary statecraft, we are also talking about the structural violence that makes the execution of this power legible, such as that of white supremacy, heteropatriarchy, transphobia, and capitalism.

15. Egla Martínez Salazar, *The Global Coloniality of Power in Guatemala.* (New York, NY: Lexington Books, 2014): 9. Martínez Salazar writes within the coloniality of power school of thought, which is primarily based in Latin America. Canonical scholars from this school include Maria Lugones, "Heterosexualism and the colonial/modern gender system," *Hypatia*, 22(1), (2007): 186-209; Walter Mignolo, *Local Histories/Global Designs: Coloniality, Subaltern Knowledges, and Border Thinking.* (Princeton: Princeton University Press, 2012); Aníbal Quijano, "Coloniality and modernity/rationality," *Cultural Studies.* 21:2-3 (2007): 168–178.

16. As Martínez Salazar illustrates in the case of Guatemala, some of the colonizer's heirs are descended from the first European families that invaded the Americas, (2014): 47. Drawing from Marta Elena Casaús Arzú (1992), Martínez Salazar notes that these heirs in Guatemala are also comprised of landed and corporate elite from Germany, Canada, and the U.S. Following historical shifts in capital accumulation, production and geopolitical power, Martínez Salazar argues that the Guatemalan oligarchy has always been transnational in nature and thus directly reflective of global power blocs: blocs that shape socioeconomic life throughout the Americas.

17. Martínez Salazar, *The Global Coloniality of Power in Guatemala*, 7. By maintaining

other words, the Invasion *continues* as a socioeconomic and cognitive process via the classification, ranking, and exploitation of people, places, and things. By framing the attendant and targeted violences of this subjectification as civil, just, necessary, or "peaceful" interventions, we add that the *politics of decency* uphold the global coloniality of power, enacting its civilizing mission as a technique of *modern* governance.

To advance this argument, we turn to an analysis of the "EPA Spill," which (re)polluted two of the major rivers sustaining the Four Corners region, the Animas and San Juan. We pay particular attention to the forces of colonial recognition that channeled political responses to its devastation. In August of 2015, government agents from the Environmental Protection Agency (EPA) "accidentally released" three million gallons of toxic waste containing poisonous metals into these rivers, while "cleaning up" the Gold King Mine in Silverton, Colorado. As a result, they ran a sickly, neon yellow and orange.[18] As the EPA was primarily responsible for this "release" of poisonous waste, local residents and politicians dubbed it the "EPA Spill."

The Four Corners is colloquially known around the world as "Indian Country" because this region is where many diverse and sovereign Indigenous nations live, such as the Diné/Navajo, Ndeh/Apache, Ute, Hopitu/Hopi, and Zuni groups and peoples. Despite its status as a global cultural heritage and tourist attraction, life in the Four Corners is shaped by staggering poverty and environmental devastation. For instance, Gold King Mine had been releasing waste into the San Juan and Animas Rivers since the late 1800s. A coalition of residents in Silverton actually barred the EPA from previous cleanup efforts because "locals feared that the stigma would destroy tourism along with any possibility of mining's return."[19] As tourism and resource extraction

control over the means and modes of capitalist production, as well as those that guide the mechanics of mainstream political representation, Martínez Salazar maintains that the colonizer's heirs enact and enforce a rule that replicates coloniality as a global terrain of struggle (2014): 7.

18. Jonathan Thompson, "When our river turned orange: Nine things you need to know about the Animas River mine waste spill," *High Country News*, August 9, 2015, https://www.hcn.org/articles/when-our-river-turned-orange-animas-river-spill.

19. Thompson, "When our river turned orange."

are two of the only viable capitalist markets in the Four Corners, they are protected at mortal expense and in the name of economic development. Still, as resource extraction makes more money, it dominates the economy. For example, the land surrounding the Four Corners' most profitable tourism jewel, the world-renowned archaeological site of Chaco Canyon, is currently being fracked. This fracking has increased the already "giant methane gas cloud" recently identified by NASA *from space* and under which people from this area are forced to live, including poor whites.[20]

As starkly noted by Simon Ortiz, the Four Corners has long borne the heavy burden of being a national sacrifice area, a zone of colonial impunity and violent capital accumulation, in both a contemporary and historical sense.[21] Ortiz insists that the systems of governance implemented by Spain in the sixteenth century, and by what he calls the "American Occupation" of the Southwest in the late nineteenth century, share uncanny similarities that support his contention.[22] For example, Ortiz points out that both regimes framed Indigenous lands and peoples of the Southwest as "savage" or in need of the "civilizing" touch of Euro-American ways of knowing, worshipping, and ordering the world. This juxtaposition ensured that there "was no need for conspiracy to steal and defraud; rather there was a national goal to fulfill and godly purpose to be done."[23] By drawing from these imperial logics to transmute the Southwest into a national sacrifice area, Euro-American power has long been consolidated in the Four Corners, in the "godly" name of decency or the civilizing mission. The Four Corners is thus consequence and manifestation of the politics of decency: politics rendered intelligible due to what Martínez Salazar characterizes as the global coloniality of power.

The populations hardest hit by the EPA Spill were already negotiating the daily crises of coloniality in the Four Corners. In

20. Julie Dermansky, "Fracking Boom Expands Near Chaco Canyon, Threatens Navajo Ancestral Lands and People," DeSmogBlog, January 22, 2015, https://www.desmogblog.com/2015/01/22/fracking-boom-expands-near-chaco-canyon-threatens-navajo.
21. Simon J. Ortiz, Woven Stone (Tucson, AZ: The University of Arizona Press, 1992), 361.
22. Ortiz, *Woven Stone*, 31.
23. Ortiz, *Woven* Stone, 349.

FIGURE 1: BILLBOARD ADVERTISING NURSING SERVICES TO FORMER DINÉ MINERS IN THE FOUR CORNERS REGION, MANY OF WHOM ARE SUFFERING THE HORRIFIC CONSEQUENCES OF URANIUM EXPOSURE. *YÁ'ÁT'ÉÉH* IS A GREETING IN DINÉ, ROUGHLY TRANSLATING TO "IT IS GOOD" AND/OR "HELLO" IN ENGLISH. IMAGE COURTESY OF THE AUTHORS.

national sacrifice areas, "it is survival that is at stake."[24] Poor and working-class Diné, Hopi, Latinx, Ute, and Anglo peoples living alongside the San Juan and Animas—upon reservation lands and in reservation-border towns like Farmington, New Mexico—fully rely on these rivers for livestock care, irrigation, agriculture, daily life needs.[25] Hard on the heels of the EPA Spill, some Diné farmers committed suicide.[26] Other towns have long paid the price of the oil and coal extraction driving the production of national energy. The sky in Waterflow, New Mexico is always a toxic, yellow color and the smell of burning coal in the air chokes the eyes and throat. People from the Four Corners also suffer from various cancers and other health problems because they live in a national sacrifice area (see Figure 1). This terrifying reality is the *dynamic materiality* of the global coloniality of power; the continued influence of Euro-American notions of progress and profit over contemporary life;

24. Ortiz, *Woven Stone*, 360.

25. Diné is generally the preferred term used by peoples who have been otherwise described as "Navajo" by the settler colonial state.

26. Betsy Woodruff, "Navajo blame EPA inaction for suicides," *The Daily Beast*, January 3, 2016. https://www.thedailybeast.com/navajo-blame-epa-inaction-for-suicides.

the "decency" of the reinvigorated civilizing mission.

Russell Begaye, former President of the Navajo Nation (2015–2019), gestured towards this materiality and continuity when he stated that the EPA Spill compounded "his people's already significant historical trauma."[27] Despite President Begaye's awareness of this trauma, his administration, as well as mainstream Anglo organizing in the area, focused upon utilizing the EPA—a bureaucratic arm of the colonial state—as a mechanism for redress. That is to say, in the face of the absolutely *indecent* and obscene track record of American occupation in the Four Corners, many stakeholders relied upon the established legal and political parameters of colonial recognition for reparations. They wanted the EPA to publicly apologize; they wished to sue the EPA; they demanded public meetings with the EPA; they asked that the EPA provide the Four Corners with clean and treated water.[28] They sat in hard steel chairs in various community centers across the US Southwest until their bodies ached. They listened to politician after politician, scientist after scientist, in a desperate and completely understandable quest to somehow make life more livable in the Four Corners

EPA spokesperson Nancy Grantham, in response to requests for assistance made by President Begaye and his administration, stated:

> We [the EPA] have a long-term relationship with the Navajo Nation and the agency is committed to working collaboratively with the Tribe on response activities related to the Gold King Mine release. The EPA and the Bureau of Indian Affairs (with EPA funding) provided over 1 million gallons of livestock and agricultural water, and nearly 8,500 bales of hay, to Navajo communities along the San Juan River.[29]

In what some Indigenous peoples noted was a horrifying parody of the small-pox ridden blankets once given to their ancestors by American colonial agents, in an early act of biological terrorism and warfare, the abovementioned water was delivered

---

27. Wodruff, "Navajo blame EPA inaction for suicides."

28. Bruce Finley, "Gold King one year later: Colorado's mustard-yellow disaster spurs plans for leaking mine," *The Denver Post*, July 24, 2016, https://www.denverpost.com/2016/02/13/colorado-counts-on-gold-king-to-spur-cleanup-of-leaking-old-mines/.

29. Woodruff, "Navajo blame EPA inaction for suicides."

to Diné and Hopi peoples in contaminated tanks. Specifically, a trucking company currently involved in fracking throughout the Four Corners delivered this water in the same tanks they used to transport natural gas.[30] In a highly publicized interview, President Begaye ran his finger along the inside of one of these water tanks, showed its blackened and oily surface to the press, and began to weep.[31]

We do not tell this story to critique a governmental official. Nor do we tell this story to make it seem as if a "pure" political subject exists that allows for *any* easy moral distinctions between "perpetrator" and "victim" of colonial state power. Instead, we seek to illustrate the folly of relying upon or partnering with this state for sociolegal intelligibility, recourse, and comfort. We understand *a politics of indecency* as one solution to these troubling issues: as something that rebukes colonial recognition, by any means necessary, with the long-term goal of dismantling the global coloniality of power and its attendant sacrifice areas. A politics of indecency understands that this power promises contaminated blankets, contaminated waters: to a sick and dying people, a sick and dying earth. A politics of indecency rejects the socially acceptable part of the colonizer's heir to initiate or continue collective processes of reorienting to power, the earth and all life-forms, by creating strategic and global alliances with those who share this abolitionist vision and "impossible" political imagination.

One way to formulate these politics and vision is to unwaveringly position the earth and its peoples, lands, waters, and all creatures as vibrantly alive, dynamic, extant, animate and thus *beyond* containment, capture, or transformation into capital, Euro-American forms of biological and political power, and Euro-American notions of progress. This positioning overturns the hegemonic capacities of "decency" by rejecting colonial recognition at its economic, historical, and cultural cores. As Ortiz notes, by embracing this worldview:

---

30. Valerie Richardson, "EPA draws ire of Navajo Nation after water arrives in dirty oil tanks," *The Washington Times*, August 20, 2015, https://www.washingtontimes.com/news/2015/aug/20/epa-draws-ire-navajo-nation-after-water-arrives-di/.

31. Richardson, "EPA draws ire of Navajo Nation."

Only then will we truly understand what it is to love the land and people and to have compassion. Only when we are not afraid to fight back against the destroyers, thieves, liars, exploiters who profit handsomely off the land and people, will we know what love and compassion are. Only then . . . will we know life and its continuance.[32]

Of course, for many Indigenous people in the Four Corners, this shift in consciousness—the abolitionist line of flight—remains an ongoing political, cultural, and historical process.

For example, following the EPA Spill, various Indigenous-led groups fostered community-wide conversations about colonial state power in the Southwest as part of their continuing organizing work Some of these groups facilitated teach-ins across the Four Corners, which framed the EPA Spill as one of the many horrific ramifications of colonialism in the region. Others organized and participated in epic walks across the Four Corners to document the devastation of American occupation, such as resource extraction.[33] These groups bring attention to the inviolable vitality of the earth, by positioning themselves as defenders of the land, rivers, and water. In so doing, they provide a rallying point for a diverse array of allies to stand in solidarity with this unfolding historical consciousness: a consciousness that continues to manifest upon other occupied Indigenous lands and nations, such as in North Dakota. As the well-being of the earth and its life-forms are increasingly being placed above that of the murderous state, the global coloniality of power currently faces some very important challenges.

NECROPOLITICS AND THE COLONIAL STATE

Following our premise that the politics of decency is generated by and extends the global coloniality of power, we now explicate some of the embodied nuances of this power as it is consolidated, circulated, and executed by the state. We engage in this analysis to illustrate how the colonial state relies upon the politics of decency

---

32. Ortiz, *Woven Stone*, 363.

33. Lyla Johnston, "Young Navajos stage 200-mile journey for existence," *Indian Country Today Media Network*, January 1, 2015. Available at http://www.idlenomore.ca/young_navajos_stage_200_mile_journey_for_existence.

to kill people. The colonial state utilizes decency as a technique of governance in order to create and manage populations, coding certain embodied subjects as especially threatening. These so-called "threats" become central targets for state-sanctioned violence, subjugation, and imprisonment. Consequently, we argue that decency articulates what Achille Mbembe terms *necropolitics*: the use of power to determine what parts of the population must die in order for other forms of life to be cultivated.[34]

Drawing from the 2016 US presidential election, we illustrate the various necropolitical techniques for targeting, disarming, mutilating, and destroying bodies vis-à-vis the deployment of decency. In doing so, we advance our argument to burn down decency as a starting point for insurgent political praxis, as under both a fascist and so-called "decent" political leader, the operations of the state remain intimately and lethally tied to brutality.[35] As the election and change of power suggests, resistance must center upon the colonial state itself, and not upon the particularities of any regime.

To understand how decency reflects necropolitics in action, we turn to a brief discussion of the theoretical moorings and concepts shaping our understanding of Mbembe's work. Necropolitics emerges from Foucault's concept of biopolitics, rooted in the maximization and cultivation of particular forms of life in the service of state, capital, and power.[36] Foucault describes the ways in which

---

34. Achille Mbembe, "Necropolitics," *Public Culture* 15 (1), 2003: 11–40.

35. In post-Trump America, two kinds of distinct rhetoric about contemporary politics have emerged. The first is that Trump's regime represents a wholly new kind of leadership, the likes of which have never been seen. The second is that his regime is a continuation and logical outcome of increased militarization, migration, and economic destitution, trends that started in the wake of World War II. Both explanations seem insufficient to explain the current political landscape, with its willingness to give a voice to the most vile of opinions. Neoliberalism operates by way of consent, albeit a manufactured consent based in economic privatization, and the collusion of state and capital. Fascism, by contrast, is meant to signify a nationalist, violent, concentrated form of authoritarian governance with a strong leader. The American check on these forms of power has consistently been articulated as representative democracy through voting, term limits, and Constitutional authority vested in the courts. As has always been clear, these checks are insufficient for marginalized populations, and do little to ward off either fascism or neoliberalism.

36. Michel Foucault, *The History of Sexuality, Volume One: An Introduction* (New York: Vintage Books, 1978).

practices, techniques, and technologies of the state manipulate flows of power to account for the operations of human discipline and state sovereignty simultaneously, to create a population that is at once knowable and a target for manipulation. In a slight dissension, Giorgio Agamben places biopolitics in relation to what he calls the state of exception, in which solely the state exists in the domain of sovereignty and bodies are under constant threat of extraordinary violence.[37] Sovereignty is exerted precisely at the moment in which the state can kill with impunity on behalf of the population: the sovereign wields violence with the right to kill. Agamben suggests that the collision of the sovereign state and biopolitics continuously inform each other, in terms of just "who" the state can kill with impunity (and thus how the state of exception is articulated). We add that much of the latter process emerges via the politics of decency; how one conducts themselves as measured against the virulent standards of white supremacy, heteropatriarchy, and capitalism. Agamben suggests it is unhelpful, even dangerous, to create a politics regarding those who can be saved and those who can be left-behind. To do so facilitates a false notion of inclusion, in which "decent" subjectivities are incorporated into the body politic, while others are made to exist in a state of exception (i.e., incapable of decency).

Mbembe shows that necropolitics always informs what appears to be state acquiescence via the state of exception. By asking under which conditions necropolitical practices come to be exercised, Mbembe highlights the centrality of the work of death (necropolitics) to the organization of modern power. We take Mbembe's concerns very seriously in terms of thinking about abolition as a political project precisely because we see decency as the fertile ideological ground for the exercise of necropolitical conditions, the work of death. It is not only the state that must be incinerated (in its nefarious presence everywhere and nowhere), but also its juridical, political, and embodied schemas of representation that effectively determine which populations will be the beneficiaries

---

37. Giorgio Agamben, *Homo Sacer: Sovereign Power and Bare Life* (Palo Alto: Stanford University Press, 1998). See also: Joseph Pugliese, *State Violence and the Execution of the Law: Biopolitical Caesurae of Torture, Black Sites, Drones* (London: Routledge, 2013); and, Susan Stryker, "Biopolitics," *TSQ: Transgender Studies Quarterly* 1, 1–2 (2014): 38–42.

of state power (i.e., the "decent fellow"), and which populations will be killed by its policing, security, and military apparatuses. In sum, we understand these determinations as hinging upon civility (its preservation and enactment) for juridical legitimization.

As Mbembe argues, race and/or racism play a central role in this legitimization. He says: "After all, more so than class-thinking (the ideology that defines history as an economic struggle of classes), race has been the ever present shadow in Western political thought and practice, especially when it comes to imagining the inhumanity of, or rule over, foreign peoples."[38] Of course, we also understand gender identity and sexuality as intertwined representational forces that determine the limits of political vitality and likewise organize decency as necropolitics. Crucially, Mbembe's argument highlights that proximity to decency, such as via whiteness, has limits. As long as the state controls the means of representation, decency will always be coded as white masculinity, and all else considered disposable aberrations. To be rid of the white, masculine standard by which all else is measured, the regime of representation that we outline here must be burned.

A historical exploration of state-sanctioned terror, genocide, and violence is central to this argument. Mbembe points to slavery as a clear instance of "biopolitical experimentation," describing enslaved subjects as experiencing a triple loss that creates a shadow subject: "loss of a 'home,' loss of rights over his or her body, and loss of political status,"[39] resulting in inevitable social death. Paradoxically, the slave was needed for labor, thus placing them within a liminal and animal-like category: alive, but less than human. By relegating slaves to subhuman status, some of the enduring techniques of modern biological and political management were established and created the foundations for legal institutions, medical knowledge, and the persistent discourses of racism.

Despite the allegedly colorblind US criminal justice system, dedicated to supposedly ensuring civility or decency on the national front, formulations of criminality and terrorism continue to be decided along fault lines of race, one's proximity to Blackness

---

38. Mbembe, "Necropolitics," 17.
39. Mbembe, "Necropolitics," 19.

and animality. Entire categories of people must continually prove their innocence, allegiances, and humanity, their "desire" to be saved by the good graces of whiteness, so that they will not be made to die. Particularly in the instance of terrorism, entire nations are called into question for their "savagery," existing always as a threat originating outside the United States. Thus, "the sovereign right to kill is not subject to any rule in the colonies. In the colonies, the sovereign might kill at any time or in any manner. Colonial warfare is not subject to legal and institutional rules."[40] Locations of apartheid, occupations, war, and the logics of martyrdom and survival, all demonstrate acute examples of sovereignty, terror, and necropower insofar as they mark the limits of political and institutional recourse.

The 2016 US presidential election only further evinces these processes and legacies of colonial state power. On the surface, it might seem like decency, as a hegemonic construct, has reached its limit. President Trump and his white supremacist followers openly and loudly embrace various means of violent and horrific disposal for those marked as "terrorists" within and outside of US borders. Calls to build a wall, alongside "lock her up" and Muslim registries, remind us of the dire consequences of indecent, nonconsensual relationships to US nationalisms. Global economic structures have given way from neoliberal pseudotolerance to extreme and blatant fascism, presented as the iron fist needed to correct "security" issues such as "illegal" migration, terrorism, drug cartel violence, and economic recessions.[41] Even though this panoply of violence generally targets the same populations (women, people of color, Indigenous peoples, poor people, and migrants), we do not overlook the mainstreaming of hate speech, hate crime, and open discrimination that Trump embodies and circulates. In the face of these trends, which increase the established mores (i.e., racism and misogyny) undergirding state-sanctioned violence on

---

40. Mbembe, "Necropolitics," 25.

41. Neoliberalism and fascism are not as distinct as their common definitions may suggest and both are possible under US democracy. Since the rise of neoliberalism, the transition from "difference" to "diversity" has resulted in the normalization of difference based on its proximity to whiteness, heterosexuality, and upward mobility. Difference is evaluated based on its offerings to the generalization of the US as a benevolent nation.

an exponential level, many moderates and liberals are still calling for the population to "respect the office" as we sit by and wait to vote again. "Progressive" politicians and stakeholders continue to vilify those who violently oppose Trump (such as "anarchist" inauguration day protests in contrast to the Women's March), coding this dissent as a threat to democracy and the "peaceful transition of power"—more so than Trump and his incoming cabinet's deadly policy goals. Cue the *politics of decency*.

Calls for civility, such as those to "respect the office of the President," work to silence political protest and normalize hateful rhetoric within mainstream discourse, all the while shoring up the representational parameters of white supremacy and heteropatriarchy. These calls reflect the unseen necropolitical negotiations shaping the recuperation, resuscitation, and rescuing of decency as a technique of governance, the state of exception legitimizing the brand of fascism promised by Trump. While neoliberalism offered pseudotolerance, "multiculturalism," and rights-based structures to marginalized populations (at the same time, killing these populations via the prison-industrial complex or war or poverty), the populist fascism offered by Trump marks a resurgence of visible, tangible, undeniably rabid white nationalism.

This nationalism also signals the structural excesses and dependencies of decency, in terms of highlighting the dynamic and emanating necropolitical conditions of *contemporary* state-sanctioned violence. From the beginning of his campaign to ongoing cabinet picks, Trump focused on removing "official" protections and direly increasing the odds of death that poor people, women, migrants, Indigenous people, and people of color face in the US. This reversal centered upon and recycled a troubling nostalgia for a white America that never was and never could be. Still, this nostalgia ultimately expresses the politics of decency, as it romanticizes the restoration of white masculine empire in the name of "Making America Great Again." That is to say, decency and the recalibrated civilizing mission very much shaped Trump's campaign approach and eventual win, albeit through the deployment of reconfigured rhetorical and juridical vehicles. "Make America Great Again" is a call to arms for white nationalists, a swift rewriting and recasting of the genocidal foundations of America, in order to shore up continued vitriol and hate. MAGA operates and resonates so strongly because it is based upon historical fiction, and therefore continually must be reiterated, legislated, and re-presented.

No matter how "decent" one acts, no matter how well one tries to meet the norms and expectations of the colonial state, certain raced, classed, and gendered people are always-already marked for state-sanctioned death. Thus, the colonial state must remain the target of abolition, as it is from this location that the distribution and management of life originates, where the unseen necropolitical negotiations that make decency legible as a relation of rule are revitalized, reconfigured, and rearticulated.

TOWARD LIBERATION: UNTANGLING DECENCY AND FREEDOM

We now turn to a discussion of freedom, in terms of its function as both an ideology and an abolitionist goal. Our entry point for this examination is how the concept of "freedom" has been rendered a weapon, through which the global coloniality of power circulates, by ever privatizing care through the logics of personal responsibility, accountability, and decency. We end by calling for a return to "freedom" that can dismantle the colonial state and enact a profound abolitionist liberation from the regimes of death shaping life in the US (and, arguably, around the world).[42]

Under current regimes of power, the possibility and potential for freedom, especially as understood and theorized by "progressive" stakeholders, is a foreclosed promise. Freedom, in its current political formulation, is entirely monopolized and overcoded, ensuring only the power of the colonial state. Freedom is synonymous with a "decent life," in which one is only "free" to act if they choose among a list of state-sanctioned ways of being. If one chooses otherwise, freedom is altogether revoked through incarceration, loss of rights, and loss of privacy. In particular, identity as the foundation for rights-based claims furthers the state's capacity to negotiate the terms of justice and silence the more radical calls

---

42. We use the term "abolitionist liberation" to distinguish said liberation from freedom, as an ideology of the powerful and the complacent.

against its power. In granting small-scale "victories," especially to those specific groups that adopt the norms of coloniality, the state only perpetuates larger institutional violences. Successful access to decency vis-à-vis identity is only possible when treading on the backs of "indecent" subjects. In effect, these subjects make the politics of decency legible because they remain the conceptual targets of the recalibrated civilizing mission.

In fact, these limits signal why abolition is a necessary and crucial tactic for achieving meaningful and lasting liberation, "freedom," from contemporary necropolitical practices and regimes of colonial governance. Jacques Rancière articulates this through the concept of "wrong," which he says is the foundation of both politics and processes of subjectification, as all subjects are formed through their relation to the state and its unequal distribution of equality.[43] Politics emerges through moments of dissatisfaction and class fractures that the state can never possibly contain, and rests on an equality that can never be truly enacted.[44] Rancière defines political activity as "whatever shifts a body from the place assigned to it or changes a place's destination. It makes visible what had no business being seen, and makes heard a discourse where once there was only a place for noise."[45] Thus, while the wrong is the product of politics, it is also critical to the enactment of liberation.

At the heart of any assertion of equality is the wrong that preceded it: the wrong that is the foundation for the unequal distribution of power throughout society. Under the current regime, freedom is an empty signifier, "the empty property of any political subject."[46] It is only under new terms, and specifically, terms of abolition that freedom can come to fruition. Democracy, often argued as the political form that offers the most equal of terms, fails to offer anything but a "theatrics of dispute" for justice.[47] Only a total and full break with the colonial state offers any hope for the

43. Jacques Rancière, *Disagreement: Politics and Philosophy* (Minneapolis, MN: University of Minnesota Press, 2004), 22.
44. Rancière, *Disagreement*, 16.
45. Rancière, *Disagreement*, 30.
46. Rancière, *Disagreement*, 77.
47. Rancière, *Disagreement*, 62.

now hollow concepts of equality and justice. In other words, the wrong must be expressed via a radical politics of indecency, and entirely bypass the "decent" notions of equality or justice espoused by the colonial state. These concepts are foils for the recalibrated civilizing mission, and thus continue a long and horrifying legacy of genocide and state-sanctioned terror: a legacy that made the US the "bastion" of democracy that it is today. We imagine a radical democracy as foundational to abolitionist liberation. Abolition shifts the meaning of freedom from *freedom from* violence to *freedom to* make demands, live equitably, and guarantee a right to life.

The political fallout of recent events in the global arena has stressed the ways in which everyday existence is made always already susceptible to exceptional violence and environmental disaster, and has continually strained the limits of social theory and activism, alike. The expression of indecency and indecent politics will necessarily cut transversally through, across, and around previously authorized boundaries of embodiment and desire. However, it might also burn it all down. To burn down the systems and representations that seek to learn the language of liberation could, and should, mean a societal transformation capable of destroying the ills and wills of the state. Félix Guattari says: "We should permit nothing to distract us from discovering the ways and means for irreversible social transformation, without which we will enter into an escalation of fear and despair on a whole new scale."[48] We cannot emphasize the importance of this intervention enough, in terms of thinking about insurgent political praxis: *the irreversibility of abolition must be the goal.*

CONCLUSION: BURN IT DOWN

Abolition entails a much broader project than merely the end of the state. Abolition also requires a dismantling of all of the ideological moorings of colonial power, a burning down of the spheres of representation that privilege a docile decency as the ideal form of comportment and civic participation. State rule has its own

---

48. Félix Guattari, *Soft Subversions: Texts and Interviews 1977–1985*, Sylvère Lotringer (ed.), Chet Wiener and Emily Wittman (trans.), Introduction by Charles J. Stivale (Los Angeles, CA: Semiotext(e), 2009).

seductive ruses of power and recognition including the very tangible benefits of protection, access to some of the necessities of life, as well as providing an affective sense of belonging or the desire for the same through the adoption and internalization of its codes for decency and/or proper citizen-subject behavior. While the state makes particular ways of living and comforts possible, it does so always at the expense of others. As we stressed throughout this article, to acquiesce to the state is not, *in any way*, passive. The price paid for the maintenance of decency is exacted in blood. In the short term, we understand that life is made livable by embracing the representational, juridical, and economic mores of the colonial state and by carving out small spaces of refuge or alternative ways of being within the shadows of empire. Still, we find this approach ultimately untenable in terms of fostering the continuance of all life on this planet.

Thus, we end on a call to action. The time to materialize an abolitionist future is *now*. Just as the state is diffuse, immaterial, psychological, and institutionalized, so too must be the politics of abolition. Abolition demands the burning down of the state, but also the destruction of the colonial ties that bind our politics, economics, well-being, and sociality. Abolition must be enacted at the personal, political and social levels, with the trust and acknowledgement that those micro-revolutions will build and sustain each other. If the state is no more than the sum of its actions, abolition is no more than the sum of its fires. To refuse order, decency, respect and civility, we must move through the flames towards our collective liberation. It is in this spirit that we dedicate our article to all of the insurgent dreamers, warriors, and knowledge keepers risking their lives every single day, in the service of imagining, bringing forth, and fighting for the emancipation of planetary life. Thank you for your vision, wisdom, courage, and beauty, for daring to invoke the power of fire to cultivate the impossible: a new world.

IS MARXISM RELEVANT?
SOME USES AND MISUSES

David Gilbert

Imperialism is piracy... reorganized, consolidated and adapted to the aim of exploiting the natural and human resources of our peoples.

[N]obody has yet made a successful revolution without a revolutionary theory.

—Amilcar Cabral[1]

One of my biggest joys and most valued activities is corresponding with younger-generation—by now it's generations—of white antiracist activists. Most of them identify as anarchist or antiauthoritarian, but knowing my history, often ask what I think about Marxism. These activists have been mightily turned off by the examples of Marxist-Leninist (M-L) organizations in the US, which are characterized by dogmatism, sectarianism, and heavily top-down internal power dynamics. Political "debate" frequently devolves into each side plucking competing quotes from Marx or Lenin or Mao—as though that proves anything. Perhaps worst of all, many predominantly white and male "Marxists" use powerful

---

1. Both quotes are from *The Weapon of Theory* (1966). Amilcar Cabral was the leader of the independence struggle in Guinea Bissau/Cape Verde Islands and was assassinated in 1973. While not necessarily calling himself a Marxist, he made brilliant use of the historical materialist method, along with his grounding in African traditions, to create an invaluable contribution to revolutionary theory on a world scale.

PHOTO OF DAVID GILBERT BY BRENO ALTMAN

terminology to insist that fighting white and male supremacy is "secondary" to the class struggle and that opposing homo- and transphobia is irrelevant.

Those examples are rightly rejected by radicals rooted in love for, and commitment to, the liberation of oppressed and exploited humanity. But what led many of my generation to embrace Marxism, in sharp contrast to the above misdirections, was the reality that most of the exciting revolutions that were sweeping the Third World (what's now called the Global South) were led by M-L parties—not Marxism as some musty catechism from nineteenth-century Europe, but rather as a living tradition being applied and developed by modern Third World revolutionaries.

A blanket dismissal of Marxism runs the risk of losing some important building blocks for analyzing the nature and vulnerabilities of capitalism. My experience during more than fifty years in the struggle has shown that those who were able to sustain activism over the long and difficult haul often had some foundation in theory and in a sense of history.

What follows is not an argument for or against Marxism as the defining framework for activism, and it certainly isn't an attempt to provide an overall or in-depth explanation.[2] Instead I want to talk about a few broad concepts that I found very useful

---

2. While I asked friends to send me the few passages I quote, I haven't otherwise read the books in some thirty or more years.

and still seem very relevant today. Often these ideas are markedly different from the more visible versions put forward by various predominantly white and male Marxists. (For brevity's sake I'll refer to those whom I feel distort the analysis in this way with quotes: "Marxists.") Before getting into the heart of this paper, I'll briefly review the path that led me to study and then try to apply Marxism.

LETTING IN THE SUNLIGHT

Coming of age in the US in the 1950s, I was reflexively anticommunist. The roar of the propaganda and "education" that engulfed us was reinforced by my distaste for the repressive East European regimes. Moving into the 1960s, my belief in US democracy was shattered, first by the inspiring Civil Rights Movement, then by the inexcusable US war on Vietnam. As I learned more, I became outraged that our government systematically crushed democratic movements in the Third World in order to impose brutal dictatorships in league with US business interests. By the time I started college in 1962, I was already on the road to committing my life to activism.

The political science classes that dealt with the basis and legitimacy of government relied on the myth that "men" (as they said) came together to agree on a social contract. Frustrated, I found a radical graduate student who recommended Karl Marx and Friedrich Engels' *The German Ideology* (1845). They started with real human needs and activities—to produce for survival under primitive conditions. Those challenges led to certain divisions of labor. The way people came together to do this, in turn, shaped social relations. Their analysis explicitly included reproductive labor (the bearing and rearing of children and all that goes into caring for people in what we would now refer to as "household work"). This book certainly didn't resolve all the issues but it was a real beginning.

My next reading was Marx's *Economic and Philosophical Manuscripts of 1844*. There was a lot to love there, especially his concept of "species being." A big part of my identity, and therefore my feelings about myself, is that I'm a member of a species. That connection means that anything that harms or degrades other people also diminishes my sense of self—who I am as a human being. Our species' relationship to the rest of nature is also crucial to how I see myself. Having been surrounded by the darkness of the dominant ideology, these readings were like opening the shutters and letting in the sunshine.

Of course, it's an anomaly to name a school of thought based in historical development and collective struggle after an individual. But the word is used to stand for a specific, penetrating approach that looked at society from the standpoint of the oppressed majority, that saw class opposition and struggle as a central dynamic, that had an incisive critique of capitalism and that, very importantly, went beyond a Utopian vision to having an analysis of actual conditions and developments within capitalism that could lead to socialism becoming a real possibility.

The starting point for understanding society wasn't some mythology about God's will or pure reason or social contracts. First and foremost, people had to engage in practical activities to ensure survival and build a basis for a way of life. Social relations, ideas, and culture developed out of that primary experience. But Marx recognized that it wasn't a one-way street—once those ideas and values arose they in turn influenced how we conducted our practical activities.

Mainstream social science usually works by breaking things down to their smallest elements and then examining those in isolation. Many things can be learned that way. Marxism usually reveals a lot more by looking at how the elements interact, with an emphasis on *process*, or the development of the whole. Standard social science often projects the future by extending current trends on a straight line, with the same direction and slope. Marx saw that real world dynamics often involved oppositions and tensions that could, at certain key points, erupt into dramatic changes. For Marx, understanding the world was interactive; knowledge first and foremost was generated out of our efforts to live in the world. His method of starting with material reality but recognizing that ideas in turn could influence practical activity has been called "dialectical materialism," which can sound (and I found) pretty imposing. For myself, I preferred the term "historical materialist" to stress the centrality of understanding current reality through looking at the process of historical development.

But it wasn't the books alone that led me, that led many of us, to come to consider ourselves Marxists. In Students for a Democratic Society of the mid-1960s we flew both the black and the red flags. What tipped, what shifted the balance, was what was happening in the world: revolutions. More than a dozen were raging, and they embodied the hope of reshaping the world in a humane way. Almost all of these revolutions had a strong base in the oppressed of their countries, were pushing for fundamental change, and were led by M-L parties. It wasn't an academic or ossified Marxism but rather a vibrant, evolving analysis that provided guidance for real revolutions in progress. By the late 1960s, perhaps in too rote a fashion, we too proclaimed ourselves Marxist-Leninists.

RELATIONS OF PRODUCTION

A standard but misleading characterization of Marxism is that it's all about class. Race or gender or LGBTQ+ concerns may (or may not) be seen as important, but at the heart of capitalism and central to overthrowing it is the opposition between wage labor and capital. Some social movement activists in turn have tried to argue for the crucial role of their struggles by saying, "race is class" or "sexuality is class."

To me, the best starting point for analyzing society is Marx's "the totality of [the] relations of production," from the Preface to the *Critique of Political Economy* (1859). He zeroed in on the relationship of wage labor and capital. Naturally, as insightful as Marx was, his perspective wasn't magically untethered from being a European male. What's even more relevant to his focus was the tremendously dynamic economic and social role industrialization was playing in mid-nineteenth-century Europe. But as I understand the sum total of the relations of production, they involve a lot more.

Patriarchy preceded capitalism and provided a big part of the foundation for it. Then capitalism incorporated the subordination of women to massively exploit their unpaid reproductive labor—a giant portion of the world's work—and to impose lower pay in jobs. Homo- and transphobia have been key, often vicious, means of enforcing patriarchy along with the terribly pervasive violence against women.

Imperialism is also a fundamental relation of production with its super-exploitation of the labor force and the rip off of entire nations' and continents' natural resources. At home, the US was built on the foundation of white supremacy—with people of color in effect internal colonies—and this is a totally central and defining relation of domestic production.

And while I'm not sure exactly how to phrase it, imperialism's rapacious plunder of humanity's—along with that of all forms of life—common wealth in nature is also critical to defining today's economic and social reality. Because Marx emphasized the development of the forces of production, he is often caricatured as an advocate of unbridled industrialization. In reality, as John Bellamy Foster and others have shown, Marx had a penetrating and still useful critique of capitalism's "metabolic rift with nature," the way capitalist agriculture and industry have damaged and destroyed nature.

All these gigantic structures of ruthless oppression are fundamental to how the ruling class both maintains its power and extracts the massive profits that are the Holy Grail and core necessity for capitalism. We can see these different forms converge in how the most exploited workers, often in toxic industries, are women in the Global South. For example, those employed in the firetrap garment factories of Bangladesh, working seventy-hour weeks and getting paid $73 a month.

Even more than an astute textual analysis, this fuller and more applicable understanding of Marx was mainly a response to the world we live in. By far the leading, most revolutionary struggles of the day were the national liberation movements in the Global South. Within the US, genocide and slavery were the foundation of the society and continue to structure political developments. Those of us steeped in antiracism became painfully aware of the history of promising radical movements within the US—labor, populism, women's suffrage—that got coopted with concessions to whites at the expense and exclusion of people of color.

The system is like an airplane in that it fully needs wings and a body and an engine to be able to fly. Patriarchy, imperialism, white supremacy, class exploitation and environmental havoc intersect and reinforce each other in many ways but cannot be reduced to any one of them. Such a reduction would lead us to miss the scope of demands and mobilizations needed to build toward revolution, to fail in grasping the importance and complications of putting together coalitions, and to deny the necessity of struggling against the ways we have internalized class/race/gender privilege and arrogance. On the other hand, recognizing the essential roles of all these areas can help us expand the number of people and range of struggles that can work together to overthrow this mega-destructive system.

WAGED AND UNWAGED LABOR

The advent of capitalism was marked by a change in the characteristic way the ruling class extracted value from those who do the work. Under feudalism wealth was based on the land, and serfs and peasants had to turn over a major portion of the product of their labor to the lords. The exploitation was very visible in the days of the week they worked on the lord's estate and/or the portion of their product they turned over to him. Under capitalism that exploitation is masked in that workers "get paid for their labor" to produce commodities that are sold. But in reality the worker gets paid less than the value of what he or she produces; that difference is the surplus value kept by the capitalists, which is the basis for profits and can also be distributed for other non-work income such as rent and interest payments.

A basic way capitalism keeps wages low and undermines workers' ability to fight onerous conditions is what Marx called "the reserve army of labor": the unemployed and underemployed, as well as other potential pools of labor such as peasants (small farmers) being driven off the land. Thus, official unemployment figures way understate the number of potential job seekers. With so many people looking for jobs, those who have them and need them to support their families are in precarious positions that severely weaken their bargaining power. The size of the reserve army will vary according to economic and political conditions, but unemployment can never be eliminated under capitalism.

While the burgeoning role of wage labor characterized the emerging industrial production, the exploiters haven't been at all purist in their relentless search for profits and have incorporated, on a vast scale, other forms of labor, including women's domestic work, slavery, and peasants who produce commodities for the world market. Many of the "Marxists" saw the emblematic form—wage labor—as the whole story, the only one that creates surplus value. Marx understood that slavery and plunder were used by capitalism to extract a steep rate of exploitation and wrote (in *Capital*, Vol. I), that capitalism came into the world covered in blood and gore as it was born out of "the discovery of gold and silver in America, the extirpation, enslavement and entombment in mines of the aboriginal population, the beginning of the conquest and looting of the East Indies, the turning of Africa into a warren for the commercial hunting of black skins. . . ."

In the 1960s, we read Eric Williams' *Capitalism and Slavery*, which showed that the slave plantations in the Caribbean were the greatest sources of the profits that financed England's vaunted industrial revolution. (For a more recent and thorough description of that reality, see Walter Johnson's *River of Dark Dreams: Slavery and Empire in the Cotton Kingdom*.)

Similarly, Marx and Engels articulated, although didn't develop, the role of reproductive labor. Contemporary authors like Angela Davis, Silvia Federici, and Selma James have shown the giant role that reproductive labor plays in generating surplus value. If those who did the domestic work were paid, even just at minimum wage, the cost of maintaining the current and raising the next generation of workers would go up astronomically, and the capitalists would have to pay out much higher wages to cover that. Women's unwaged contribution to surplus value is cashed in at the point of lower wages to those in paid jobs. In addition, the oppression of women is a basis for much lower wages when in the job market, with the global average of women's wages only 52 percent of men's.

Even the old form of peasant (small farmers in the Global South) labor is used by capitalism. They may not be paid in wages but their products enter the world market at very low prices for the benefit of the transnational corporations (TNCs) in the Global North—either to provide cheap raw materials or to be processed and then resold at much higher prices. These products from the Global South sell at much lower prices relative to the labor involved than high-end products from the North. Overall the exchange is highly unequal.[3] Those who considered peasant labor as extraneous to capitalism missed this major, very profitable transfer of value via unequal exchange. In addition, there are still some 45 million human beings in 167 countries held in the thrall of outright slavery.

The "Marxists" say that the workers in the Global North are the most exploited because they have such a high level of productivity—but that is largely a product of technology, a social product associated with the accumulation of capital that has come from many sources. In those instances where such technology is employed in the Global South, workers who typically make one-tenth the wages have similar levels of output. For example, a study of autoworkers showed that those in the US are 18 percent more productive than their counterparts in Mexico, but are paid fourteen times (1,400 percent) more.[4] Similarly, if the differences were based on higher productivity in the North, then the prices on those advanced goods would have fallen relative to the Global South's labor-intensive commodities. In reality, the long-term trend in relative pricing has gone in the completely opposite direction.

In addition to these more traditional forms of labor, modern imperialism has engendered a burgeoning informal sector—those whose efforts to survive occur in areas totally outside of any government regulation or oversight. As subsistence agriculture has declined and poverty has risen in the rural areas of the Global South, hundreds of millions of people have migrated to the cities, often living in sprawling, makeshift slums, in their own slapped-together housing, with very little in the way of sanitation

---

3. Because of the stark power differential in who runs the global economy, we sometimes refer to the imperial nations as the "centers" of the system and the Global South as the "peripheries."

4. Zak Cope, *Divided World Divided Class: Global Political Economy and the Stratification of Labour Under Capitalism* (Montreal: Kersplebedeb, 2012), 241.

or other services. They become a source for completely unprotected and deleterious sweatshop labor. Even more of them live by scavenging in garbage dumps or abandoned buildings or by other recycling activities. They sell the items they find cheaply, thus lowering costs for industry or for consumers, which lowers the wage needed for survival of the workers' families. Probably the most important function of the informal sector for capitalism is that their desperation means an additional and very deep layer of the reserve army of labor.

In short, slavery, peasant labor, and women's domestic work (and now along with aspects of the informal sector) are all invaluable—and completely essential for the survival of the system— sources of capitalist profits.

CONTRADICTIONS OF CAPITALISM

Marx is most noted for his penetrating analysis of capitalism, much of which is still relevant today. His standpoint is alongside the oppressed, eloquently expressed in his vivid description of how capitalism was born dripping in blood and gore and in his biting exposé of the hellish conditions—increasingly being imposed on women and children—in Europe's factories.

His critique went beyond the brutal physical level with his explanation of alienation. Those whose labor produces society's wealth are pitted against each other by how the system generates competition to get and hold the jobs desperately needed to feed their families. Then, they have no control or even say over what gets produced, regardless of their community's needs. In fact, the more they produce the more they enhance capital's power over them. Thus, the workers are alienated from one another, from the product of their labor, and as we saw before, from their species being.

I'll resist the temptation to attempt—which would undoubtedly be unsuccessful—a brief explanation of Marxian economics, and instead try to offer a few broader points. Establishment economists, then and now, usually extol how well the system works. Marx elucidated how imbalances and instability were built into the system. And, in fact, many economic crises and upheavals have occurred. Most importantly, Marx saw these contradictions as driven by the class nature of society: the control by a small minority and their compulsion to accumulate capital can lead to all kinds of dislocations.

Some "Marxists" have reduced his analysis to a kind of iron law for a "falling rate of profit," which would inexorably lead to depression and revolution. But for Marx that was a *tendency* with various possible countermeasures. The same goes for capitalism's difficulty in selling all that it produces, at least at the expected prices. The measures to counteract these tendencies can lead to new problems.

Capital was not a work of narrow economic determinism. Instead, capitalism as an exploitative class system creates and intensifies many economic tensions which in turn can give rise to various arenas of class and social struggle. Since the nineteenth century, capitalism has developed new methods and structures—highly irrational and inhumane—such as a deepened and more integral penetration abroad and the mushrooming of waste sectors, like the sales effort, the military industrial complex, and finance at home. All of these create new or additional terrains for political struggle.

IMPERIALISM

Capitalism was a global project from the beginning, with the plunder of the Americas, Africa, and Asia providing huge amounts of capital. But several qualitative structural changes developed at the end of the nineteenth century that captured the attention of Marxists such as Vladimir Lenin and Rosa Luxemburg. Capitalism had become highly monopolized—or more accurately oligopolized, where a handful of giant firms dominate an industry—with finance capital playing a leading role. In addition to the long-standing plunder, imperialism now meant that capitalist production was more organized on a global level.

Investments in the peripheries became crucial for the centers to control the extractive industries that provided key raw materials. Many products of peasant labor were now exchanged on the world market, for use in Northern industries. With Southern labor paid at a pittance compared to the North, these new investments were highly profitable. These exploitative terms also kept raw material prices low, thereby lowering capital costs for Northern industries. This way of organizing production and guaranteeing the sanctity of investments became so essential that imperial powers fought world wars, and many smaller ones, over who controlled various highly lucrative Southern territories.

Reaping such vast riches, the imperialists were able to provide significant benefits to maintain the loyalty of their home working classes, such as the consumer society in the US and the welfare states in Europe. In the US these benefits piggybacked on top of the longstanding privileges most white workers had relative to Blacks and other people of color. For the thirty years following World War II there was a tacit pact that a large sector of white male workers could enjoy a rising "standard of living" as long as they supported the US imperial mission. Now, since the late 1970s, real wages have not been rising, and that's led to a change in the dominant politics from the old maintenance of passivity to more of a deflecting of white working-class anger away from the ruling class and toward the racial "other"—immigrants (often seen as Latino/a), "criminals" (seen as Black), and "welfare queens" (seen as Black women).

To me, the best term to name the current system is "imperialism." That underscores the global organization of production, with its high rate of exploitation and the horrendous violence used to maintain it. A defining aspect of imperialism is a polarization of wealth and power, more precipitous than the Grand Canyon, with its main divide between a few controlling centers, the banks and the TNCs in the US, Europe, and Japan, and the three-quarters of humanity who live in the peripheries. In today's world, the sixty-two richest individuals own as much wealth as the 3.6 billion people who constitute the poorest half of humanity.[5] Additionally, the class polarization within each of these arenas is steep, with elites in the Global South who collaborate with and benefit from imperialism, and with many who are oppressed in the North. The oppression and exploitation of women, while the forms may vary, are central in both arenas.

---

5. In addition to yearly income, wealth includes all assets, ranging from cars to stock holdings. The inequality of wealth is a lot greater than that of income and also more telling for life prospects.

Given these realities we can continue to look to the Global South for the fiercest battles and strongest leadership for change. At the same time, the center/periphery divide underscores the reasons that the struggles of people of color within the US, a country built on genocide, slavery, and the theft of Northern Mexico, are so central. In addition, the very rapaciousness of the system is the driving force for a reckless and now extremely dangerous destruction of the environment.

While "imperialism" might be the best, it's not an adequate way to name the system unless we're explicit about how it's been built on and incorporates patriarchy and class rule; how it's defined by the sum total of the relations of production. We have to be clear about naming and fighting all the major forms of oppression.

NATIONAL LIBERATION

The four decades that followed World War II were the most exciting and promising in world history—the era of national liberation. The imperial powers, exhausted by that cataclysmic war, could no longer maintain the dam holding back the floodwaters of uprisings for independence in Africa and Asia. The weakened colonial powers regrouped with a strategy of neocolonialism, following the example of the US in Latin America. They were willing to grant formal independence—a new flag and a native president—as long as they could continue to dominate the economy.

But many of the decolonization efforts, along with movements in Latin America, weren't settling for that. They got to the root of their problems by fighting for their nations' labor and resources to be redirected away from enriching the TNCs and back to the needs of the home populations. These national liberation movements faced fierce attacks. Usually the only way they had a chance against awesomely superior military technology was to fight a "people's war," making use of guerrilla tactics and developing an active base among the majority of their people—peasants, workers, women, youth, minorities.

From 1949–1979 such movements won in China, Ghana, Tanzania, North Korea, Algeria, Cuba, Vietnam, Laos, Cambodia, Angola, Mozambique, Guinea-Bissau/Cape Verde Islands,

Zimbabwe, and Nicaragua. Similar struggles were raging in the Philippines, Eritrea, and several countries in Latin America, while others were emerging in Palestine, Namibia, South Africa, and Northern Ireland. This range, the number of people involved, the startling victories against superior military power were breathtaking; they also provided inspiration for a proliferation of radical movements within the US, Europe, and Japan.

What made this unprecedented wave all the more earthshattering was the qualitative difference from all past revolutions where one elite replaced another (e.g., the bourgeoisie overthrowing the feudal lords). Now we had the "wretched of the earth," the most direly oppressed and the vast majority of humankind, rising up and reshaping the world in a more equitable and humane way.

As opposed to simply formal independence, the revolutionary movements were characterized by: 1) a goal of economic independence; 2) a commitment to ending illiteracy and poverty; 3) being prepared to wage guerrilla war; 4) mobilizing the oppressed majority; 5) having a formal commitment (although more limited in practice) to women's emancipation; 6) expressing solidarity with other such struggles around the world; and 7) seeing the possibility for solidarity and radical movements within the imperial nations. Almost all the struggles with such programs were led by Marxist-Leninist parties.

Events in the real world seemed to contradict established theories. Traditional Marxists had held that socialist revolution could not happen in such economically backward countries. The prerequisites for socialism were seen to include advanced industry, an educated population, and a more or less unified working class that comprised the majority of the population. The countries in the peripheries were economically impoverished, with widespread illiteracy, and usually comprised of a small working class and a large peasant majority. So it wasn't just Northern "Marxists" but also many communist parties in the Global South that asserted that socialism could not be on the agenda until these countries first had a bourgeois revolution led by the national capitalist class.

Some more realistic and creative Marxist-Leninists refuted the conventional wisdom because waiting for the bourgeois revolution was like waiting for hell to freeze over. As Che Guevara and others explained, the realities of imperialism had demolished the road to capitalist development in the Global South. Not only did imperialism extract vast wealth that these countries needed for development, but it also channeled economic activity away from building the home economy and instead toward exports that benefited the TNCs—the extraction of raw material and low-level, labor-intensive manufacture. Most of the local elites were closely tied to imperialism, so there was no strong national capitalist class to lead a bourgeois revolution. The unforgiving nature of this structure of exploitation was enforced by more than 50 US interventions since the end of World War II to overthrow or block Southern regimes that tried to redirect economic activity toward domestic needs.[6] The Soviet Union was another important factor. Under incredible pressure, it had devolved, in my opinion, into more of a bureaucratic state than a socialist society. Nonetheless, the USSR opposed US hegemony and provided significant military and economic aid to many national liberation movements.

The national liberation movements couldn't wait for a bourgeois revolution that would never happen, but for all the earlier stated reasons they weren't in a position to achieve socialism. Instead, their historic task was, as Mao Tse Tung put it, "New Democracy" (the Vietnamese called it "National Democracy") to accomplish the progressive tasks of the bourgeois revolution: reclaim self-determination and a national direction for production, "Land to the Tiller[7]," the emancipation of women, universal education, political experience and participation for the masses of people. Since these New Democratic revolutions were based in the lower classes, the reforms would be more thoroughgoing and entail giant social advances—and the changes would be structured to be most favorable to lead into the next stage, the transition to socialism.

---

6. During this time, Monthly Review Press in New York became the de facto source for literature on how imperialism kept these countries impoverished. For example, Andre Gunder Frank's analysis of "the development of underdevelopment" was featured on the cover of *Monthly Review*, Vol. 18, No. 4 in September 1966. See https://monthlyreviewarchives.org/index.php/mr/article/view/MR-018-04-1966-08_3

7. Editors' note: "Land to the Tiller" is a 1970s US-backed Vietnamese land reform designed to redistribute land to farmers. However, it was intended for the US to take peasant support away from the Vietcong during the Vietnam War.

How could impoverished peripheral countries feel that they had any chance at all against the imperial Goliaths? A strategy to win emerged out of the realities on the ground, such as with Che's "two, three, many Vietnams." Even the mighty imperial octopus couldn't wage multiple wars abroad against simultaneous popular revolutions. The very extent of its lucrative outreach was also its vulnerability because the arms could be chopped off, eventually draining the blood needed to sustain the head. This approach was having dramatic success. At the same time, Black and other people of color rebellions, along with a number of emerging radical movements within the US, challenged the system with an additional and debilitating internal front.

NATIONAL LIBERATION AND SOCIALISM

By 1980, a dozen revolutions had taken power, while similar struggles were raging in a dozen more. In contrast, even while there were some vital struggles, there hadn't been a single working class revolution in Europe or the US. This overwhelming empirical reality didn't deter Northern "Marxists" from insisting that the working classes in the advanced countries would make the revolution. While also calling themselves "Leninists," they did not incorporate Lenin's analysis of the impact of imperial profits on the home working class, an obstacle that had only grown, immensely, since Lenin's day.

Those of us who understood the priority of solidarity with national liberation—not simply because they were struggles for social justice but even more as the route to weakening imperialism enough to break open revolutionary potential at home—tended to be too facile about a direct road to socialism. Looking back, it's clear that the promising strategy of "two, three, many Vietnams" hasn't defeated imperialism and that even the liberated countries are a far cry from socialism. On the most negative side, a few have devolved into dictatorships, most prominently North Korea, while Cambodia was taken over by genocidal criminals.

In almost all other cases, the victories meant dramatic advances for the people with the launching of successful mass literacy campaigns, establishing health clinics in rural areas, and advances for women's rights and participation. Inevitably, some of these rights were eroded once the new regimes consolidated power.

China has become an economic powerhouse, something that would have been impossible if it had remained under the imperial thrall, but at the expense of intense exploitation of its working class and growing inequality. In many ways it seems to be a state capitalist regime. For the other liberated countries, while there have been important social advances, there's been precious little in the way of achieving autonomous and thriving economies, or even having a conscious and mobilized majority playing a determining role in political and economic decisions. Assessing what happened merits a book, at least, in itself. Here I'll just mention some of the factors, under two broad categories: the assaults by imperialism and underdevelopment's legacy of damage and distortion.

Imperialism doesn't just give up once the revolutionary movement seizes state power. As with any extortion racket, it exacts brutal and visible punishment on those who try to opt out in order to show they won't achieve a better life for their people. That's why long after the US realized it would have to withdraw from Vietnam, it continued its unprecedentedly massive bombings and chemical ecocide. Some farmland there still can't be used because of the danger of unexploded bombs that lie buried in the ground, even though these are just a tiny percentage of all the bombs dropped. And Vietnam still is dealing with the tragedy of babies being born with birth defects due to the residue of Agent Orange in the water supply.

Cuba has been perhaps the most promising example of mass participation, free education through graduate school, excellent medical care for all, and a magnificent internationalism that played a key role in defeating both Portuguese colonialism and the apartheid regime in Southern Africa. But Cuba has had to deal with incessant CIA-sponsored invasions, assassination attempts, and economic sabotage—all of which push the government to become more repressive—on top of a crippling economic blockade.

Nicaragua, Angola, and Mozambique's dramatic advances in literacy, health and women's rights were soon beset upon and then severely set back by CIA-sponsored terrorists who, amid wholesale attacks on civilians, went after village health and educational workers in particular. In addition, imperialism will do anything in its power, with its bountiful assets, to promote internal antagonisms based on tribal or ethnic or religious differences. This basic divide-and-conquer strategy is used not only against revolutionary governments but also against any Southern regime (and also Yugoslavia in Europe) that doesn't fall into line with the dictates of the world market and US military domination.

If the only obstacles were sabotage and terrorist attacks, the mass-based revolutions would have prevailed, but the newly liberated nations were also being strangled by economic embargoes and the tyrannies of the world market. Embargoes can mean that these still-poor countries can't get the spare parts needed to keep the limited machinery they do have up and running and can only access sorely needed medications at exorbitant prices. Small, poor countries can't develop such technologically advanced sectors overnight. And in many ways, they still have to function in a capitalist world market where the centuries-long trend has been for businesses in the centers to extract raw materials and labor-intensive goods from the peripheries.

The inequities of the world market compounded with the ravages of underdevelopment not only constrict economic advances but are also reflected in society. While the revolution may have launched successful literacy campaigns, only a small elite has the level of technical skills key for organizing production and the state. Internal class divisions and patriarchy are still major forces. Despite some inspiring examples of solving problems through mass participation, the tremendous pressure to get the economy going leads to reliance on an elite with managerial skills.

Meanwhile the military attacks evoke a consolidation of the repressive capabilities of the state. In a situation where social and economic advances are being stymied, some formerly self-sacrificing cadres become susceptible to corruption from the blandishments of the TNCs seeking to re-implant their tentacles into these still juicy Southern morsels. This formidable series of barriers doesn't mean that the road to socialism is impossible, but it sure is a complication, contested, difficult route. National liberation struggles, against all apparent odds, made dramatic advances and inspired a vision of potential world revolution, but we're still a long, long way from socialism.

REVOLUTIONARY VISION

The prospects for humanity are not as grim as our historical and contemporary problems would imply, and Marxist theory can be helpful in unlocking today's revolutionary potential. The "Marxists" were wrong in insisting the revolution would be made by the working classes of the imperial nations. Those of us inspired by how the national liberation movements lit up the world were overly optimistic about their potential to debilitate imperialism and move quickly to building socialism. In a way, both errors came from a failure to recognize how much capitalism is a world economy, even while political realities necessitated fighting these battles out on national terrains. Today's world is characterized by a major contradiction between the now-global organization of production and the continuation of political and cultural formations on the national level.

Marx saw that capitalism was moving in a global direction. In *The Communist Manifesto* (1848), he writes, "The need of a constantly expanding market for its products chases the bourgeoisie over the entire surface of the globe. It must nestle everywhere, settle everywhere, establish connections everywhere." Marx's *Capital* was intended to be the first part of a series of works (never completed) projected to end with a volume on the world market. But Marx's own views were mixed and in flux as to what degree globalization would bring industrialization to the peripheries or alternatively exploit them for agricultural products. Similarly, while not uniform, much of his writing implied a vision that workers of all nations, genders, and ages would increasingly find themselves in similar situations: poorly paid and unskilled appendages to the relentless machines of industrial production, with their jobs and lives made increasingly precarious via a large reserve army of labor. In contrast, the world today is one of multiple and tremendous variations in life experiences, income, power of workers in different jobs and locations. The biggest divide is between North and South, but within each of these spheres there's a multiplicity of divisions and fragmentations in workers' roles and circum-stances. To assess this situation, it helps to first correct a prevail-ing, gross misconception about Marx's theory of revolution.

Mainstream political science when I went to college, and probably still today, dismissed Marx's theory of revolution in about one paragraph. The refutation went that it was based on his pre-diction of the immiseration of the proletariat: capitalism's drive to lower wages, the way advanced machinery eliminated jobs, and the periodic economic crises would all push the conditions of the workers down to bare subsistence or below. That, supposedly, was the situation that would lead the proletariat to rise up. But clearly, the professors would intone, the workers have never been better off. Maybe that has to be modified now with stagnating real wages since 1980, but most people with jobs in the US are not being pushed below subsistence level and many sectors are still living fairly well.

The standard truisms are radically untrue in two basic ways:

1. Capitalism is a global economy, which undermines the very survival of the vast majority of workers, who reside in the Global South (along with many in the Global North)–whether small farmers and agricultural workers, laborers in mines and factories, or the hundreds of millions in the informal sector eking out existences in sweatshops or scavenging in garbage dumps. R. Jamil Jonna and John Bellamy Foster estimate the global reserve army of labor as 2.3 billion people.[8] Some 4.3 billion, 60 percent of the world's population, live on less than $5 a day, 1.2 billion of whom are living on less than $1.25 a day. For these billions of human beings life is precarious indeed.

2. Marx's theory of revolution was never based simply on im-miseration. If oppression were enough, it would have been the peasants who overthrew feudalism. They did have many

---

8. R. Jamil Jonna and John Bellamy Foster, "Marx's Theory of Working-Class Precariousness: Its Relevance Today," *Monthly Review*, vol. 67, no. 11 (April 2016),https:// monthlyreview.org/2016/04/01/marxs-theory-of-working-class-precariousness/. The authors provide a much fuller and more nuanced discussion than mine of the concept and how it plays out in the global economy.

heroic rebellions, but back then it was the bourgeoisie who led the revolution that created the new society. The reason was that new forces of production had been emerging involving dynamic trade routes and a proliferating number of commodities made in workshops. Feudalism, with power and control residing in landed estates, became a barrier to this growing trade and "manufacture" (initially meaning produced by hand). The bourgeoisie was the revolutionary class because they could reorganize society in a way that unchained this emerging commodity and trade-based mode.

As capitalism matured, it in turn created increasingly social forces of production. Large numbers of people were brought together to work in giant factories. Since a varied number of processes had to be coordinated, communication and transportation systems were created that closely connected people across nations and continents. For Marx, the central contradiction of capitalism was between this increasingly social production and the prevailing private appropriation, the control of it all by a small minority for their own profit. As this tension grew, it got expressed in society in a range of ways—economic crises, wars, labor struggles, political upheavals. The workers who produced the wealth found themselves in increasingly precarious circumstances.

The proletariat was the revolutionary class because they were the social class; they were the ones who could reorganize society on the social basis needed to overcome the mounting crises and move forward. Even though they had to compete against each other for jobs, they were the ones brought together, in large numbers and with increasingly complicated interaction, to work together. In addition, as they faced harsh conditions, they learned to join together in collective action to form unions, carry out strikes, become politically active. In one way, this emergence was qualitatively different from all past transformations: for the first time in history the revolutionary class consisted of the vast majority and the most exploited. They embodied the potential for reorganizing society on an egalitarian basis that would eventually abolish class divisions altogether.

SOCIALIZATION VS. FRAGMENTATION

Today, socialization of production has proceeded to an almost unimaginable degree. When you buy an iPhone, the coltan ore was mined in the Democratic Republic of the Congo; over a hundred different components were made in countries such as South Korea, Singapore and Japan; the parts were assembled in China; the apps were written in Silicon Valley; the advertising campaign designed on Madison Avenue; the financing arranged on Wall Street; and the call-in service centers set up in Mumbai. Indeed, one of many ways this arrangement is very antisocial is the environmental costs of all the global transports involved.

But the same example shows how capitalism has moved in exactly the opposite direction of putting workers of all nations and backgrounds into a common situation. We now have unprecedented fragmentation with a mind-numbing variety of different roles, pay levels, statuses, circumstances. Patriarchy and white supremacy provide major structural differences, but that's not all. Each of the blocks of this prison has a number of different floors and cells within it—giving us a multiplicity of divisions and subdivisions. We've noted that rulers assiduously cultivate tribal, ethnic, and religious antagonisms. In addition, even within the working class of a given nation, there are major differences in role, pay, and status ranging from high-tech honchos to home health aides. In some ways the high rates of exploitation of people of color and women throughout the world support the pay and status of large swaths of workers in parasitic sectors in the centers—like advertising, finance, the military-industrial complex, the criminal justice apparatus—engendering their backward sense of superiority and thereby their loyalty to the system.

In the US, a clear political recognition of the multiple ways people are oppressed and how they intersect emerged out of the women of color movement in the late 1970s. Some critics felt that such an articulation was divisive and ran counter to the universality of all people, or at least of the vast majority who were working class. (Of course most of these women of color were working class.) Certainly, what's now called "identity politics" can be divisive if and when it shifts the focus from fighting the system as a whole to simply having comfortable cultural enclaves and when it's centered in distinctions from other oppressed sectors. At the same time, it's healthy and necessary for those who are oppressed to be the ones who articulate their issues and aspirations and how those different oppressions intersect various people in a range of ways. The white and male dominated unions and political organizations were not universalist. Real unity, real universalism must be built from the bottom up. Raising those concerns isn't divisive; what's divisive, and perniciously so, is racism, sexism, elitism, homophobia, transphobia, ableism.

Activists with this perspective have articulated that our fight is against capitalism, white supremacy and patriarchy—which is a good way to capture those pernicious structures that reinforce each other. But we need to be explicit that our framework isn't simply within the US; we are fighting a global system of imperialism, which ruthlessly exploits three-quarters of humankind while also recklessly destroying the environment.

TOWARD A HUMANE AND SUSTAINABLE FUTURE

Our situation today entails the most colossal contradiction between social production and private appropriation. We have the integration, involving almost instantaneous means of global communication, of the efforts of hundreds of millions of workers controlled by the mega-rich few who push the majority to mere subsistence or below and who wreak havoc on the earth as a habitat for humanity and countless other species. The macabre irrationality of the system is expressed in inexcusable waste alongside massive deprivation, incessant wars, periodic economic crises, the breakdown of earlier generations' sense of community and comity, and more. Never have we had a greater ability to meet human needs and yet never have so many needlessly suffered.

The challenge for revolutionaries is to build unity on a principled and lasting basis. That hasn't been achieved by denying differences. The long march to human liberation must smash through each of the many walls of oppression. Nor can we rely on economic depressions to do the job for us. History has shown that the imperial rulers can take white working-class frustrations from economic stress and redirect the anger by means of fascist scapegoating of the racial "other."

The current situation is dangerous and daunting, but not cause for despair. If we don't fight, we're doomed. If we do fight, we have a chance, especially given all the unpredictable twists and turns of history. As ferocious as imperialism may be, it's also unstable and volatile. The great, if far from fully tapped, power on our side is that the vast majority of people have a fundamental and increasingly urgent interest in revolutionary change. I'm certainly not able to outline a grand strategy, but I want to mention a couple of key elements, some initial wisps that are potential precursors toward forming the mighty, cleansing wind we need.

Overall, I don't think we're still in the era of national liberation. The challenges of moving out of underdevelopment may be too much for small and/or poor countries given imperial attacks and the inequities of the world market. One counterstrategy would be to build regional blocs—say much of Africa or of Latin America—to be big enough to largely replace investments and trade from the North. Given the range of political regimes and interests involved, forming such a bloc is extremely difficult. And imperialism has targeted any government that leads in that direction, regardless of whether it is authoritarian (e.g., Qaddafi in Libya) or democratic (e.g., Chavez in Venezuela).

I still believe, emphatically, that the front line of struggle is between imperialism and the peoples of the South. That's where the horror of contemporary capitalism is most glaring, where the consciousness has been highest, where the confrontations have been the most intense. Although we don't hear much about them in the corporate media, thousands of promising Indigenous, women's, environmental, food sovereignty, and workers' (very much including China) struggles are in motion around the world.[9] A few examples include women's cooperatives reclaiming land for local food needs in the Rishi Valley in southern India; the Mangrove Association fighting to protect the environment in Lower Lempa,

---

9. A number of such struggles are briefly described in the 2016 *Certain Days: Freedom for Political Prisoners* calendar. Every year the theme changes; in 2016 it was "Internationalism, Solidarity and Global Struggle" [when this essay was first written] and in 2020 it was "Knitting Together the Struggles."

El Salvador; the democratic and women-empowering Rojava Revolution in northern Syria; the Unist'ot'en Indigenous encampment resisting Canada's tar sands and fracking projects; community efforts to develop food sovereignty in Kenya; and the Via Campesina union of peasants and small farmers from seventy-three countries. I don't know how this myriad of little rivulets might come together to form a mighty stream, but they are beginning to irrigate the soil for revolutionary shoots to grow.

Within the US in this period, Black Lives Matter is especially needed and exciting. We also have a range of other promising efforts on the environment, the criminal justice system, LGBTQ+ equality and more. We're still grappling with how to form a vision that brings together these disparate efforts as well as with how to build organizations that are both democratic and effective, even when under intense pressure.

The two needed elements I'll mention are that all forms of oppression have to be challenged and that internationalism is a necessary cutting edge. Whatever we can do to blunt the attacks emanating from our country can make a big difference for embattled movements in the Global South. Far from solidarity being 'us' deigning to help 'them,' it's their struggles that are cutting out a path toward a more humane and sustainable world for all of us. The mounting catastrophe of climate change—mainly caused by profligacy in the North but most lethal in the South—is an issue that can unite all the oppressed against this clear and present danger.

CONCLUSION

Many of the examples of Marxist-Leninist formations make it tempting to echo Marx in saying, "I'm not a Marxist."[10] I'm not either, if Marxism is understood as a pat dogma, as small sects vying to claim leadership of the movement and carrying out political debates by citing opposing quotes from old texts, and especially when it's used as a "revolutionary" rationale for continuing white and male domination. At the same time, I would encourage today's activists not to lose a treasure trove in both method and

---

10. As reported by Engels, Marx said this when in the midst of a frustrating political struggle with some sectarian French Marxists.

many specifics of analysis by dismissing Marxism out of hand. Of course, there are still many unresolved issues. One in particular that has divided anarchists and Marxists is form of organization. I didn't address that above because I don't have much that's helpful to say, except that so far both models seem inadequate to me.

The question looming over us is how to overcome the multiplicity of stratifications, fragmentations, and antagonisms that divide the vast majority of humankind who are oppressed and exploited. This challenge requires engaged, thoughtful practice and creative thinking by all of us. Regardless of whether one is steeped in Marxism, the reality is that we face the gargantuan earthquake fault of the contradiction between social production and private appropriation. The global forces that are now in play are of such magnitude that the continued control by a few whose main goal is profit constitutes an existential threat for humanity. The challenge is to overcome the divisions. To do so in solidarity with the Global South is crucial, to make a difference in their prospects and at the same time for us to be able to advance at home.

Given how world capitalism is hurtling toward ecological crises, we can join Marx's, "There's a world to win" with "There's a world to save!"[11]

---

11. With big thank yous to Dan Berger, Terry Bisson, Kathy Boudin, Chris Dixon, Sara Falconer, Laura Foner, Naomi Jaffe, Karl Kersplebedeb, Vicki Legion, Elana Levy, Rob McBride, Molly McClure, Hilary Moore, Alexis Shotwell, and Victor Wallis.

OUT OF THE SHADOW OF CASTE
AND INTO OUR CONSCIOUSNESS

Priti Gulati Cox

Nobody is me, there are many like me. My life has no worth in my country's popular consciousness and my violators roam freely. I am a Dalit, an Adivasi, and no upper-caste hands hold signs with our names.

I live and die and am reborn in their shadow....their calculating minds, their violent arms, their rapist's thighs, their trampling feet. This soil was once my fertile soil and I walked upon it. Now their collective usurpation has replaced it with chemicals and concrete. And I lie upon it, my feet pointing up at their mind's gods, waiting to be recognized as a victim of their discrimination. My hands' actions contradict my dignity and humanity. These are not my arms, but some upper-caste's other two arms. A mechanical bonus pair, like the Hindu goddesses. A surplus, to be manipulated any which way. My fate is as old as the Hindu scriptures that gave me these wretched arms, and their usurpers have evolved. My once-sympathetic Shudra comrades, born of Purusha's feet are now the postnineties neo-Brahmins that stomp on my assertive words of equality with neoviolence.

I show up sometimes as the spirit of unity and solidarity in Declaration of Empathy petitions, but I am still the more than three hundred thousand defeated hearts of the World Conference against Racism, Racial Discrimination, Xenophobia, and Related Intolerance, which failed to recognize me as a victim of descent-based discrimination. Maybe my place is at the back of those 'I Am' signs, scribbled in invisible ink: Nobody is Me, There Are Many Like Me.

DEMOCRACY AGAINST REPRESENTATION

A RADICAL REALIST VIEW

Paul Raekstad

A concept is a brick. It can be used to build a courthouse of reason.

Or it can be thrown through the window.

— Brian Massumi[1]

The New Democracy Movement started something that we're still seeing play out around the world. Since the Arab Spring, the Movement of the Squares, Occupy and beyond, radical movements have been calling for "democracy." In areas as diverse as Tunisia, Egypt, Greece, Spain, and the United States, "each of these movements has brought democracy into question."[2] Marina Sitrin and Dario Azzellini go on to write:

> A uniting agenda is that of challenging rule by politicians: we can govern ourselves. Movement participants around the world believe that representative democracies are not democratic, and that established politicians and political institutions should not be trusted. Instead, most of the new movements

---

1. Brian Massumi, "Translator's Introduction," from Giles Deleuze and Felix Guattari, *A Thousand Plateaus: Capitalism and Schizophrenia* (Minneapolis: University of Minnesota Press, 1987), xii.

2. Marina Sitrin and Dario Azzellini, *They Can't Represent Us!: Reinventing Democracy From Greece to Occupy* (London: Verso, 2014), 10.

practice forms of direct democracy in public spaces. . . . In this way, the political, economic, and social spheres are no longer separated. In fact, this practice is grounded in a long global history. . . . Nevertheless, the embrace of direct and participatory democracy is one of the most strikingly novel aspects of today's global movements.[3]

Similarly, Jerome Roos and Leonidas Oikonomakis write that by "refusing to align themselves with any political party or ideology," the movements "challenged the legitimacy of prevalent power structures," revealing "a profound crisis of representation in democratic capitalist society."[4] In so doing, these movements repeated calls for a society ruled for and by the people—in the same way that earlier revolutionary organizations called for "social democracy."[5] Paradoxically to some, these movements also claimed to reject representation and their more radical members used to

3. Sitrin and Azzellini, *They Can't Represent Us!*, 10; see also Jerome Roos and Leonidas Oikonomakis, "They Don't Represent Us! The Global Resonance of the Real Democracy Movement from the Indignados to Occupy," in *Spreading Protest: Social Movements in Times of Crisis*, (eds.) Donatella della Porta and Alice Mantonini (Essex: ECPR Press, 2014), 117–136.

4. Roos and Oikonomakis, "They Don't Represent Us!," 118. This essay focuses on movements like the Movement of the Squares and Occupy, which the authors have some experience with and about which a lot has been written. Having said that, a great number of other very important movements also have (among other things) a radical democratic politics at their core, such as Nouvel Debout, Black Lives Matter [see Keeanga-Yamahtta Taylor, *From #BlackLivesMatter to Black Liberation* (Chicago: Haymarket Books, 2016)], and a variety of movements and organizations covered by what Chris Dixon has called "the antiauthoritarian current of North American social movements" [in *Another Politics: Talking Across Today's Transformative Movements* (Oakland: University of California Press, 2014).] I don't know whether the argument of this article will be relevant to all of these, and in any case that's a decision that can only be made by people and movements themselves. This article addresses itself to any and all contemporary anticapitalist and antistate movement participants that are considering, among other things, using a radical concept of democracy as part of their critique of contemporary society, and it wants to avoid labeling or deciding exactly who might or might not count as part of this. To the extent that various groups and activists are interested in a radical concept of "democracy" that can be used to critique the basic structures of our society—including but not limited to capitalism and the state—I'm hoping they find it to offer some interesting ideas and suggestions.

5. For instance, many early revolutionary Marxist parties called themselves "Social Democratic," and the revolutionary anarchist organization Bakunin founded before joining the First International was called the "International Alliance of Socialist Democracy."

reject states altogether—a keystone of many contemporary liberal understandings of democracy.

How can we make sense of this and what can we, as partici-pants in contemporary movements, learn from them today? This article tries to contribute to that development by reconstructing an idea of what I think we should take "democracy" to mean, how we can use this concept to make sense of the critique of rep-resentation prominent in many recent and contemporary radical movements, and examine how it can help to guide social change and the practices seeking to bring it about.[6] My investigation will be "realist" in the sense that it contributes a piece of political the-ory that seeks to make sense in terms of and guide real politics.[7] In this view, real politics is fundamentally about how human actions and interactions are organized, coordinated, and carried out. More precisely, it centers on three related questions: (1) the agents and contexts of political action; (2) the timing of such actions; and (3) their motivation, justification, and legitimation.[8] The main goal of this article is to develop and defend a radical concept of democracy that's drawn from the ideas and practices of a range of radical movements today, which can help to further make sense of and guide our politics. Despite first appearanc-es, I will argue that a coherent conception of democracy can be found—a notion of democracy as collective self-rule—and that it can be a powerful tool for understanding and critiquing the shortcomings of contemporary societies as well as for guiding our efforts to overcome them.[9]

---

6. This article is written from the perspective of a participant in some of these move-ments, particularly in Britain, with experience from the student movement, Occupy, and the radical labor movement, as well as a couple of different libertarian socialist organiza-tions. None of this gives me any particular position or authority from which to be writing this, but the question of democracy as a political value of and for radical movements keeps coming up, and I would like to present some useful ideas in that regard.

7. See Raymond Geuss, *Philosophy and Real Politics* (Princeton, NJ: Princeton University Press, 2008), and Paul Raekstad, "Two Contemporary Approaches to Political Theory," *International Critical Thought*, Volume 5, Issue 2 (2015): 226–240.

8. See Geuss, *Philosophy and Real Politics*, Part I.

9. Let me stress that my purpose here is to develop a *concept of democracy* to be used for certain evaluative and practical purposes. I am not attempting to say anything de-tailed about certain kinds of things (e.g., certain institutions) that may or may not call themselves "democracies."

WHAT IS DEMOCRACY?

The modern concept of democracy is vague, complicated, and often contradictory. It's associated with a variety of different things: the ancient and radical enlightenment idea of the collective self-rule of a group of people; the idea of voting for your rulers and administrators, or at least some of them; the acknowledgment and securing of certain political freedoms like speech, press, conviction, et cetera; and it is associated with a variety of other values such as freedom, equality, and solidarity. It would be very odd if all of these things occurred together, either always or in general. I think this is one of the reasons why a lot of everyday usage of the term as well as a large amount of the academic—especially normative and philosophical—literature on democracy conflates and confuses a variety of different things. In particular, much of the contemporary philosophical or political-theoretical work on democracy simply assumes—absent evidence or argument—that letting people vote for representatives is sufficient for them to have real powers to determine their governments' deliberation and decision making.[10] As we have seen, this is precisely what many participants in contemporary social movements reject, and as I'll discuss below, it's demonstrably false.

Can we, in spite of this, reconstruct a clear meaning that makes sense for, and is relevant to, the ones we see in contemporary radical movements? I think that we can, provided we don't try to do the impossible: analyze the word as it is used and assume that we have to come up with a definition that fits every single

---

10. Sometimes this is made explicit by normatively focused philosophers, and other times it's an unstated assumption. Richard Arneson, for instance, writes, "The vote in a serious political election is one among many that together determine rules that constrain citizens' conduct and life options in obvious and palpable ways. The vote gives each citizen of a democracy a tiny bit of the political power a dictator or powerful monarch possesses." [See Richard Arneson, "Defending the Purely Instrumental Account of Democratic Legitimacy," *Journal of Political Philosophy* 11 (2003): 125.] Similarly, Ronald Dworkin claims that, in modern states, the vote guarantees a degree of political influence to all people. [See Ronald Dworkin, *Sovereign Virtue*, (Cambridge, MA: Harvard University Press, 2003), 202.] And also, see Thomas Christiano, who writes, "it is because voting power is widely distributed that public deliberation on a wide scale exists at all." [Thomas Christiano, "The Significance of Public Deliberation," in *Deliberative Democracy*, eds. James Bohman and William Rehg (Cambridge, MA: MIT Press, 1997), 251.]

intuition and application of it. Instead, what I'll try to do here is to refine or develop *a concept* of democracy that is coherent, usefully connected to much of its past and present usage, that avoids the naïve identification of democracy with either representative or direct institutional forms, that usefully captures what many contemporary radical movements want to do with it (such as critique contemporary states and capitalism), and that can answer the objections put forward by critics.

My starting point for developing a concept of democracy is the traditional definition of democracy as the collective self-rule of a group of people. In Europe, this word and its concept originate in ancient Greece, with discussions about how to structure independent cities, the *polis*. There were, according to ancient Greek thinkers, three main ways in which a polis could be structured. A polis could be a monarchy, an aristocracy, or a democracy. This is fundamentally a question about who holds power within the polis. If one person holds all of the power within the polis it is a monarchy, if a minority of people—the few—hold power within the polis it is an aristocracy, and if all people—the many—hold power within the polis it is a democracy.[11]

This concept is taken up by the radical Enlightenment tradition from Spinoza through to Marx, but now gets expanded to thinking about issues of how to organize human societies on much larger scales.[12] For these ancient and radical Enlightenment thinkers, democracy refers to the collective self-rule of a group of people. A society is a democracy if and only if all of its members rule; if they do not, it is either a monarchy or an oligarchy. Democracy, in this sense, is a question of power—it's about who has it and who doesn't.

---

11. For proper discussion of this and more, see: Herman Mogens Hansen, *The Athenian Democracy in the Age of Demosthenes: Structure, Principles, and Ideology* (Oxford: Basil Blackwell, 1991).

12. See Jonathan Israel, *Radical Enlightenment: Philosophy and the Making of Modernity 1650–1750* (Oxford: Oxford University Press, 2001); *Enlightenment Contested: Philosophy, Modernity, and the Emancipation of Man 1670–1752* (Oxford: Oxford University Press, 2006); *A Revolution of the Mind: Radical Enlightenment and the Intellectual Origins of Modern Democracy* (Princeton, NJ: Princeton University Press, 2009); and *Democratic Enlightenment: Philosophy, Revolution, and Human Rights 1750–1790* (Oxford: Oxford University Press, 2011).

It was this notion of democracy the US founding fathers had in mind when they modeled their new constitution on the political structure of the British Empire, with the explicit aim of *preventing democracy*, and the debt cancellations they feared would follow. Instead, they wanted a republic, a "balanced" form of government really ruled only by and for wealthy white men, and feared the burgeoning democratic movements they saw around them.[13]

The systematic exclusion and suppression of key segments of the population—in particular people of color, working-class people, and women—persisted as a pillar of a republic built on slavery and settler colonial genocide.[14] One important part of this is what's sometimes called the "Wages of Whiteness," described by W. E. B. Du Bois as follows:

> It must be remembered that the white group of laborers, while they received a low wage, were compensated in part by a sort of public and psychological wage. They were given public deference and titles of courtesy because they were white. They were admitted freely with all classes of white people to public functions, public parks, and the best schools. The police were drawn from their ranks, and the courts, dependent upon their votes, treated them with such leniency as to encourage lawlessness. Their vote selected public of officials, and while this had small effect upon the economic situation, it had great effect upon their personal treatment and the deference shown them.[15]

Joel Olson writes, on this view, the "wages of whiteness literally pay off in terms of higher wages, two-tiered wage scales, exclusive access to certain jobs, and informal unemployment insurance," along with ensuring "access to land, capital, and markets to those who can afford them" and granting "whites an elevated

13. See Woody Holton, "'Divide et Impera': 'Federalist 10' in a Wider Sphere," *The William and Mary Quarterly*, 3rd ser., 62, no. 2 (2005): 175–212; David Graeber, *The Democracy Project* (London: Allen Lane, 2012), Chapter 3; and Ellen Meiksins Wood, *Democracy Against Capitalism: Renewing Historical Materialism* (Cambridge, Cambridge University Press, 1996), especially 204-237.

14. Patrick Wolfe, "Settler colonialism and the elimination of the native," *Journal of Genocide Research*, Volume 8, Issue 4 (2006): 387–409.

15. W. E. B. Du Bois, *Black Reconstruction in America 1860–1880* (New York: The Free Press, 1998), 700–701.

social status."[16] Furthermore, "[t]his devil's bargain has under-mined freedom and democracy in the US ever since." [17] What is sometimes called "white democracy" can be viewed as one part of an elite-led effort to prevent democracy. "White democracy" is no democracy at all. Even today, David Graeber writes, "there's nothing that scares the rulers of America more than the prospect of democracy breaking out."[18]

Looking back, there is reason to think these efforts were suc-cessful. Even after extending suffrage and (a few) basic political rights to women, people of color, and the area's few remaining original inhabitants, the latest evidence suggests that the majority of the United States' population has little influence on their rep-resentatives' actions—unlike a wealthy minority who strongly and consistently assert their influence. Martin Gilens and Benjamin Page conclude their study examining the ability of different seg-ments of the US-American population to affect government action with the following observation: "when the preferences of econom-ic elites and the stands of organized interest groups are controlled for, the preferences of the average American appear to have only a minuscule, near-zero, statistically nonsignificant impact upon public policy."[19]

They go on to suggest "that majorities of the American pub-lic actually have little influence over the policies our government adopts," and this means "America's claims to being a democratic

---

16. Joel Olson, *The Abolition of White Democracy* (Minneapolis, MN: University of Minnesota Press, 2004), 13.

17. Joel Olson, "Whiteness and the 99%," October 23, 2011, available at https://libcom. org/library/whiteness-99-joel-olson.

18. Graeber, *The Democracy Project*, xiv. Note that the sense in which Graeber here uses the term "democracy" is one according to which the past and present United States is not a democracy. In Graeber's view, the elites are not scared of the kind of republic the United States was or is but of democracy in a different sense to do collective self-gov-ernment—a sense that he believes does not accurately describe the political structure of the United States.

19. Martin Gilens and Benjamin I. Page, "Testing Theories of American Politics: Elites, Interest Groups, and Average Citizens," *Perspectives on Politics* 12, no. 3 (2014): 575. We shouldn't think of this as unique to the US though, since these findings have recently been replicated in the Netherlands as well. See, for example: Wouter Schakel, "Unequal policy responsiveness in the Netherlands," *Socio-economic Review*, April 21, 2019, https://academic.oup.com/ser/advance-article/doi/10.1093/ser/mwz018/5475880.

society are seriously threatened."[20] Note, the claim here is not that constituents are rarely or never aligned with the actions of their representatives in the contemporary United States. Nor is the claim that these representatives are entirely unaffected by the wishes and preferences of their constituents as a whole. Instead, the claim is that only a minority of wealthy constituents and interest groups has any significant effect on what the US government does, at every level of government. Based on a conception of democracy as collective self-rule, this cannot be considered democratic.

The idea of democracy as collective self-rule was carried on into the early socialist movement. In his younger, pre-socialist years, Marx advocates democracy in this sense, writing that unlike other forms of society, in "a democracy the constitution, law, i.e. the political state, is itself only a self-determination of the people and the determinate content of the people."[21] Its "formal" principle is therefore identical with its "material" principle,[22] meaning that the institution that claims to rule for and on behalf of the community of individuals really does so.

For the early Marx, this entails a re-appropriation of humans' social essence. As I have argued elsewhere, this entails:

> the various social forces created by, and inherent in, human society are no longer wielded by alien powers external and opposed to that of the vast majority of the population – whether these powers be those of a capitalist economy over workers in it, those of an absolute monarch over his or her subjects, those of a privileged feudal nobility over their serfs, etc. Instead, these social powers are taken over by the body of the people, subjected to their rule, and thereby transformed into powers under their own command.[23]

When Marx becomes a socialist, he retains this radical democratic core, adding specifically economic elements to do with overcoming

---

20. Gilens and Page, "Testing Theories of American Politics": 577.

21. Karl Marx, "Critique of Hegel's Doctrine of the State," in *Karl Marx: Early Writings* (London: Penguin, 1992), 89.

22. Marx, "Critique of Hegel's Doctrine of the State," 88.

23. Paul Raekstad, "The Democratic Theory of the Early Marx," *Archiv für Geschichte der Philosophie* 99: 4 (2017): 458.

the capitalist division of labor, instituting a participatory form of economic planning, and distributing goods and services according to needs. For the later Marx, a future socialist society is supposed to be "the true *appropriation* of the *human* essence through and for man; it is the complete restoration of man to himself as a *social*, i.e., human, being."[24] Socialism is able to achieve this because it makes possible "universally developed individuals, whose social relations, as their own communal [*gemeinschaftlich*] relations, are hence also subordinated to their own communal control."[25] In this sense it is the case that in "a real community the individuals obtain their freedom in and through their association."[26]

Marx was far from alone in this. Early revolutionary anarchists such as Bakunin also used the language of democracy, for example, when naming one of their groups the "International Alliance of Socialist Democracy." As Graeber writes on the connections between democracy and anarchism, "Anarchism does not mean the negation of democracy—or at least, any of the aspects of democracy that most Americans have historically liked. Rather, anarchism is a matter of taking those core democratic principles to their logical conclusions."[27] Anarchism—along with libertarian strands of Marxism and social ecology—take principles of collective popular self-rule through participatory assemblies to

24. Marx, in *Karl Marx: Early Writings*, 348. See also Paul Raekstad, "From Democracy to Socialism: Then and Now," *Socialist Register* 54 (2017): 263–274.

25. Karl Marx, *Grundrisse: Foundations of a Critique of Political Economy* (London: Penguin, 1973), 162.

26. Karl Marx and Friedrich Engels, *German Ideology, Part 1 and Selections from Parts 2 and 3* (New York: New World Paperbacks, 1970), 83. The link between Marx and radical Enlightenment thinkers is far from new—see Albert Igoin, "De l'ellipse de la théoriepolitique de Spinoza chez le jeune Marx," *Cahiers Spinoza* 1 (1977): 213–228; Alexandre Matheron, "Le Traitéthéologico-politiquelu par le jeune Marx," *Cahiers Spinoza* 1 (1977): 159–212; Etienne Balibar, *Spinoza and Politics* (London: Verso, 2008); Miguel Abensour, *La Démocratiecontrel'État: Marx et le momentmachiavélien* (Paris: Éditions du Félin, 2004); and Stathis Kouvelakis, *Philosophy and Revolution: From Kant to Marx.* (London: Verso, 2003)—but is often insufficiently appreciated. For instance, in his early democratic period Marx makes extensive notes on Spinoza (see Marx and Engels, *Gesamtausgabe*, vol. IV: 1, 233–276), and throughout his life he was an avowed fan of many radical-democratic writers such as Helvétius, Diderot, and Goethe. His conception of democracy is basically identical to the one he discusses in his notes on Spinoza's *Tractatus Theologico-Politicus* (see the *Gesamtausgabe*, vol. IV: 1, 240–241, 785).

27. Graeber, *The Democracy Project*, 154.

their logical conclusion by working for a society where people collectively self-rule their lives and society in these ways.

Now, it is well known that there is no single Marxist or anarchist conception of democracy. Different Marxist and anarchist thinkers have many differing conceptions of, views on, and arguments for and against what they call "democracy." In large part this is due to the shifting meaning of the term "democracy" throughout the nineteenth and twentieth centuries. When the early Marx called for democracy, when Bakunin called his organization, the "Alliance for Socialist Democracy," and when Graeber writes of anarchism as taking democratic principles to their logical conclusion, what they mean by "democracy" is precisely collective self-rule, where this is not associated with modern representative states with universal suffrage. In the first two cases this is because such states don't yet exist, and the association between "democracy" and modern representative states has not yet developed, and in the last instance Graeber is using a concept of democracy to advocate replacing states altogether.

The term "democracy" gradually became associated with modern representative states, first in the United States and then spreading worldwide. Graeber writes that it "was between 1830 and 1850 that politicians in the United States and France began to identify themselves as democrats and to use democracy to designate the electoral regime, even though no constitutional change or transformation of the decision-making process warranted this change in name." This "cynical ploy" was widely successful, and the result was that soon all candidates began to refer to their electoral systems as "democratic."[28] As a result of this, during the late nineteenth and early twentieth centuries Marxists begin to make distinctions between "bourgeois" democracy and "proletarian" democracy, and anarchists begin to reject "democracy" outright.[29] In so doing, they reject the representative states they oppose; needless to say, they are in no way giving up on their goals and ideals of collective self-rule. Today, there are disagreements among

---

28. Graeber, *The Democracy Project*, 169–170.

29. For a number of contemporary examples, see CrimethInc's series "The Anarchist Critique of Democracy" here: http://www.crimethinc.com/blog/2016/03/16/series-the-anarchist-critique-of-democracy/.

Marxists, anarchists, and other radicals about whether the term "democracy" is best reclaimed in a more radical sense useful for critiquing modern society, or abandoned as too associated with modern state structures. The point of this article is to argue that the former is a viable project, and to suggest that this is best done by defining democracy in terms of the collective self-rule of a group of people. I think that much of this idea remains in the way we think and speak about "democracy" today, and it's this I want to argue is useful for contemporary radical movements.

There are three main reasons why this conception of democracy is useful for contemporary radical movements: (1) it is an already-existing evaluative concept with significant emotional and political power; (2) the ancient and radical idea of democracy as the real rule of the people, by the people, for the people is still a part of the confused amalgam that is its everyday concept; and, (3) it is not a merely procedural criterion for a process, decision, or action; it makes strong, valuable, and substantive demands for the reconstruction or replacement of our basic economic and political institutions, and as such sits nicely alongside other valuable concepts like equality and freedom.

This conception of democracy is something that we might call a conception of institutional *substance*, as opposed to institutional *form*. It is an instance of institutional *substance* in the sense that it lays out a description or requirement a society or institution needs to fulfill in order to be considered a democracy—i.e., is it or is it not an institution featuring collective self-rule? It does not, however, specify the precise institutional *forms* through which this is instituted or brought about—i.e., how does the collective self-rule happen? It does not, for instance, say anything specific about voting procedures, whether decisions are taken by simple majority vote, supermajority vote, consensus, and so forth.[30] This is an important point, because it allows

---

30. Three examples bring this out really well. First, Aristotle, for instance, terms both his contemporary Athens, which overwhelmingly operated according to direct voting and selection by lots as democratic, and at the same time applied the term "democratic" to other institutional forms, such as Solonian Athens, which he believed elected people to offices through votes, while being able to hold them to account when necessary (see, for example, his *Politics* in Aristotle, *The Basic Works of Aristotle* [New York: The Modern Library, 2001], 1247a15–18) and Mantinea, in which offices were appointed by elected representatives (in turn elected by the whole people), again in

this concept of democracy to avoid the impasse of identifying it with either the representative forms of the modern state apparatus or the direct models of, for example, ancient Athens.

NEITHER DIRECT NOR REPRESENTATIVE DEMOCRACY

This focus on substance over form gives us reason to move away from the question of direct or representative institutional forms. On the one hand, representative state formations—often labeled "representative democracies"—are one of the things that many radical movements want to reject as fundamentally undemocratic in nature.[31] On the other hand, purely direct models—either consensus or by direct assembly voting on every issue—have problems with numbers and scale.[32] This is a serious dilemma: If we identify "democracy" with representative forms like modern states, the critique of the state and representation in many radical

---

Politics (1318b21–35; see also 1281b). It only makes sense for Aristotle to talk about these institutional forms as "democratic" if we don't read him as identifying democracy with direct, delegated, or representative forms specifically, but instead with a common institutional substance they help to instantiate. Second, at one point Thucydides writes that during the leadership of Pericles "what was in name a democracy was in practice government by the foremost man," i.e., a monarchy. [Thucydides, *The History of the War of the Pelepponesians and the Athenians* (Cambridge: Cambridge University Press, 2013), 130.] Such a statement is only possible if democracy is not associated with any specific forms (which did not change during the period he's writing about) but rather with substance, i.e., who really has power, who really determines deliberation and decision making. (As an aside, this is not particularly plausible, since, as Thucydides notes just before this quote, the Athenian assembly did turn against him and even fined him on one occasion, which is not the sort of thing that happens when there's a single undisputed ruler). Third, when Marx advocates democracy in the above sense, he is actually sensitive to the potential complications involved in delegation and representation, and explicitly notes that the important question is not delegation or direct voting per se but rather the extension of real participation in society's deliberation and decision making. [See Karl Marx and Friedrich Engels, *Gesamtausgabe* (Berlin: Dietz Verlag, 1975), vol. I: 2, 130, and 133; and see also I: 1, 285.] Again, this only makes sense if he is thinking of democracy in terms of institutional substance rather than institutional forms. [See Raekstad, "The Democratic Theory of the Early Marx."]

31. See, for example, Mark Bray, *Translating Anarchy: The Anarchism of Occupy Wall Street* (Alresford Hants: Zero Books, 2013); Graeber, *The Democracy Project*; Roos and Oikonomakis, "They Don't Represent Us!"; and Sitrin and Azzellini, *They Can't Represent Us!*

32. See Bray, *Translating Anarchy*, 39-110, for an anarchist critique of this; defenses in Marianne Maeckelbergh, "Horizontal Democracy Now: From Alterglobalization to Occupation," *Interface: A Journal for and about Social Movements* 4, no. 1 (2012): 207–234; and Graeber, *The Democracy Project*, Chapter 3.

movements falls apart by definition; if we identify it only with strict direct forms like ancient Athens or large direct assemblies that eschew delegation of any kind, then we risk advocating something that arguably cannot scale to modern societies with millions of people.

Defining democracy in terms of institutional substance (is it or is it not an institution featuring collective self-rule?) rather than institutional forms (how does it do it?) avoids this dilemma. When the question of democracy is about collective self-rule, we don't have to assume that either representative or direct structures of whatever kind are democratic by definition, and this has significant advantages. As I'll argue below, it gives us a good definition from which to argue that representative states are not democratic, which is a powerful argument.

There are other advantages as well. First, by distinguishing between substance and form we can advocate something we value and care about—collective self-rule—and criticize institutions for failing to live up to it, without assuming that what we value is necessarily instantiated in only one kind of way. Instead of assuming that both representative and direct institutional forms are "democratic" in some hazy and necessarily incoherent sense, or that only direct institutional forms of some very specific kinds can be democratic at all, it becomes an open empirical question whether any particular institutional forms are democratic or not.

This means that we can potentially use this concept of democracy to criticize any kind of institutional forms for failing to be genuine instances of democracy as collective self-rule, and there are cases where that is important. For example, even a direct vote among a small group of people could fail to realize collective self-rule if wealthy individuals were allowed to threaten or bribe people to vote one way or the other. Or, take an example of strict consensus decision-making where one person consistently blocks every proposal (without the group throwing them out or moving to a form of supermajority, etc.). Here too there is a failure for certain institutional forms to instantiate genuine democracy as collective self-rule. In both these cases, distinguishing clearly between a substantial conception of democracy as collective self-rule and the institutional forms that may or may not realize it allows us to avoid having to say that they are democratic (directly or otherwise) when, in those cases, they clearly are not democratic in any sense that we value and care about. Direct institutional forms may of course be the best and most reliable way of securing democracy in the sense I'm advocating, but this is something that should be argued for in a clear and factual way.

Another advantage of defining democracy in this way is that it makes it harder for political opponents of contemporary radical movements to misrepresent what they are advocating. By advocating "direct democracy," it often seems to those uninitiated that what is being advocated is simply huge assemblies where everyone present either votes on each and every issue or seeks to achieve consensus on each and every issue—often with the added assumption that this was all there was to the workings of the Athenian polis and to how the Greeks thought about it. This is harmful to the movement because it leaves it vulnerable to the seemingly solid objection that contemporary societies, which are not only more complex but much larger in scale than any ancient Greek city-state ever was, simply cannot be organized adequately along such lines. This, of course, is not actually a good argument, since even those advocating consensus forms of decision-making allow for delegation in some sense. Even the most ardent advocates of direct and consensus modes of deliberation and decision-making, such as Marianne Maeckelbergh and David Graeber,[33] point this out in their discussion of "spokescouncils," and in their advocacy of the spokescouncil model over simply having huge consensus assemblies (as happened in much of Occupy in the United States). The point I want to emphasize here is that when things like "direct democracy" are advocated, this is usually interpreted to mean institutional forms that do away with delegation altogether, which immediately makes it seem unrealistic and therefore unappealing. Defining democracy in the substantive terms I'm advocating avoids this confusion from the outset.

---

33. Graeber, *The Democracy Project*; and Maeckelbergh, "Horizontal Democracy Now." This also goes for other advocates of what they call "direct democracy," such as Murray Bookchin, who is explicit about advocating a confederalist model. See, for example, Murray Bookchin, *The Next Revolution* (London: Verso, 2015).

Defining democracy in this way also has a third advantage. It helps us to see more clearly how what we are advocating relates meaningfully to what other thinkers—in ancient Greece, in the radical Enlightenment (such as Baruch Spinoza, Denis Diderot, and Mary Wollstonecraft), and in early socialism (Marx included)—were doing when they advocated "democracy." The concept of "democracy" that they used, was typically much more radical and very different from what modern liberals euphemistically term "representative democracy," yet without explicitly talking about "direct democracy." If we also make the common erroneous assumption that there are two kinds of "democracy"—direct and representative—then we end up erroneously assuming that everyone has to be talking about either a direct model (such as the ancient Greeks, but as we've seen that's often not what's meant) or something like an idealized representative state. Murray Bookchin, for example, does this when he writes, "the word *politics* itself contains the Greek word for 'city' or *polis*, and its use in classical Athens, together with democracy, connoted the direct governing of the city by its citizens."[34] This reading is incorrect since it wrongly assumes that the Greeks were using "democracy" in the same way that Bookchin uses the term "direct democracy." To take just three examples from Aristotle, he called not just post-Cleisthenes Athens a "democracy" but also Solonian Athens, which he believed elected people to offices through votes, while being able to hold them to account when necessary. Likewise, he called Mantinea, in which offices were appointed by elected representatives (in turn elected by the whole people), a democracy as well.[35] Neither Solonian Athens and Mantinea were strict "direct democracies" in Bookchin's sense, so the Greek term cannot mean what he thinks it does. Since Bookchin assumes that people talking about "democracy" *must* be talking about "direct democracy" or "representative democracy," and since the Greeks couldn't have been talking about the latter, he thinks they must be talking about "direct democracy" in his sense. Within this framework of assumptions, it becomes impossible to understand what

---

34. Bookchin, *The Next Revolution*, 11–12.
35. See note 126.

the Greeks meant, since it runs together ideas about institutional substance and institutional forms. This thwarts our ability to understand the past and to draw on its useful radical content (while also, of course, criticizing it for its shortcomings).

Finally, thinking about democracy in substantive terms helps to open the way for a serious and much-needed debate on the institutional forms we want to aspire to in a future society, and that we want to try to implement in contemporary organizing. Any modern society and organization beyond a certain size arguably requires a degree of delegation. Since the advent of modern libertarian socialist movements, the question has been, how do we ensure that these delegates enable society's collective self-rule rather than thwart it? In ancient Athens, the question was solved by drawing officials by lots, rotation, and direct voting on all major issues.[36] Among anarchists and other libertarian socialists historically, the answer has typically involved tools like mandating delegates; frequent rotation of delegates; putting in place mechanisms whereby delegates must report back and explain themselves to their lower-level assemblies; and systems of immediate recall. And for many of the Occupy encampments across the United States, the Global Justice Movement, and others, it has involved consensus modes of deliberation and decision-making (often with forms of supermajority as fallback options if and when necessary), spokescouncils, and a host of sophisticated tools to ensure that deliberation reaches an acceptable consensus.[37] In any case, this is a debate we need to have on a clear conceptual basis. I think the best way of doing this is to first try to be clear about what we want to achieve by our institutions and organizations and then try to determine which institutional forms achieve this best as a matter of fact.

In addition to these advantages, conceiving democracy in terms of collective self-rule also gives us good foundations from which to mount powerful critiques of both the contemporary state and capitalism.

---

36. See Hansen, *The Athenian Democracy in the Age of Demosthenes.*

37. Here, David Graeber, *Direct Action: An Ethnography* (Oakland: AK Press, 2009) is invaluable.

DEMOCRACY AGAINST REPRESENTATION

How can this conception of democracy be used to critique the state and capitalism? As mentioned above, the most solid empirical evidence available shows that in the world's most well-known representative state, the United States, the majority of the population has no influence on the state's actions. Do we have any reason to assume that things are better anywhere else? Is there any good evidence to indicate it?

Consider how representatives in contemporary states actually operate:

> In [so-called] liberal or representative democracy, the 'representatives' do not have to comply with what they or their party promised during elections, or what their party program says. Once they are elected, they do whatever they want (or what the economic elites want), and do not have to justify themselves to the people who voted for them. There is no accountability for decisions, even not if they do the exact opposite of what they promised while campaigning. Supporters of liberal democracy try to hide these circumstances by saying that the elected representatives should act 'according to their conscience' regardless of the stance of the electorate or their party. This not only turns the supposed 'representation' into a joke, but also obviously transforms the campaigns into fairytale contests.[38]

Consider also how states frequently act contrary to popular opinion on crucial issues: the widespread, and deeply unpopular, imposition of austerity throughout Europe today; the moves to transfer state power to increasingly secretive and unaccountable transnational institutions like the European Union, the International Monetary Fund (IMF), et cetera; the widespread surveillance and repression of popular movements; Trade in Services Agreement (TiSA), Transatlantic Trade and Investment Partnership (TTIP), and their like; or the deeply unpopular neoliberal imperial warfare we've seen create humanitarian disasters across the Middle East. These things are all deeply unpopular, but what the population wants seems irrelevant to what the state does—except insofar as such opinion generates actions that force it to do otherwise.

---

38. Sitrin and Azzellini, *They Can't Represent Us!*, 41–42.

The fact that such things are possible illustrates precisely that modern representative states are not institutions within and through which the people really participate in deliberation and decision-making in any meaningful way. Modern states are therefore not, according to the definition I've been discussing, democratic. In very rudimentary terms, this shows how we can begin to critique the modern state on the basis of the concept of democracy as collective self-rule. Modern states and the politicians that staff them are not at all vehicles for their citizens' collective self-rule. Their claims to democratic legitimacy are founded on false assumptions. As one participant in Greece put it, "This is not democracy. We have no power. We don't make decisions."[39] We have enough here to come up with a useful distinction between delegation and representation, even though they are often used synonymously in popular parlance. Delegation can be defined as the act of selecting a group or individual that claims to speak and act on behalf of a group of people. There is nothing inherently undemocratic about delegation in this sense; delegation is one conceptually possible means through which a group might rule itself collectively. By contrast, the sense of "representation"—defined as the act of selecting a group or individual that claims to speak and act on behalf of a group of people without those people being able to significantly affect their actions—is rejected by many radical movements as undemocratic. The reason this is undemocratic is obvious: if the people being "represented" lack the power to affect what their supposed "representatives" do, then it is simply impossible for the latter to be a vehicle through which the former rules itself collectively. But the power of democracy as a critical concept goes further than this.

DEMOCRACY AGAINST CAPITALISM

The focus on institutional substance that I am arguing for also moves a radical discussion of democracy away from narrow and fetishistic liberal confinement of the question of democracy to the polity or the state. It moves the debate to where it belongs: to the deeper questions about the nature of power in decision-making structures, thereby enabling one to critique the decision-making

---

39. Cited in Sitrin and Azzellini, *They Can't Represent Us!*, 41.

structures in any aspect of society.[40] As such, it is a concept that can more readily be used to criticize not only representative state structures but also things like the capitalist economy.

Under capitalism, people are not allowed to control their working lives or the wider economy in any meaningful way. The vast majority of people have no say in what their workplace does (e.g., the things it makes or the services it provides), how their workplace goes about doing it, and who benefits from it and how. They have no control over who gets hired or fired, whether their workplace gets moved abroad to exploit cheaper and more easily oppressed labor, whether to maximize profits in the hands of a tiny clique of shareholders who store it in tax havens, or whether to invest society's surplus into sustainable industries or gamble them away on the stock market. Unlike states, modern-day corporations don't even pretend to feature any form of meaningful public input into the way they're structured, and myths of "consumer sovereignty" are universally unsupported and frankly ludicrous.

A movement for democracy, in the sense discussed here, can also say something substantial about what to do about this state of affairs. It can and should insist on a fundamental restructuring of all social institutions in such a way that their participants collectively control them by fully participating in deliberation and decision-making. To do this would require rejecting a cornerstone of modern representative states: the division between the economic and the political. Sitrin and Azzellini make this point well in *They Can't Represent Us!*:

> Modern democracy [here, representative states] being founded upon the separation of the economic, political, and social spheres, the economy and society are excluded from democratic governance. Yet this separation is inextricably linked to the idea of representation: the government's powers being limited to the political sphere and focused primarily on guaranteeing individual rights and civil liberties (including the right to private property), political participation is kept at arm's length from economic and civic life. Political participation is necessarily indirect. Thankfully, other forms of democracy are possible.[41]

---

40. See István Mészáros, *The Necessity of Social Control* (New York: Monthly Review Press, 2015).
41. Sitrin and Azzellini, *They Can't Represent Us!*, 51.

THREE OBJECTIONS AND REPLIES

If this concept of democracy is basically coherent and useful, we now need to see if it can respond to some prominent criticisms. Specifically, this section considers the arguments that calling for democracy is bad, because: (1) it involves defending something that exists that we shouldn't be propping up, such as hierarchical representative states; (2) it involves obscuring and hiding oppression and social contradictions; and, (3) it avoids the critical question of the collective power of the people.[42]

First, do calls for "democracy" necessarily end up propping up things that shouldn't be, like modern states? From an anarchist perspective, the CrimethInc. has recently argued that when we understand participation in assemblies, networks, collectives, and so forth "as *democracy*—as a form of participatory government rather than a collective practice of freedom—then sooner or later, we will recreate all the problems associated with less democratic forms of government,"[43] thereby coming to reinforce forms of hierarchy and domination the authors claim to be inherent in, among other things, modern representative states. Writing from a self-proclaimed Marxist perspective, Jodi Dean similarly argues that calling for democracy "is a defense of the status quo, a call for more of the same"—that is, more of the representative capitalist state.[44] It's worth noting that Dean provides no argument or evidence for her claims that *this* is what participants in Occupy mean or meant by their calls for "democracy," "real democracy," and so on. Similarly, CrimethInc leaves out the possibility that we can think of "democracy" in a sense different from the one they go by, avoiding the conclusions they fear.

---

42. Focusing on these three connected arguments necessarily leaves out one or two other important critiques of using democracy for radical politics, such as that of Uri Gordon, "Democracy: The Patriotic Temptation," May 26, 2016, http://www.crimethinc.com/blog/2016/05/26/democracy-the-patriotic-temptation/.

43. See CrimethInc, "From Democracy to Freedom," April 29, 2016, https://crimethinc.com/2016/04/29/feature-from-democracy-to-freedom.

44. Jodi Dean, *The Communist Horizon* (London: Verso, 2012), 57–58. This might seem anti-authoritarian, but in her later work *Crowds and Party* (London: Verso, 2016), she explicitly argues that oligarchy is necessary for any large-scale organizing, thus rejecting the core Marxist commitment of universal human emancipation through proletarian self-emancipation, on which, see Paul Raekstad, "Democracy, the Party, and Self-Emancipation," *Critique* 45: 4 (2017): 599–611.

Their critiques of using democracy as a radical critical concept in general only makes sense if we assume that "democracy" necessarily involves accepting the rule of some people over others in some way, people who are usually selected through election. This assumption is false. First, many democrats explicitly want to avoid electing anyone to anything, as was the case in ancient Athens, where only generals and a few financial officers were elected—and that was considered an exceptional concession. Other ardent democrats like Spinoza and the early Marx advocate democracy, but they define it entirely differently. Similarly, it's clear that many of the participants in the Occupy and other radical movements like the Movement of the Squares in Spain and Greece—many of them libertarian socialists—call for "democracy" precisely as a way of criticizing the state and advocating its abolition. In fact, these claims directly contradict what some of its most prominent participants and commentators write, such as David Graeber,[45] Mark Bray,[46] and Marina Sitrin and Dario Azzellini,[47] and which the latter support with a huge amount of personal experience, evidence, and argument. Obviously, this doesn't just mean more or better state representation. The critics could reply that there can be no coherent concept of "democracy" that does this, but as this article has argued, defining democracy in terms of collective self-rule is coherent, can make sense of (at least some of) how that term is used in radical movements, and can be used to critique both the state and capitalism.

Does democracy, and calls for democracy, necessarily obscure oppression and social contradictions and avoid the critical question of collective power? Paul Z. Simmons argues that democracy (and calls for democracy) "functions as a mask for coercion, making horror palatable while producing unbearable consequences for the individual, for the species, and for the planet."[48] Whereas,

---

45. Graeber, *The Democracy Project*.

46. Bray, *Translating Anarchy*.

47. Sitrin and Azzellini, *They Can't Represent Us!*

48. Paul Z. Simmons, "Rojava: Democracy and Commune," May 19, 2016, http://www.crimethinc.com/blog/2016/05/19/rojava-democracy-and-commune. He goes on to discuss how experiments in Rojava may be turning democracy from a worthless and outdated principle into one worthy of contemporary anarchist theory, and then goes on to talk about the commune.

in contrast, Dean writes that the Left's usage "of the language of democracy now avoids the fundamental antagonism between the 1 percent and the rest of us by acting as if the only thing really missing was participation."[49] Moreover, the Left "should be committed to the collective power of the people," which Dean claims that calls for democracy avoid.[50]

Again, we can see why critics think this only if we assume that the liberal definition of democracy, or something very close to it, is the only one available. Only if we start by assuming that democracy entails the rule by some over others does it make sense to say that advocating "democracy" obscures real issues of collective power.

If we think about democracy in terms of collective self-rule, however, the question of power is placed front and center. If we define democracy in terms of collective self-rule in any area of social life, then any advocacy of democracy will inherently draw attention to the contradictions between the ruling minority and ruled majority, since this contradiction is above all a contradiction of power and interests. If we don't collectively rule our societies, then who does? And in whose interests do they do so? The 1 percent are the 1 percent because they have the power necessary to become so and stay so. The 99 percent do not rule and do not control our societies, either their polities or their economies, and this critique is right at the core of many contemporary radical movements. If we understand democracy in a radical way, democracy is the antithesis to minority rule. This is the way democracy was thought of throughout much of the term's history, and it remains an important and central ingredient in the existing mishmash of ideas and usages of the term. If we understand democracy in a more precise way as collective self-rule, then we can do exactly the opposite of what these critics suggest. Instead of obscuring the question of collective power, understanding democracy as collective self-rule can help to put it front and center of our theory and practice. Taking democracy seriously need not obscure the contradictions between the rulers and the ruled; it tells us that we need to abolish them.

---

49. Dean, *The Communist Horizon*, 57–58.
50. Dean, *The Communist Horizon*, 60.

CONCLUSION

I have argued that we should think of democracy as the collective self-rule of a group of people. This is a clear and coherent definition that does what I and (I think) many other participants in various parts of contemporary radical movements and organizations want it to. As we have seen, this definition is by no means a new one, but has a long history of being part of struggles for freedom and equality. This article is thus an attempt to help the normative self-clarification of a wider social movement. Ultimately, its usefulness is not something that can be argued for in any piece of writing but something that must be proved through the role it manages to play in ongoing political practice. If we want democracy to be realized in the basic institutions of society, then we need movements and organizations that function on the basis of collective self-rule. The fact that this has been happening is one of the most encouraging developments of recent years.

I've focused on how this relates to issues of polity and economy because they're the ones most talked about when it comes to discussions of "democracy," and because they're the ones I'm at all qualified to say something about. Contemporary social movements and struggles for democracy are about much more than just this: they tackle head-on the traditional oppressions and exclusions of women, people of color, LGBTQ+ people, and more. These struggles are hugely influential and important, and these too can make use of a radical concept of democracy (among many others). As one contemporary expert writes, the "role of democracy as a political value" in the modern world is to "probe constantly the tolerable limits of injustice, a permanent and sometimes very intense blend of cultural enquiry with social and political struggle."[51] "The true definition of democracy is merely one prize at stake in those quarrels."[52] I think it is one worth taking seriously.

---

51. John Dunn, *Setting the People Free: The Story of Democracy* (London: Atlantic Books, 2005), 171.

52. Dunn, *Setting the People Free*, 172.

ABOLITIONIST DEMOCRACY

FEAR, LOATHING, AND VIOLENCE IN THE 2016 CAMPAIGN , WITH NOTES FOR 2020 AND BEYOND[1]

Joy James

Any chronic illness is a curse . . . . the nature of the beast is a complete loss of control—of your emotions, of your intellect, your instincts, your common sense—basically your sense of yourself, a really frightening aspect of this insidious disease.

—Deborah Danner, "Living with Schizophrenia"[2]

FEAR AND LOATHING

The dread that Deborah Danner—a sixty-six-year-old Black woman living in the Bronx—had concerning herself, family, society, and police meant that her prescient fear of becoming a fatality of poorly trained, indifferent, or hostile police became reality on October 18, 2016. Nude in her apartment, armed with a baseball bat, she confronted a police officer who chose his revolver over his Taser.

The electorate, more often than not, has limited capacity to focus on the anxiety and death of people like Danner. As a casualty outside mainstream citizenry, her presence dissipates into a frightened political persona coping with dread and depression

---

1. Editors' note: James's intervention was originally written in the height of the 2016 election and is updated here to extend a critical understanding of the prevailing issues animating abolition democracy and the pitfalls of electoral politics for 2020 and beyond.

2. Deborah Danner, "Living With Schizophrenia," *New York Times*, October 19, 2016, https://www.nytimes.com/interactive/2016/10/19/nyregion/document-Living-With-Schizophrenia-by-Deborah-Danner.html.

generated by the US' current political leadership. A fear-based presidential election in which significant numbers of gendered, racial, and economic elites feel the sting of anxiety is the new normal in US democracy.[3]

Unprecedented levels of unease and combativeness among Americans who consider themselves valued citizens obsess over whether this democracy remains "the greatest nation on earth" or will be dragged into chaos and dustbins by immensely unpopular presidential rivals. In 2016, Hillary Clinton and Donald Trump were disparaged for betraying *electoral* democracy. Yet, few note electoral democracy's dependency upon captivity, exclusion, and consumption. Electoral democracy values structure that is stable and predictable, in spite of bureaucratic inertia, corporate-written policies, celebrity politicians, and deceptions safeguarded by secrecy. In electoral democracy, wealth controls access and benefits—quality health, dignified work, safety—to determine who is electable, although the "electable" is not viewed as inherently desirable or even respectable.

Like all presidential candidates, Clinton and Trump were not demonized for advocating the abolition of prisons, slavery, white supremacy, poverty, sexual violence. Despite their ideological differences, they were in agreement that they are not abolitionists. Abolitionist democracy, based in real and imagined freedoms from captivity and fear, was a dark horse candidate in 2016— campaigning to destabilize the master-mistress/slave relations— and is even more so the candidate haunting the 2020 elections.

Political rivalries define US democracy, but the battles extend beyond party affiliation. Electoral democracy has contested abolitionist democracy, dismissed it as too radical, impractical, and impatient, a "spoiler" in elections. The differences between the two are stark. Electoral democracy does not seek equity; rather, it seeks "winners" (free citizens who are ideological compatriots) and not "losers" (those locked up or locked out of social and political power). Abolitionist democracy, on the other hand, challenges structures of confinement in a quest to transform the non/subhuman

---

3. NPR's WNYC and *The Nation* chronicle this in their coproduced podcast "The United States of Anxiety." Available at https://www.wnycstudios.org/podcasts/anxiety.

into a citizen who controls not only their votes but also how their bodies are treated.

Compassion and ethics expressed during elections prioritize agency and citizenry through the voter (working within systems that she does not control) and victimization of those targeted by prison systems, exploitation. Elections recognize struggles against indignity, captivity, violence, and demands for protection or self-defense. Channeling them into strategies for winning office, electoral democracy refashions political protests as campaign props (e.g., the DNC informed staffers through [leaked] emails to chant "Black Lives Matter!" at the July 2016 Democratic National Convention while avoiding substantive policy and advocacy to end anti-black violence).[4] Abolition probes the boundaries of violence—legally or illegally enacted with impunity—in order to discover democracy's fault lines and the extent to which some of its predatory characteristics and practices need to be abolished. Electoral democracy maintains that the political will of the people is expressed in its elections. Yet, the political will of (some) of the people is also expressed in police violence that targets citizens denied full rights.

It is significant to recall that, in 2015, distressed by the rebellions and riots following Freddie Gray's homicide while in the custody of the Baltimore police, President Barack Obama asserted that he could not "federalize" or control the police. This signaled the limits of reform (body cameras, trainings, community review boards). If the police are like the ballot (ballots with bullets) then they are an expression of the "will of [some] of the people"—but not those people who are disproportionately violated or killed by police. With or without mental illness, people like Deborah Danner had been outvoted in electoral democracy by the social workers, advocates, and police who regulated and eventually terminated her life.

Police use an unofficial acronym "NHI" ("No Humans Involved") for murder victims who are African American, prostitutes, and the drug afflicted.[5] This is political speech or campaign rhetoric.

4. Julia Craven, "Leaked 2015 Memo Told Dems: 'Don't Offer Support' for Black Lives Matter Policy Positions," *Huffington Post*, August 31, 2016, https://www.huffpost.com/entry/dnc-black-lives-matter-memo_n_57c6f80de4b07858f1072ca.
5. Zachary Wigon, "The L.A.P.D. Didn't Catch an Alleged Serial Killer for 30 Years.

Electioneering determines social life and social death. Police fail to find and grieve with the kin of the deceased (aka "NHI"), or adequately investigate their murder, because this political speech nullifies their civic and governmental duty. NHI is its own political campaign that is embedded in US electoral democracy, as policing sectors conflate Blackness with criminalized labor and/or disease.

This starting point—that no humans are involved in democracy—is an aspect of policing in democracy that elections can dismiss or diminish as electoral reforms conflate power with policy and voting with ethics. Progressive politics admirably oppose voter intimidation; racist "voter fraud" charges; felon disenfranchisement; biased redistricting or gerrymandering. The law has not recently worked for progressivism. Civil rights protections were gutted in 2013 *Shelby County v. Holder*; and, "shadow" political parties or patrons were expanded through 2010 *Citizens United v. Federal Election Commission*.[6] In addition, progressivism seems to avoid the need to abolish structures in order to safeguard against captivity.

ELECTORAL DEMOCRACY VS. ABOLITIONIST DEMOCRACY

Electoral democracy has distinct factions that suggest ideological differences are the sum total of the game. During the last campaign season, in progressive quarters, Senators Bernie Sanders and Elizabeth Warren decried that US democracy is "rigged" by corporate wealth and politicians who lack a moral compass. In the liberal-centrist mainstream, Hillary Clinton, and to a degree Joe Biden, adapted progressive populism for campaign victories, deploying the virtue of critics who wield influence as post-primary surrogates.

In conservative-reactionary factions, Donald Trump rages against a "rigged" system to channel fascist, rebel yells (with

---

Is It Because the Victims Were Black?" *Vanity Fair*, December 18, 2014, https://www.vanityfair.com/hollywood/2014/12/tales-of-the-grim-sleeper-nick-broomfield.

6. Myrna Pérez, "After 'Shelby County' Ruling, Are Voting Rights Endangered?" *Brennan Center For Justice*, September 23, 2013, https://www.brennancenter.org/our-work/research-reports/after-shelby-county-ruling-are-voting-rights-endangered. John Dunbar, "The 'Citizens United' Decision and Why It Matters," *The Center for Public Integrity*, October 18, 2012, https://www.publicintegrity.org/2012/10/18/11527/citizens-united-decision-and-why-it-matters.

"Second Amendment solutions"). Former president Barack Obama has stated that "one of the few regrets" of his presidency is that citizens have increasingly come to view democracy as being "rigged," due in part to their exclusion from power and resources, and admonished Trump for "whining" about potential and perceived "unfairness" to him, as leader of the so-called free world. None of these sectors (or the mainstream conservatives repudiating Trump) recommends abolitionist democracy as part of the architecture for the future, i.e., as a form of democracy that should rival if not supplant electoral democracy's focus on declaring a victory without having waged a battle against captivity.

The 2016 campaign-as-evil-twin of the 2008 election shredded the historic optimism that we made a sizable dent in white supremacy. The soaring rhetoric of "Hope," "change we can believe in," and transcending "race" (abstracted from racism, poverty, mass incarceration/slavery, executions) is beyond lost in this political moment. For decades, both parties opportunistically campaigned as tough-on-crime and pro-police. Embracing either "law and order" or "reform," or some mixture of the two, Democrats and Republicans adhere to policies engineered by corporations, governance, nonprofits but not communities. Democracy's foreign and domestic arenas include foreign wars that cannot be "won" (thousands of civilians die by drone strikes, twenty US veterans commit suicide daily, and national debt increases); and "pay-to-play" candidates who preside over decaying roads, bridges, schools, and affordable housing.

The electoral struggle between the "pragmatist" and the "demagogue" becomes apocalyptic so that the (not-so) good must triumph over evil (and down-ballot candidates), as we vote our *fear and loathing* but not our conscience (in a society where dominating beats ethics).[7] The 2020 Campaign, just as the previous one, shows how creepy it is to live captive to fear and disgust, held by forces that "lead" as they derail or threaten your life. Distressed, detained, and imprisoned people are intimately familiar with those feelings.

---

7. Hunter Thompson's *Fear and Loathing on the Campaign Trail '72* focuses on Richard Nixon and George McGovern's presidential contest; however, McGovern first had to defeat Congresswoman Shirley Chisholm in the primaries, and move to the right of her anti-racist and anti-sexist platform opposing the war in Vietnam and poverty.

"OCTOBER SURPRISES"

In US elections, October Surprises are events that influence the presidential contest. This October, there was the tragedy of Danner's killing; Trump's "sex tape"/Town Hall denial of assaults/alleged victims' public testimonies. (Trump deflected from his personal immunity in sexual assault by (re)demonizing the falsely accused Central Park 5, exonerated through DNA after a racist 1989-1990 interracial rape prosecution during which Trump advertised in the *New York Times* for the death penalty for the black and Latino children.[8]) In October, Wikileaks' released hacked emails belonging to 2016 Clinton presidential campaign chair John Podesta and the DNC, revealing Clinton's Wall Street speeches that contradict her borrowed progressivism from primary rival Bernie Sanders, and Democratic elected officials attempting to control or corral their more radical party members.

October Surprises included a gift from Ava DuVernay's Netflix documentary *13th* to abolitionist democracy. *13th* dissects slavery and mass incarceration (and features clips of Clinton and Trump promoting racist and classist planks to fortify imprisonment and criminalization). The documentary references political prisoner/fugitive Assata Shakur, a former Black Panther Party member targeted by the illegal FBI counterintelligence program. Angela Davis and Van Jones describe how the US government violently persecuted activists, including Shakur, and used political imprisonment to stalk and derail liberation movements. Yet, neoslavery and political persecution remain discredited topics in a campaign where candidates bemoan their "victimization" by or in the media. Town halls allowed citizens to raise questions while missing opportunities to ask about the relationship of slavery and consumption to mass incarceration; and police violence and torture (including, Mumia Abu-Jamal's medical mistreatment) as forms of political practices and campaigns; and the role of political dissidents such as Shakur and Edward Snowden in expanding democracy despite self-serving FBI/NSA narratives.[9]

---

8. Goldie Taylor, "Donald Trump Keeps Smearing the Long-Since Exonerated 'Central Park Five,'" *Daily Beast*, October 7, 2016, https://www.thedailybeast.com/goldie-taylor-donald-trump-keeps-smearing-the-long-since-exonerated-central-park-five.

9. Rachel Wolkenstein, "Mumia's Fight for Medical Treatment," *Free Mumia*, January

So much of the discourse about criminalization came to focus on the candidates themselves. Remember the "Lock her up!" chants that were popular at Trump rallies and the debates: Clinton's private server, missing emails and legalistic mea culpas were seen as FOIA evasion. Trump's sexual predator immunity card was voided by those outraged that white women had been violated. These events overshadowed the agency of the imprisoned and their attempts to expand and develop democracy through abolitionism.

On September 9, 2016, imprisoned activists went on strike and presented their own political platforms for an abolitionist democracy.[10] They are calling for the elimination of the exception clause for slavery in the 13th amendment. As members of communities excluded from electoral democracy, with little to no protections of first amendment rights and access to familial and communal kin, they offered political visions that exceed the political capacity of most politicians and voters. Their outline for abolitionist democracy, particularly in the demand to rewrite the 13th amendment in order to serve the common good, provides new architecture, one that surpasses conventional politics and social justice advocacy. The 13th Amendment is not central to any major or minor party candidate because abolitionism is not the foundation of their party or platform. Those striking against prison labor as slave labor, and the indignities of captivity, define the scope and potential of democracy by liberation from its most predatory practices. When news of incarcerated people-citizens making demands that would benefit all Americans was disseminated weeks after the strikes began, this became the greatest October Surprise, at least for abolitionist democracy.

18, 2016, http://www.freemumia.com/2016/01/report-on-mumias-court-hearing/.

10. "Announcement of Nationally Coordinated Prisoner Workstoppage for Sept 9, 2016," *Support Prisoner Resistance*, September 9, 2016, https://supportprisonerresistance.noblogs. org/post/2016/04/01/announcement-of-nationally-coordinated-prisoner-workstoppage-for-sept-9-2016/.

THE PITFALLS OF WHITE
LIBERAL PANIC

Dylan Rodríguez

There should be no shock at the success of White Nationalist revival. A fog of liberal-progressive panic seeps across the closest quarters, oddly individualizing what some inhabit as a *normal and collective* disposition of familiarity with emergency under conditions of constant bodily and spiritual duress. In the living room, kitchen, office, school, cafe, park, dorm room, gym, and library there is a steady sad din: How did this happen, Why such hate, There are so many of them, What will happen to our country, Will I be threatened, My uncle and neighbor lied, What does the world think of us, I do not feel safe, What do we do now, Who will protect *those people* from *them*, How could this happen my god my god . . .

Wrapped up in the noise, it is worth reminding that this alleged descent into new chapters of state-induced racial and sexual terror is not reducible to the serial reprehensible (though completely unsurprising) tweets, assaults, and grandstanding of the new President. There are some who understand, because their wisdom is inherited, that the terror he embodies is both long-standing and carried in the thrust of a Civilization's futurity. This guy was always here, he is the persona his predecessors possessed but disguised so well (*though you never fooled me, you assholes*), and many of those in the throes of liberal-white-people-panic *know this deep down* because their revulsion to him is driven by a hatred of the intimate, the familial, and maybe the same.

I must admit: i¹ suspect some of them are incapable of seeing and feeling past themselves, their own bodily integrity, this isolated moment in a long, long history. The way they are spinning into prescriptions of how and why "we must resist" this *particular* abhorrence not only domesticates the liberal white riot, it threatens an infiltration of imagination in dislocated quarters that are accustomed to their negligence and generally thankful for their absence. The white misery desires multicultural company. Some of the ones panicking in public (online, on the mic, onscreen) are ready to tell the rest of us what to do, how to feel, and when to move—when in truth, if they felt so motivated, they would realize that their greatest contribution might be to shut the fuck up and get out of the way, because there has been some well thought out, beautifully imagined, wild shit going on for years now, and some of it entails anticipation of their demise along with—because they are part of—the abhorrence.

And those of us doing this kind of work (teaching, singing, organizing, playing, conspiring . . . i will plead the Fifth) have long realized that the lines we draw (such as the one i am replicating here) are never so clean, that we cross them because they always cross us, and it never feels good until we get back to the other side.

Here we are again: there are rapists, there are thugs, unruly women, incorrigible queers, "marauders in the streets" (as the new President's far more liberal predecessor Barry Goldwater once said) who must be neutralized, humiliated, *violated* in the bask of national vanity. It is to elevate to the level of assumption that the subjection of Black people to unbreaking proto-genocidal state violence is a generalized template through which other-others are periodically audited. To be undocumented is to be Brown or Black, and if others might fall into this category, it is only by misfortune of official nomenclature. "Grabbing pussy"

---

1. Exemplified by such revolutionary practitioners as Assata Shakur in *Assata: an Autobiography* (1987; Chicago: Lawrence Hill Books, 2001), the use of "i" suggests a first-person identification that departs from notions of the free-willing, self-determined, rational (white and Western) modern subject, and instead gestures toward the historical forces of subordination and degradation that form *practices* of "human being" and "identity" as confrontations with genocidal racism, racial colonialism, human chattel, and displacement."

is no longer a phrase that white women and old white men (or crusty-ass others) can condemn as the repulsive lyrical flourish of "those rappers" (whose names they rarely know), now that it has become the regular orientation of a ruler's impulse-order.

Elsewhere you see the people's fugitive broadcasts of the racist police threat, usually carried out by white cops, but sometimes by Black and Brown ones, even and especially under the Watch of The Former Black President. (If they could kill this way under him, what will they be capable of doing now?) Can we say that a certain Hope is dead, and there must again be vigilant suspicion of what some mean by Change?

Should we admit, now, that the "postracial" moment was a precursor (rather than a provocation) to a white populism that bizarrely insists on its nonraciality while it projects GIFs, memes, and clumsy puns invoking monkeys, taco bowls, and the Prophet Muhammad? It is stranger still that old terms—racism, misogyny, homophobia, sexism—have flooded the national discourse as if *this* spectacle, *this* candidate, *this* President is the catalyst of a doomsday that has in fact been long present in the seemingly limitless reach of white (male) entitlement to degrade, humiliate, and assert dominion over the field of zero consequences.

The morbid-cynical joyride of (white . . . multiculturalist?) liberal panic is neither merited nor, for some of us, fathomable. One could learn lessons from the twenty-somethings in my classroom—Black, Brown, a few white, working-class and lower-middle class, queer and trans, one degree (or less) removed from an incarcerated and/or undocumented loved one—who do not lament a damn thing, and are simmering with urgent questions about the necessity of artful, collective rebellion against an order. They are invigorating a truth that some older, wiser heads have generously shared for years: that to live within an everyday understanding—and embrace—of emergency is to thrust liberal panic to the margins of an indulgence. It is to say, without a hint of "i told you so" smugness or exaggerated rage, that such a political-cultural recalibration to the White Supremacist Normal (however absurd this version may be) is *always to be anticipated.*

The question is never "if," it is "when" and "to what extent." The problem, every fourth year, is never one of electoral outcome, it is one of political culture and the nuances of repression and fleeting opportunism that may follow.

Despite outward appearances, Barack Obama, Hillary Clinton, and Donald Trump are first cousins swaying to rhythms of progress and reaction, united by a commitment to negotiate and *relate* to the fact of white nationhood. President Obama will be remembered fondly in the liberal-national memory as the glimmering preface to an unexpected descent into the eighth *bolgia* of an American Hustle. But what is most remarkable about this moment is not the instantaneous implosion of an electoral/governing regime nor the anticipated onslaught of official attacks on basic civil and sexual freedoms. Rather, it is the possibility that every radical accusation against the United States Empire and the complex monolith of "White America" that could once be easily dismissed as paranoid and extremist, hateful and "reverse racist," or even treasonous and "terrorist" is now reckoning sober consideration as being, at the very least, *on to something*.

Undoubtedly, the audacity of hope, the optimism of change, and the belief in the transformative possibilities of symbolic-charismatic leadership divined from the Executive Branch of the US nation-building machinery should die a lonely death here, and should not be revivified anytime, ever again. Liberal panic amidst proto-fascist ascendancy is the symptom of an insistent belief in the long-debunked narrative of (with apologies to the rest of the Américas) an American possibility that shines with justice and shared joy in the spoils of "White Being."[2]

Panic never lasts long, and once it dissipates, there is therapeutic (mal)adjustment to yet another new normal. The modalities of sanctioned resistance to the worst of the normal become common, tolerable, negotiable, and finally ignorable. Civil society (that is, *this* civil society) again reveals the non-negotiable terms of being human (in fact, of "human being") in a rush to reconvene a spirit of nation, though possibly many more Other humans than at any time in the last half-century will refuse the call, despite the seductions of compulsory corporate diversity and official

2. Casey Goonan and Dylan Rodríguez, "Policing and the Violence of White Being: An Interview with Dylan Rodríguez," *Propter Nos*, 1(1), https://trueleappress.com/2016/08/30/policing-and-the-violence-of-white-being-an-interview-with-dylan-rodriguez/.

multiculturalism. It is not worth the time and energy, because the moment forces yet another reckoning with that which cannot be assumed: health, home, rights, respected personhood, and at times the future itself. *They don't understand, will never understand, what it means to carry this stress, and those of us who do must talk about it as incitement on our own, complex terms. It is always killing us, slowly and quickly, but maybe now is their time to suffer.*

An insurgency imperative accompanies a revival that is White Nationalist in origin, and white supremacist-misogynist in form. It is a different kind of invitation, one that thrills in living against, creating for, refusing the impossible, renarrating the "practical," catalyzing collective genius to shift a historical script. As always, this is nothing new, although it might make sense to inhabit the thing as if everything is still to be done.

TEAR DOWN WHITE SUPREMACY

Jesus Barraza and Melanie Cervantes

AS THE US OLIGARCHY EXPANDS ITS WAR, MIDDLE-CLASS WHITE PEOPLE MUST TAKE A SIDE

Robert Nichols

The United States has always used war and theft to build its power and wealth. There has never been a single decade of US history in which this hasn't been true. For Native Americans and African Americans, this has always been pretty obvious, since they have been the primary targets. Their labor and their land have fed the nation for centuries.

This plunder has had *fast* and *slow* versions. In the fast version, state power (usually the military and police) has been used to kill people and steal from them. In the slow version, people have been forced into unequal and unfair working and living conditions. When people cannot effectively control the conditions of their own employment, they can work their lives away and find themselves no better off in real terms because, for every dollar they make for themselves, they are making two for their bosses.

This system has historically been held together, in part, because the wealth that has been generated by this dual-track plunder has been distributed outward and downward to a significant section of the middle-class white population. Middle-class white people (such as myself) find that, while we always have something to complain about, our experience of the United States isn't so bad. It seems like a relatively stable, fair, prosperous country, with a decent system of laws and government.

However, over the last few decades, the unspoken agreement amongst the white middle class and the very wealthy has been breaking down. The wealth that is generated by the hundreds of millions of working people is no longer reaching even the middle-class white world. It is shifting upward to an ever-smaller group of super billionaires. People have an intuitive sense that this is unfair. These ultra-wealthy oligarchs do not work billions of times harder than the average store clerk, teacher, or factory worker.

Whom have we blamed? The political class. There is now a widespread crisis across the liberal-democracies of the "West," because people no longer trust their political elites to work in their interest. They see these political elites as removed from the reality of the average person, and as trying merely to benefit themselves. By and large, they are right.

The ultra-wealthy oligarchs of the world have picked up on this and are doing something very smart—they are getting on the bandwagon. They are using this as an opportunity to simply remove the middleman. Whereas the political class used to mediate between the middle class and the ultra-rich (constraining them somewhat, while distributing some of the wealth back downward to us), the billionaire class has used this crisis as an opportunity to simply remove the "politicians." They are working to totally merge the corporate and political worlds, and will now rule directly, no longer needing the 'politicians' as their managers.

In my view, this is what the Trump administration represents: a coup d'état by the ultra-elite billionaire oligarchs, who have effectively eliminated the political-managerial class that used to sit between us and them. Trump's cabinet, the wealthiest in history, is staffed almost exclusively by billionaires and millionaires.[1]

There are—at least—two consequences of this: the old war-and-theft system is: *speeding up* and *widening*.

They are shifting from the slow mode of plunder to the fast one. Despite all the talk about "small government," this administration is building up the massive state power that is needed to forcibly control, arrest, and deport millions of poor and working-class

---

1. Juliana Goldman, "Donald Trump's Cabinet richest in US history, historians say," *CBS News*, December 20, 2016, https://www.cbsnews.com/news/donald-trump-cabinet-richest-in-us-history-historians-say/.

people. They have to do this because, no matter how wealthy they are, a few hundred people cannot rule over the billions of humanity without direct force. So the war is moving back into its "fast" phase.

In doing this, however, they are also catching a larger and larger segment of the total population in their net. As I said, the United States has always been in a kind of low-level war against Native Americans and African Americans, but this has been spreading to include Latinos, Muslims, LGBTQ+ communities, migrants and refugees, environmentalists, feminists, even scientists and journalists. All of these groups now face direct suppression and control by the Trump administration.

Here is where a great opportunity can be found. Now that the war and theft is speeding up and spreading outward, it is catching up many more people, including many of the white-middle-class people who used to think that they were safe from all that kind of thing. The big question will be: what will we middle class white people do? Will we fight only to return to the old system, that is, to return to the "slow war" period, the time when people of color were exploited and dominated, with (some of) the benefits trickling down to us? Or will we stand with those people who have *always* been fighting this system against the authoritarians and oligarchs in order to produce a new and more universally just system? What side are we on?

AGGRIEVED WHITENESS

WHITE IDENTITY POLITICS AND MODERN AMERICAN RACIAL FORMATION

Mike King

Race has always been the fundamental political contradiction of our society. White supremacy in the United States has been challenged and has evolved a great deal, as has the society in which it is embedded, since the initial formulaic construction of racial social ordering. From the conception of the American racial system in the US South in the early 1600s to the current moment of mass incarceration, unequal education, and persistent state and vigilante violence, white supremacy has been challenged but also refashioned, repackaged, and reproduced. This article argues that aggrieved whiteness is a historically new facet of US racial formation, cohering as an approach to race politics after the civil rights movement and gaining material and ideological support throughout the neoliberal era. Furthermore, social wage retrenchment in the neoliberal era and the concomitant fivefold expansions of state expenditures throughout the criminal justice system are symbiotically entwined with aggrieved whiteness and its political mobilization.[1] This politics became far more vocal, visible, mobilized, and violent[2] during the Obama presidency, as economic crisis, burgeoning class inequality, social atomization, and a lack of responsive political institutions became more acute. Aggrieved

---

1. Paula Ioanide, *The Emotional Politics of Racism: How Feelings Trump Facts in an Era of Colorblindness* (Stanford, CA: University of Stanford Press, 2015).

2. Charles Kurzman and David Schanzer, "The Growing Right-Wing Terror Threat," *New York Times*, June 16, 2015, https://www.nytimes.com/2015/06/16/opinion/the-other-terror-threat.html.

whiteness was central to Trump's election, and its ideas have been core tenets of his presidency.

Aggrieved whiteness is a pillar of contemporary US racial formation, linking the material political projects of neoliberal carcerality[3] with racial representations and identities. Michael Omi and Howard Winant define the ideological connective tissue between material inequality and socially constructed racial identities as a "racial project":

> A racial project is simultaneously an interpretation, representation, or explanation of racial dynamics, and an effort to reorganize and redistribute resources along particular racial lines.[4]

Racial projects are sociohistorical products of the material conditions and political conflicts of particular eras. They connect racial attitudes to ideological structures and political processes, in order to mobilize political actors in efforts to reorder racialized power relations in society. These projects are more than individual attitudes or viewpoints, but they do include an affective component. The racial project of aggrieved whiteness organizes white public feelings toward specific material ends of racial redistribution of power, wealth, and social standing in the era of neoliberal carcerality.

Attitudes of white racial resentment are longstanding. The two primary politico-economic and ideological trends differentiating the racial project of aggrieved whiteness from earlier conceptions of white political identity are neoliberalism and individualistic identity politics. Contemporary resentment attitudes (and the broader ideology and politics of which they are a part) are now affectively attached *to* and articulated *through* the assumptions, values, beliefs, and objectives of a neoliberal political terrain. This terrain is defined by a carceral/warfare state that privileges security over previous obligations toward the general social welfare, within an increasingly atomized and unequal

3. Politically, defined by the substitution of social welfare provisions with racialized increases in policing and prisons within an economic context of deindustrialization and rising class inequality. See, for example: Ioanide, *The Emotional Politics of Racism*; Lauren Berlant, *The Queen of America Goes to Washington City* (Durham, NC: Duke University Press, 1997).
4. Michael Omi and Howard Winant, *Racial Formation in the United States: From the 1960s to the 1990s* (New York: Routledge, 1994), 56.

society where government revenue and expenditures have consistently been understood through racialized dog-whistle racial politics.[5] Contemporary white racial resentment also differs from past eras of resentment in how it is articulated through normative dehistoricized and nonmaterial identity politics. The racial project of aggrieved whiteness is oriented toward reconstructing white racial hegemony through: a) positing a post-racial social order, in which evidence of material racial inequality is explained through meritocratic individualism, and b) defining efforts to recognize or address real material racial inequality (through government policies or through social movements) as a form of social injustice that systematically disadvantages whites. While the ideology of white supremacy, and white resentment as a subset of that ideology, are by no means new, their ontological grounding within a political context of presumed post-racialism allows white victimhood politics to be popularly expressed as simply the unbiased pursuit of group interests. The politics of aggrieved whiteness has been mutually constituted by racialized neoliberal-carceral restructuring and the subjectivities of race and class that they coproduce.

Throughout the years of the Obama presidency, aggrieved whiteness became more ideologically cohesive through the covert and overt political mobilization of its adherents in the Tea Party and "Birther" movements, and then most visibly through Donald Trump's candidacy and electoral victory.[6] This politico-ideological project asserts that white citizens in the US are racially subjected and structurally discriminated against by powerful forces which limit their life chances due to their whiteness. Despite clear and persistent sociocultural and politico-economic structures of white supremacy, that serve to privilege rather than oppress white people, a politics of aggrieved whiteness has nevertheless become increasingly prevalent. The politics refashion "bootstraps" arguments that individualize and dehistoricize real racial disadvantage for people of color, elevating a diverse list of

---

5. Ian Haney Lopez, *Dog Whistle Politics: How Coded Racial Appeals Have Reinvented Racism and Wrecked the Middle Class* (New York: Oxford University Press, 2014), 66–69.
6. Samuel Sommers and Michael Norton, "Whites See Racism as a Zero-Sum Game that They Are Now Losing," *Perspectives on Psychological Science* 6, no. 3 (2011): 215–218.

racialized scapegoats which demand punitive containment, and amplifying longstanding white racial resentments to affirmative action and welfare. Aggrieved whiteness is a white identity politics aimed at maintaining white sociopolitical hegemony. For example, by challenging efforts to combat actual material racial inequality, while supporting heavily racialized investments in policing, prisons, and the military, and positing a narrative of antiwhite racial oppression loosely rooted in an assortment of racialized threats.

Public opinion polls suggest the prevalence of aggrieved whiteness beliefs. A Public Religion Research Institute poll found that 44 percent of all Americans and 61 percent of Tea Party supporters in 2010 thought that discrimination against whites was just as great as discrimination against racial minorities.[7] A Pew Research poll taken in August 2014—two weeks after the killing of Mike Brown in Ferguson, Missouri—revealed that "about seven in ten whites (71%) expressed a great deal or fair amount of confidence in local police to treat Black and white people equally, compared with just 36% of blacks."[8] When asked about the Black Lives Matter movement, respondents to a September 2015 PBS poll revealed, "59 percent of whites think it distracts attention from real issues."[9] These polls illustrate the extent to which white majorities identify themselves as racialized victims, a politics that goes beyond a simple resentful reaction to the election of the first mixed-race president, or blowback to emerging Black social movements. These polls reflect more than persistent individual biases or longstanding projected fear among white respondents; they highlight the much broader and paradoxical ways in which white supremacy has become fundamentally linked with a subject position of victimhood.

---

7. Robert Jones and Daniel Cox, "Old Alignments, Emerging Fault Lines: Findings from the 2010 Post-Election American Values Survey," http://publicreligion.org/site/wp-content/uploads/2011/06/2010-Post-election-American-Values-Survey-Report.pdf.

8. Bruce Drake, "Divide Between Blacks and Whites on Police Runs Deep," Pew Research Center, April 28, 2015, http://www.pewresearch.org/fact-tank/2015/04/28/blacks-whites-police/.

9. Margaret Myers, "Race Relations in U.S. at a Low Point in Recent History, New Poll Suggests," *PBS*, September 21, 2015. http://www.pbs.org/newshour/rundown/race-relations-low-point-recent-history-new-poll-suggests/.

Within the existing racial formation in the United States, aggrieved whiteness has become the public face of modern white supremacy—a contradictory identity through which white political and economic dominance is maintained through rolling back the limited racial progress of the civil rights movement under the auspices of meritocratic fairness. The ideology of white supremacy has evolved over time, and is composed of sets of ideas articulated together to give coherence to dominant racial ideas, practices, and political subjects.[10] Racial stereotypes, racialized public emotions, assumptions about social structures and relations, and contemporary political mobilizations are articulated (and rearticulated) to provide ideological coherence for the existing racial formation, and identities for people living within it. Articulated through existing racial stereotypes, post–civil rights attitudes of resentment, New Right racialized antistatism and neoliberal carcerality, in addition to recent mainstream political movements overtly situated around white identity, aggrieved whiteness has become the hegemonic racial project within the contemporary US' racial formation.

The fact that aggrieved whiteness is not firmly rooted in fact or rational logic (i.e., economically, politically, and socially white Americans as a social group consistently benefit rather than suffer from racial inequality) does not differentiate it from previous sociopolitical white supremacist claims (i.e., the white man's burden, eugenics, the culture of poverty). Therefore, I will not go to great lengths to illustrate the extent of white privilege in the United States, nor the factual baselessness of this projected victimhood. My aims in this article are to provide a rough sketch of the politics of aggrieved whiteness in contemporary US politics and society, and to begin an analysis of the two major intersecting social contexts through which this politics has emerged.

---

10. Omi and Winant, *Racial Formation in the United States*, 53–61; Stuart Hall, "The Whites of Their Eyes: Racist Ideologies and the Media," in *Gender, Race and Class in the Media*, eds. Gail Dines and Jean Humez (New York: Sage Publications, 1995), 18–19.

ECONOMIC AND PSYCHOLOGICAL WAGES OF
WHITENESS AS SOCIOHISTORICAL CONSTRUCTS

At its most basic, race is about seeing and treating people differently in society based on historically constructed racial identities—a
reinforcing process of defining and then treating people from racialized groups as less than human. This sociopolitical structure
of race was the founding cornerstone of racialized chattel slavery,
predating both industrialization and US independence. Despite
real historical changes over time, race remains a sociopolitical
order engrained in the US state and society. It is an order that
has evolved through both challenges to the racial order by social
movements and to meet the historically determined needs of the
polity and economy.[11] Throughout its history, race has been a core
determinant of the US class structure and a political category that
organizes where and how people live, with state and vigilante violence working at different times and in different ways to enforce
a socio-geographic racial ordering of individuals and populations.

A consistent feature of the US racial order has been the intrinsic elevation of all whites—regardless of occupation, education,
wealth, or personal lifestyle—to a sociopolitical status higher than
other racial groups. This stratification was instilled and reproduced
through separate but reinforcing norms of social status (political
rights and social privileges) and economic benefit (access to work,
land, and other mechanisms for the construction of personal
wealth). The economic advantages and disadvantages directly related to race (from slavery, to Jim Crow, to the post–civil rights movement) have been accompanied by an evolving set of social privileges
produced and maintained by political structures as well as social
relations supported by various ideological incarnations of white
supremacy. W.E.B. Du Bois articulated this political and economic
stratification as a measurable set of wages (an economic wage and
a social psychological wage) understood at different sociopolitical
levels from individual consciousness to macro-level social relations.
Du Bois explains the importance of the sociopsychological wages of
whiteness as they intersect material advantages:

---

11. Loic Wacquant, "Deadly Symbiosis: When Ghetto and Prison Meet and Mesh,"
Punishment & Society 3, no. 1 (2001): 95–134.

It must be remembered that the white group of laborers, while they received a low wage, were compensated in part by a sort of public and psychological wage. They were given public defer- ence and titles of courtesy because they were white. They were admitted freely with all classes of white people to public func- tions, public parks, and the best schools. The police were drawn from their ranks, and the courts, dependent on their votes, treated them with such leniency as to encourage lawlessness. Their vote selected public officials, and while this had small effect upon the economic situation, it had great effect upon their personal treatment and the deference shown them. White schoolhouses were the best in the community, and conspicu- ously placed, and they cost anywhere from twice to ten times as much per capita as the colored schools. The newspapers special- ized on news that flattered the poor whites and almost utterly ignored the Negro except in crime and ridicule.[12]

White supremacy as a system, and whiteness as an identity within that system, are durable historical structures, but ones that can- not be reproduced without mobilizing support for race as a set of political practices that enacts white identity at the level of in- dividual consciousness and political agency. White identity and the psychological wage collected at the level of the individual— as esteem derived from a privileged racial status, self-definition through anger directed at the other, exemptions from racialized punishments meted out to people of color, or the affective connec- tion to a white racial worldview—is only realizable in and through tangible policies that publicly demarcate the significance of race by elevating one group over another. Even when ostensibly color- blind, or advanced through racially coded language, the "public and psychological wage" is contingent upon and inexorably linked with material racial inequalities produced by political structures and policies, it is not simply an ideational process at the level of individual consciousness or identity.

Drawing from Du Bois's own limited engagement with this valuable set of concepts he generated, I contend that the public and psychological wages are primarily derived in the political sphere

---

12. W.E.B. Du Bois, *Black Reconstruction in America: 1860–1880* (New York: Free Press, 1998), 700–701.

and not simply at the level of ideology (whether it be modern conceptions of race rooted in "culture of poverty" assumptions or the individual instantiation of racial bigotry). Writing within the context of Jim Crow, the "public deference and titles of courtesy" Du Bois referred to in relation to the public and psychological wage are clearly linked to juridical and sociopolitical orders. In other words, it not simply personal (or social) ascription to white supremacy as ideology, but rather white supremacy as a political process.[13] The white identity that is forged by this public and psychological wage is only possible in and through race-making institutions and policies. It is therefore crucial to examine both the socio-psychological and economic wages of whiteness at the level of individual consciousness, support and action, as well as at the level of social relations, public policy, and the impact of powerful social structures on peoples' lived realities and life chances [See Figure 1].

FIGURE 1: ECONOMIC AND SOCIAL PSYCHOLOGICAL WAGES OF WHITENESS AT THE INDIVIDUAL AND SOCIAL LEVEL

	Economic Wages of Whiteness	Social Psychological Wages of Whiteness
Individual Level	Preferential access to jobs, land, and other mechanisms for the construction of personal wealth.	Psychological esteem derived from adherence to the political ideologies of white supremacy; positive affective social definition of self (racial other as a counterpoint and target for anger, a boogeyman to fear and control).
Social Level	Bifurcated class structure; hyper-exploitation and political exclusion of Black, Latino, Native populations.	A white status to be upheld/ supported through political processes of racial inequality— including state, vigilante, and structural violence against racialized groups.

13. Du Bois, *Black Reconstruction in America*, 700.

THE WAGES OF WHITENESS IN THE NEOLIBERAL, POST–CIVIL
RIGHTS MOVEMENT ERA

The fascists are the vanguard of the white race; however, the
big problem right now is not the white vanguard but the white
mainstream.

—Noel Ignatiev[14]

A material analysis of the aggrieved whiteness project illustrates
that its protagonist, the "white victim," is ultimately the offspring
of white supremacy and neoliberalism. From its origins in the
late-1960s, laid out ideologically by Nixon and more fully enacted
since the presidency of Ronald Reagan, US neoliberal carcerality
has combined a racialized project of backlash against the gains of
the civil rights movement with social welfare retrenchment, and
the political erosion of already limited working-class institutional
power (i.e., unions). The maintenance of racial structures and the
reproduction of an economically, politically, and socially exalted
white identity has been a cornerstone of modern conservativism
and of the overall bipartisan rightward political shifts of the neoliberal era. Nixon's Silent Majority was, at its most basic, the overt
reconstitution of a cross-class racial alliance through which public
support was mobilized against the subaltern racial (but also gender, sexual, and anti-imperial) insurgencies of the moment. The
growth of bipartisan, race-making carcerality[15] in the past four
decades has been the primary political mechanism driving the reformulation of the public and psychological wages of whiteness
within post–civil rights movement racial formation.

Neoliberalism and the carceral turn were borne out of the historic economic crisis of US capitalism that first emerged in the

---

14. Noel Ignatiev, "To Advance the Class Struggle, Abolish the White Race," October
30, 1994. Available at http://www.spunk.org/texts/pubs/lr/sp001714/racetrat.html.

15. The enormous expansion of police and prisons which began in the late-1960s, predominantly targeting Black urban neighborhoods, serve the function of intensifying
the longstanding criminalization of those communities while drawing political support from suburban and rural whites. Beyond the stark material inequalities these
changes brought, ideas about race which implied inherent Black criminality and white
innocence were reformulated and strengthened to support these projects, and to define racialized subjects more broadly.

mid-1960s and reached its height economically with the "stagfla-tion" that persisted through the 1970s and into the early 1980s.[16] It was within this period of political and economic crisis, where postwar working-class power was clearly declining, that the ap-peal of racialized conservatism won over more and more of the white working class, by articulating racialized fears with dog-whis-tle economic arguments about taxes and government spending (which were manufactured crises of neoliberalism's own making).

Now, more than a generation of working-class wage stagnation and political decline (made manifest in de-unionization, deindus-trialization, social service cuts, etc.) has symbiotically coincided with a nativist white politics of carcerality and class hatred for the racialized poor who have been hit the hardest by these politico-economic shifts. What the white working class lost economically in the last five decades has to some extent been mitigated by an increase in the sociopsychological wages of whiteness. This peri-od of precariousness across much of the working class has seen many white workers align themselves racially, to varying extents, in a white-cross class alliance with a neoliberal project that was in-extricably linked to race in the United States, finding affective sol-ace and self-affirmation in the punishment of the racialized poor. In the prevailing political contexts, where the working class has limited ability to effectively demand more of the economic pie, mobilized white fear and hostility has been effectively channeled against working class communities of color, in a race-making pro-cess materially enacted through the dual movement of social state retrenchment and carceral state expansion.

This politically mobilized bigotry has cohered within a neo-liberal strategy of shrinking the social state while shifting the tax burden off of upper tax brackets onto median-wage workers. By the time of Ronald Reagan's reelection in 1984, hostility toward government and economic strain was being channeled into sup-port for lower taxes and increased investment in the police, courts, and prisons to address problems of violent crime and drugs pre-sented in clear but coded racialized arguments and policies. The

---

16. Christian Parenti, *Lockdown America: Police and Prisons in the Age of Crisis* (New York: Verso Books, 1999) 36–44.

carceral shift was created by, and has re-solidified, a white cross-class alliance that has consistently attacked the racialized poor, represented in and through discourses of crime, welfare dependence, and "unfair state support." In this era of bipartisan neoliberalism, white fear and anger have successfully been channeled downward and outward against low-income Black and Latino communities—through the war on drugs, welfare reforms, social service cuts, and costly continuous war and military interventions around the world.[17]

In a context where the working class has little ability to demand higher wages, what has emerged as a political (and ultimately economic) form of activity of the white working class has been to expand the social-psychological wage. This form of agency has been mobilized, fostered, and nurtured by the Right since Richard Nixon's Silent Majority right up to Donald Trump. Beginning with Nixon's Silent Majority, the US political right-wing alliance has been able to broaden and deepen its base of support through the affective courting of socially dominant groups who feel threatened by the prospects of social equality; this connection was truly solidified by Reagan who was able to use this strategy to capture 74 percent of the Southern white male vote in 1984, and 66 percent of white males nationally.[18]

Beyond simply manipulating white resentment and fear, this mobilization of affect has been central in turning white working-class fear and uncertainty into active support for race-making political policies that have not only sought to roll back limited civil rights gains but to fundamentally shift the American state away from Keynesian redistribution toward punitive neoliberalism, from a (modest) liberal welfarism to a corporatist carceral-warfare state.[19] This rightward shift in government policy was symbiotically fostered in and through a racialized linkage of social liberalism with threats to white, heteronormative patriarchal power. Quoting the work of Jonathan Rieder, Omi and Winant describe how the rise of modern conservatism (which has shaped both

17. Ismael Hossein-Zadeh, *The Political Economy of US Militarism* (New York: Palgrave Macmillan, 2006).
18. Omi and Winant, *Racial Formation in the United States*, 133.
19. Ioanide, *Emotional Politics of Racism*, 34–42.

major political parties in the United States for decades) is intertwined with whiteness, in and through racialized, yet publicly coded attacks on liberalism, the social wage and wealth redistribution, which draw upon centuries-old individualist tenets within American politics:

> Liberalism came to be associated with 'profligacy, irresponsibility, and sanctimoniousness,' while conservatism acquired 'connotations of pragmatism, character, reciprocity, truthfulness, stoicism, manliness, realism, hardness, vengeance, strictness and responsibility.' Liberalism was seen as beholden to minorities, for whom it provided 'handouts,' while conservatism was thought to embrace traditional individualist (and thus 'colorblind') values of hard work and sacrifice.[20]

Viewed myopically, increasing white working-class support for this fused neoliberal-carceral turn is often seen as a form of "false consciousness." It is true that the neoliberal period has been one of economic stagnation for the white working class. For many white male workers in particular, it has been a period of significant losses to their economic and sociopsychological position as feudal lords of their households, as women have both proactively and out of economic necessity spent more time laboring for a wage outside of the home.[21] But political allegiance to race has materially insulated the white working class from the full brunt of neoliberal restructuring, which conceptually must include the hyper-incarceration of urban, Black working-class populations.[22] Arguments about false consciousness fall short, not only because they fail to recognize the very real and material (including economic) benefits of supporting white supremacy but also because they assume that material racial benefits are and have historically been economically and politically minor, a position that is hard to justify when examining either US history, or the contemporary neoliberal period.

20. Omi and Winant, *Racial Formation in the United States*, 140.

21. Silvia Federici, *Revolution at Point Zero: Housework, Reproduction, and Feminist Struggle* (Oakland, CA and Brooklyn, NY: PM Press/Common Notions, 2012), 46–51.

22. Loïc Wacquant, "Race, Class and Hyperincarceration in Revanchist America," *Daedalus* 139 (2010): 74.

While it is clear that white workers' efforts to reproduce their racial privileges through a cross-class alliance with capital has historically undercut (an inherently multiracial) class struggle, the public and psychological wages of whiteness have served as a "safety net" for the white working class. While the average white worker in the neoliberal period faces very real economic hardships—such as generalized wage stagnation, job insecurity, and an overall precarious economic position compared to previous generations—they have been largely exempt from the "carceral turn" that has taken place in the same period. Relative immunity from hyper-incarceration, but also from police profiling and violence, predatory mortgages and redlining, housing segregation, and associated public education inequality, are concrete benefits and core components of the modern social and psychological wages of whiteness. The "safety net" of whiteness has helped to mitigate—both economically and psychologically—the precarity wrought by a politically triumphant neoliberalism. The instantiation of the public and psychological wages of whiteness in this context of neoliberal carcerality includes the reformulation of a white political identity, which is defined as honest, hardworking, respectable.[23] This white identity is also notably defined as vulnerable; it is imagined to be victimized—socially, politically and economically—by the stereotyped other through which it is constituted, and against which carceral neoliberalism is fully directed.

This amalgamated white conservatism is central to modern American politics, while its overt racial nature is often subsumed and veiled.[24] Aggrieved whiteness articulates a white identity of racially coded political-moral supremacy (of hard work, responsibility, and meritocratic fairness) within a worldview where this identity has been wronged by entwined forces of social liberalism and racial progress. White victimhood is a political construct birthed by conservative narratives that posit the mythical forces of liberalism imposing unfair policies designed to target, exploit, and disadvantage historically dominant groups.

23. Michele Lamont, *The Dignity of Working Men: Morality and the Boundaries of Race, Class, and Immigration* (Cambridge, MA: Harvard University Press, 2000), 60–63.
24. Haney Lopez, *Dog Whistle Politics*.

As Joel Olson rigorously traced in *The Abolition of White Democracy*, the project of white supremacy has historically relied on several social pillars, notably the durable support for, and reproduction of, a white political identity and accompanying social policies and socioeconomic practices (segregation, the carceral turn, etc.)[25] The demonization of Latinx immigrants and the criminal pathologization of Black people, Arabs, and Muslims is the other side of the coin that normalizes an elevated status for whites as a sociopolitical group. Arguments of "post-racialism" are premised upon an acceptance of the generalized othering of nonwhites by a logic of white supremacy that relies on stereotypes rooted in projected social behaviors—Black criminality (violent threat), welfare dependence (laziness), or illegal status of immigrants (job competition and syphoned social services)—and not a quasi-biological logic. White supremacy, as it exists and reproduces itself socially, relies upon sets of beliefs that are cohered through active reinforcement from a variety of social structures, ultimately given life through social allegiance rather than rational logic or empirical validity. It is the imagined behavior, values, and integrity of the other which serves as a social, political, and cultural counterpoint for the construction of a noble, hard-working, meritocratic, individualist white identity (and not biology) which animates the elevation of whites to a superior sociopolitical status today.[26] This project is wrapped up in delusions, self-alienation, projections, and fears that are never directly confronted by whites, which allow them to maintain a fabricated coherence. Paula Ioanide has definitively stated how difficult the project of uprooting these white racial investments will be: "So long as notions of national identity are predicated on the affective enjoyments of exclusivity, possessive individualism, and justified violence, the devastation caused by nativist investments is not likely to disappear."[27]

25. Joel Olson, *The Abolition of White Democracy* (Minneapolis: University of Minnesota Press, 2004), xxix.
26. Lamont, *The Dignity of Working Men*, 60–63.
27. Ioanide, *Emotional Politics of Racism*, 137–38.

EMOTION, IDENTITY, AND PROJECTION AS RACIAL
AVOIDANCE AND RACIAL CONSTRUCTION

If men define situations as real, they are real in their consequences.

—W. I. and D. S. Thomas[28]

The intensification of socioeconomic inequalities, state violence, and punitive control in the post-civil rights era has largely been achieved through the organization of public feelings rather than facts.

—Paula Ioanide[29]

The ideologies that support white supremacy have generally posited fundamental differences between politically constructed racial categories. These ideologies seek to naturalize legally differential rights and privileges, unequal access to economic resources (in terms of jobs, capital, credit, public investment), and political power (from institutional controls to cultural representations). When the ideology of white supremacy shifted in the mid-nineteenth century away from a biological argument toward sociocultural ideas about cultural inferiority (of Black, Latinx, and Indigenous peoples in particular), it was accompanied by a litany of generalizations that sought to demonize, denigrate, and pathologize racialized groups while simultaneously elevating white status and social standing.[30] Suburbanization further strengthened whiteness through the incorporation of "white ethnics," or racialized wealth accumulation and geographic segregation. Just as the "scientific knowledge" that served as a foundation for early twentieth-century eugenics can be easily refuted, so too can the modern sociological foundations of a "culture of poverty." White supremacy does not—nor has it ever been inclined to—rely on objective or empirical facts as its foundation.

Political debates around issues like welfare, crime, crack cocaine, single mothers, and affirmative action have reinscribed

28. W.I Thomas and Dorothy Swaine Thomas, *The Child in America: Behavior Problems and Programs* (New York: A. A. Knopf, 1928), 572.

29. Ioanide, *Emotional Politics of Racism*, 1–2.

30. Omi and Winant, *Racial Formation in the United States*.

racial difference and hostilities while mobilizing a dual movement of welfare state deconstruction and the expansion of institution-alized state punitiveness disproportionately directed at impover-ished or racialized groups (or both). Ostensibly "colorblind" ef-forts to get tough on crime, or the undeserving poor, intrinsically target racialized groups or are at least understood as serving that function. Once enacted, these policies and practices—and the dis-proportionate impact they have on communities of color—seem to confirm the stereotypical assumptions that drove them in the first place. When looked at objectively, they reflect confirmation bias premised on racialized grievance.

Paula Ioanide has provided perhaps the most comprehensive discussion of how the construction, recognition, and response to racialized threats is rooted in historically structured feeling and the mobilization of affect toward political action, usually framed as protection from grossly exaggerated racialized threats rather than the overt, self-aware pursuit of white supremacist political interests. Ioanide argues that these threats, presented as "simulta-neously colorblind *and* race- and gender-specific, were the central conduits for creating public desires that legitimated state and neo-liberal restructuring toward military-carceral expansion and social wage disinvestment."[31]

Modern white supremacy is perpetually energized and repro-duced, both in practice and in thought, through manufactured social panics that refashion stereotypes and myths toward new political ends (the war on drugs, gangs, terror) and through coded initiatives presented as efforts to uphold individualistic fairness (welfare reform, attacks on affirmative action or "illegal" immi-gration). These projects result in structural, epistemic, and direct violence by the state or white vigilantes directed at racial others.[32] The massive, almost exponential, expansions of police, courts and prisons since 1980 has been a process of carceral state-building[33]

31. Ioanide, *Emotional Politics of Racism*, 4.

32. Stanley Cohen, *Folk Devils and Moral Panics* (New York: Routledge, 2002), 148; Stuart Hall et al., *Policing the Crisis: Mugging, the State, and Law & Order* (New York: Palgrave Macmillan, 2013), 240–242; Mike King, "'The Knockout Game': Moral Panic and the Politics of White Victimhood," *Race and Class* 56, no. 4 (2015): 85–94.

33. Ruth Wilson Gilmore, *Golden Gulag: Prisons, Surplus, Crisis, and Opposition in Globalizing California* (Berkeley: University of California Press, 2007), 85–86.

that serves two fundamental functions: to criminalize and disproportionately punish urban, Black (historically rebellious) populations, while simultaneously producing a politically useful white identity (premised on imagined potential victimization and legitimized vengeance).

Racial identities (including white identities) have been materially reconstructed and reproduced through this affective white adherence to racialized projects felt and supported as a means of self-defense and justice, rather than being self-understood as structural bias and selective punishment. These projections serve not only to demonize "others" but also to reinvest in the public and social wages of whiteness, fundamentally reconstructing a white self-identity of respectable social standing in accordance with dominant values. Ioanide argues that within these contexts feelings consistently overshadow facts:

> The widespread social panics over the perceived threats of criminality, terrorism, welfare dependency, and undocumented immigration in the post–civil rights era are similarly dismissive of reasonable facts and evidence. Although these threats are largely based on historically repeated myths, fallacies, misrepresentations, and hyperbolic and skewed information about Black, Latino/a, Arab, and/or Muslim people, revealing the overwhelmingly fabricated nature of these threats rarely stops people from believing and fearing them anyway. Because phobic emotional responses feel immanent and crucial to survival and the preservation of one's self-identity, people who experience them tend to feel first and perhaps think later.[34]

AGGRIEVED WHITENESS IN THE ERA OF IDENTITY POLITICS

Aggrieved whiteness is a brand of identity politics designed to secure resources (in relation to both the economic and socio-psychological wages of whiteness) upon a terrain that sees political and economic resources as part of a racialized zero-sum game. The formal, legal gains made in the civil rights era (for Black people and other racialized groups but also for women and LGBTQ+

---

34. Ioanide, *Emotional Politics of Racism*, 14.

persons) have been interpreted, not as a (partial) fulfillment of a pluralistic America and an extension of equal rights, but as gains made by subaltern groups that incur political and economic costs to socially privileged groups, in this case whites.

Wendy Brown's discussion of identity politics is useful here. Brown argues that in contemporary US identity politics, political subjects define themselves through harms that have been inflicted upon them, while distancing themselves from the vaguely conceptualized power that is responsible for that subordination.[35] After the repression and subsequent wane of the radical movements of the 1960s and 1970s, the central ideological frames on the Left shifted to liberal positions of identity—inclusion, diversity, privilege—and not systemic oppression related to persistent historical systems.. With systemic analyses of oppression largely out of the public imagination, and marginal within discussions of inequality, white backlash to the advances made and attempted in the '60s and '70s began mobilizing, with its resentment cloaked in the now pervasive language and logic of victimhood.

In the post–civil rights United States, in a context of perceived political equality, the construction of race as a zero-sum game where white people are at risk of losing political and economic dominance has become hegemonic. Beyond the simple individualistic white resentment of the 1970s (typified in popular culture by Archie Bunker), today's aggrieved whiteness is expressed through a collective white subject position that feels that its pursuit of white political interests is an attempt to achieve racial equality rather than a defense of racial advantages. The fact that this ideology, politics, and assortment of public feelings find coherence within dominant post-racial conceptions of race and power has far different implications than similar white resentments in previous historical moments. The dominant slogan of the Tea Party movement of "Taking Back our Country" or the resonance of Donald Trump's "Make America Great Again" speak directly to this widespread sentiment that white people are losing political control and economic standing within a polity where social dominance is implicitly their birthright. This perceived

---

35. Brown, *Politics Out of History* (Princeton, NJ: Princeton University Press, 2001), 22–27.

loss of power and privilege (again, not reflective of actual economic data but nonetheless real in terms of white affect) has resulted in an extremely individualistic and racist defense of a past racial status quo defined by an even starker sociopolitical racial ordering. Against a backdrop of a litany of imagined racialized moochers and schemers (the "welfare queen," the "illegal immigrant" with free healthcare, the threat of Syrian refugees, etc.), aggrieved whiteness is a conservative movement in the sense that it seeks to retain white privileges threatened by the prospect of racial equality.

For the average white worker, whatever privileged economic standing they may have seems both tenuous and historically declining, threatened by real forces of economic globalization beyond their control and an imagined litany of racialized groups who have secured "preferential treatment" in the post–civil rights era at their expense.[36] The politics of aggrieved whiteness offer both an elevated social standing to be protected against a host of ready-made antagonists who can be identified, targeted, and subdued

As Brown argues, contemporary identity politics is premised on identifying oneself apolitically, as a victim defined by a harm one cannot challenge. This produces forms of self-reified victimhood that reduce political identity to an effect of power. This moralistic definition of politics and the self makes formulating a vision to overcome social injustices ultimately impossible through the adoption of an identity that is powerless, both theoretically and practically. The late-modern loss of faith in historical progress and in the state as a vehicle for fostering justice is not exclusive to the Left. The individualistic politics rooted in identity groups competing for recognition and resources that Brown critiques on the Left is part of broader political trends and an approach to politics that has increasingly been adopted by socially dominant groups to protect their privileged position in and through presenting themselves as victims.

36. On a political landscape that ignores or distorts class by interpellating much of the working class as middle class in ways that are also racially coded as white (for instance, the way in which terms like "middle class" or "Main Street" refer to white workers as a group made up of wage-earners or near middle-income salaried employees) and where the working class has little institutional political power in society or representation in government, race has increasingly been how white workers have come to understand themselves, the state, questions of taxation and government spending, and the sociopolitical landscape at large.

On a political terrain in which subjects see their identities as abject effects of history (rather than understanding themselves as agents of history) and where the structural mechanisms that produce difference and material inequality are assumed to be immutable (and thus drop out of political discussion altogether), the political identity of "victim" has been decoupled from a materialist analysis across the political spectrum. In this context, dominant groups (whites, men, heterosexuals) have adopted identity politics and posited themselves as victims—of affirmative action, political correctness, diversity, and social programs that purportedly serve to advance the social standing of nonwhite, non-male, non-Christian, non-heterosexual persons. The Men's Rights Movement and modern Christian Conservative attacks on marriage equality, reproductive rights, or secularism follow a similar pattern of victimhood as a strategy for maintaining a privileged social standing.

Aggrieved whiteness is the appropriation, by the white Right, of liberal discourses and understandings around race, which are premised on individuals and bias rather than groups and structural inequality. In the post–civil rights era, a more liberal discourse and strategy of identity politics was developed to replace the radical, structural analysis of the movements of the late-1960s. Liberal identity politics formulated wounded identities that became invested in a victimized status as a means for valuing group pain in an atomized political sphere where redistribution and justice are seen as unattainable.

In a political culture where power is not seen as relational, and questions of class and wealth are not understood as matters of exploitation or oppression, dominant groups have been able to make claims of material deprivation and victimization, the substantiating point of reference for which is previous eras in which their group's dominance was more pronounced. Aggrieved white identity politics are bolstered by mostly imagined, hyperbolic constructions of unfair advantage resulting from limited programs of affirmative action or social welfare designed to redress racialized (and/or gendered) inequality. These government policies aimed at historical structures of social inequality are understood in the parlance of white victimhood to undermine social hierarchies.

The discursive erasure of longstanding white material advantages derived from social, economic, and political relationships fundamentally rooted in white supremacy allows even limited ameliorative efforts to be cast as not only unnecessary but as a form of anti-white racial bias. Social facts and statistics about racialized material inequality, to the extent they are politically visible, are rationalized as effects of intrinsic sociocultural failings on the part of racialized groups (in regard to longstanding racist tropes of laziness, violence, manipulation, etc.), which are the cornerstones of modern US racial formation.[37] These mainstream politics of white sociocultural supremacy, usually presented in coded language in discussions of crime, poverty, welfare and employment, are the cornerstone of the aggrieved whiteness project—where any and all efforts to address material inequality are understood as upsetting a social order where whites are naturally dominant rather than privileged by systemic dynamics of advantage.

TOWARD A POLITICAL CARTOGRAPHY OF "GETTING OUR COUSINS"

Today there is still the white problem—its expectations, its power, its solidarity, its imagination. Even after the civil rights movement, whiteness stands at the path to a more democratic society like a troll at the bridge. The political task . . . is to chase the troll away, not to ignore it or invite it to the multicultural table.

—Joel Olson[38]

To all the good white folks out here, go get your cousins.

—Rosa Clemente[39]

The political task of challenging aggrieved whiteness, and white supremacy more broadly, hinges upon substantially new movements, agendas, and visions. Rational arguments about white privilege and data that illustrate real and persistent racial inequality are necessary but wholly insufficient to dismantle an

---

37. Omi and Winant, *Racial Formation in the United States*, 59–60.
38. Joel Olson, *The Abolition of White Democracy*, 144.
39. Rosa Clemente, "To all the good white folks out here..." Twitter, April 28, 2015, https://twitter.com/rosaclemente/status/593059790638620673.

affective economy entrenched in a racial project dominated by white public feelings of fear, anger, anxiety, and vengeance.[40] Racial justice requires the development of a broad-based social vision that provides security, opportunity, and an embrace of shared and equal humanity—beyond, outside, and against individualistic, racialized, and morally fragmented white democracy. Backlash politics and entrenched white conservatism have been expressed in imagined, but politically real and consequential, notions of victimhood and in concrete policies of racial subjection. These politics, and entwined psychosocial and political structures that foster racial inequality while positing a postracial order, are forged through the political mobilization of constructed white affect.

What is necessary, as part of a broader antiracist strategy/praxis is to forge a crisis of white political identity; one that does not simply demand the recognition of white privilege. Discussions about white privilege tend to revolve around liberal recognition politics, with the same problems of political self-neutralization and victim reification that Wendy Brown deconstructed almost thirty years ago. Judith Butler has recently further elaborated Brown's point, emphasizing the necessity of addressing oppression rather than injury:

> There is a difference between calling for recognition of oppression in order to overcome oppression and calling for recognition of identity that now becomes defined by its injury. . . . The transition from an emphasis on injury to an emphasis on oppression is one that lets the category of identity become historical.[41]

From the standpoint of historically defined white subjects, this means coming to terms with historical relations of oppression, which they may not have created but are nonetheless defined by. As James Baldwin so poignantly stated, most white people have tried to avoid coming to terms with history and the forms of self-realization (and/or perceived loss) this would entail:

40. Ioanide, *Emotional Politics of Racism*, 137–138.
41. Judith Butler and Athena Athanasiou, *Dispossession: The Performative in the Political* (Malden, MA: Polity Press, 2013), 87.

They are, in effect, still trapped in a history which they do not understand; and until they understand it, they cannot be released
from it. They have had to believe for so many years, and for innu-
merable reasons, that black men are inferior to white men. Many
of them, indeed, know better, but, as you will discover, people find
it very difficult to act on what they know. To act is to be committed,
and to be committed is to be in danger. In this case, the danger, in
the minds of most white Americans, is the loss of identity.[42]

Affectively, psychologically, and politically, for white people this
historical reckoning will mean recognizing that the identities that
they inhabit in their daily lives are borne out of historical legacies of
oppression. Adherence to the aggrieved whiteness political project
entails not only conscious and unconscious defense of white racial
privileges but also an ontological erasure of historically defined subjects—such as the ahistorical, individualist, and meritocratic belief
that we are all self-made subjects on an equal historical footing.

Taken at their best, all discussions of white privilege seek to
induce this historical reckoning. While there is value in white
recognition of their own privileges, an analysis or politics that
does not focus its attention on the material forces and structures
that produce that privilege (and the racial subjection of people of
color) and build a political movement for the abolition or radical
transformation of those structures, including white identity, is
ultimately flawed. White supremacy is not premised on a lack of
white recognition of the privileges white supremacy bestows upon
them; it is founded on institutional and social relations that foster differential life chances based on race. These social relations
are reproduced largely through white political support, not identity as such. While the two tend to go hand-in-hand, there is an
important distinction between racial privileges that accrue to all
white people as a result of existing historical structural relations,
and the active or nascent support for those structural relations.
At their best, discussions of white privilege are an essential first
step toward identifying those relations, how they are socially reproduced, and the political choice people who have been
socially defined as white have, to either support or oppose the

---

42. James Baldwin, *The Fire Next Time* (New York: Dial Press, 1963), 22–23.

various policies, social institutions, and mindsets that reproduce white supremacy.

For example of an oppositional project, in the 1990s, the journal *Race Traitor* helped develop a material analysis of white identity that explored the mechanisms through which white supremacy can be effectively undermined. While it has been challenged for being too agential, and perhaps strategically privileging subjects socially defined as white, there is much to be gained today by revisiting the strengths and limitations of this approach, especially in the context of discussions of identity and political praxis. The following extended quote, from the editorial statement in the first volume of the journal in 1993, gives a sense of *Race Traitor*'s political currency:

> The existence of the white race depends on the willingness of those assigned to it to place their racial interests above class, gender or any other interests they hold. The defection of enough of its members to make it unreliable as a determinant of behavior will set off tremors that will lead to its collapse . . . . The white race is a club, which enrolls certain people at birth, without their consent, and brings them up according to its rules. For the most part the members go through life accepting the benefits of membership, without thinking about the costs . . . RACE TRAITOR exists, not to make converts, but to reach out to those who are dissatisfied with the terms of membership in the white club. Its primary intended audience will be those people commonly called whites who, in one way or another, understand whiteness to be a problem that perpetuates injustice and prevents even the well-disposed among them from joining unequivocally in the struggle for human freedom. By engaging these dissidents in a journey of discovery into whiteness and its discontents, we hope to take part, together with others, in the process of defining a new human community.[43]

If "treason to whiteness is loyalty to humanity," as *Race Traitor*'s motto suggests, this project should be a richer articulation to a

---

43. "Abolish the White Race—By Any Means Necessary," *Race Traitor*, no.1 (Winter 1993), http://racetraitor.org/abolish.html. See also Noel Ignatiev and John Garvey (eds.), *Race Traitor* (New York: Routledge, 1996).

broader audience of what that humanity could be, and a challenge to people socially defined as white to make an informed choice between whiteness and humanity. At the level of political identity, and of thought and action, the proactive definition of future identities rooted in a shared humanity, materialized through everyday life practices of equality, respect and cooperation, are essential not only to undermine existing oppressive systems but also to develop alternative, viable, durable, liberatory social relations.

Reinvigorating or reworking a race traitor approach does not mean arguing that white allegiance to the white club is the "linchpin" of white supremacy. There is no singular linchpin to any durable set of structural relations. An intercommunal[44] approach to challenging white supremacy might be likened to the classic children's game KerPlunk, which begins with a multitude of pins placed through a cylinder that forms a web within the cylinder, upon which rests dozens of marbles. Success is achieved by strategically removing individual pins in order to negate the structural integrity of the pre-established web of overlapping pins that holds all the marbles (social relations) in place. Political efforts to undermine the viability of the "white club" should be understood and strategically engaged as part of a broader and interdependent set of efforts to dismantle white supremacy. We must figure out how to formulate and bring into being through practice and struggle a new identity and social role for those who are structurally defined as white in our existing society today.

---

44. The intercommunalism put forward by the Black Panther Party, probably furthest materialized by Fred Hampton and the Rainbow Coalition in Chicago before being systematically attacked by the state, offers lessons and potentially a model to be reformulated. In terms of cooperation, alliances, and coalitions among different political organizations, intercommunalism was premised on valuing group autonomy while prioritizing shared struggle and political action against common enemies, and prefiguring a new social order. Huey Newton put forward the following analysis of intercommunalism: "If we get rid of this enemy in a united common struggle it will be easy to transform this unity into a common scheme of things. We are not separate nations of men to continue the pattern of fighting amongst ourselves. We are a large collection of communities who can unite and fight together against our common enemy. The United States' domination over all our territories equals a reactionary (in opposition to the interests of all) set of circumstances among our communities: Reactionary Intercommunalism. We can transform these circumstances to all our benefit: Revolutionary Intercommunalism." [David Hilliard and Donald Weise, *The Huey P. Newton Reader* (New York: Seven Stories Press, 2002), 236.]

The abolition of white democracy requires direct challenges to both the political structures of enduring white supremacy and the political identities that reproduce and are reinforced by them. Such a process of political change succeeds in large part by imagining and articulating new subject positions, new social relations, and a new society devoid of racial hierarchies, while fostering social struggles and political crises through which people learn how to remake themselves and their world through action. In order to undermine existing oppressive structures and to foster a new social order rooted in racial justice and resilient to countervailing forces, these efforts will require a resurgence of class struggle, but must also squarely oppose oppression based on gender, sexuality, and other axes of social inequality. Resistance to marriage equality, persistent attacks on women's reproductive autonomy, and the perception of secularism as the oppression of Christians ("if people define the War on Christmas as real, it is real in its consequences") not only follow a similar pattern of privileged groups positing their oppression to maintain that privileged status, they posit identities and political positions that codetermine, cohere, and reinforce each other.

Consciousness and peoples' politics are often determined in the course of social action. Social action and politics are both driven as much by affect as they are by rational self-interest, or seemingly stable political/social identities. The abolition of white democracy involves undermining the processes through which white political identity is elevated and defended. There surely is a role for people socially defined as white to play in the process of dismantling white supremacy, though the various contradictions, tensions, and conflicts involved in this process need to be further examined and strategy more clearly defined.

ART

IN THIS PLACE 206
NILDA BROOKLYN AND ADRIEN LEAVITT

In This Place 206 is a project about gentrification and the loss of queer space and memory in Capitol Hill, a historically queer neighborhood in Seattle. Centered around the portraits and stories of eight older queer women, our project was designed to carve out physical space, both online and in person, as a way to address changing queer cultural and political landscapes from the influx of new development and to focus on the tension we each face with erasure of memory through the erasure of landscape.

Our intention in creating this body of work is to examine one small story of gentrification in Seattle by looking at the stress that new development brings through the lens of its effects on a community of older queer women in the Capitol Hill area. It is also to create a memorial to the queer history physically leaving Capitol Hill and to engage newcomers with the physical location's history.

Each woman's portrait is present to tell those new to the neighborhood: here, for this moment, you must remember me. Each image, and the images as a collective work, serves as a reminder to the viewer that cities are built upon the lost stories of those who came before us.

Our project was also documented on Instagram:
#inthisplace206

ALREADY SOMETHING MORE

HETEROPATRIARCHY AND THE LIMITATIONS OF RIGHTS, INCLUSION, AND THE UNIVERSAL

J Sebastian

INTRODUCTION

Why are we seeking rights when our movements call for justice? Rights have served as a tool of contestation to challenge exclusionary practices and differentiated treatment for various groups over the course of the development of the United States. Several historic milestones reached in the early twenty-first century represent the narrative of inclusion through rights-based struggle. For example, in 2007, the Indigenous Rights caucus of the United Nations produced a ratified document of the Declaration on the Rights of Indigenous Peoples (UN DRIP), to which many have pointed as a sign of recognition and reconciliation between Native and settler societies.[1] In 2008, Barack Obama became the first biracial president in US history, a moment that prompted liberals and conservatives

---

1. For discussion of this point, see, Lorie M. Graham and Siegfried Wiessner, "Indigenous Sovereignty, Culture, and International Human Rights Law," *The South Atlantic Quarterly* 110, no. 2 (Spring 2011): 403–427. Available at https://sogip.word-press.com/2011/04/06/article-%C2%AB-indigenous-sovereignty-culture-and-international-human-rights-law-de-lorie-m-graham-et-siegfried-wiessner/. For a critique of this line of argument, see: Haunani-Kay Trask, *From a Native Daughter: Colonialism and Sovereignty in Hawai'i*, rev. ed. (Honolulu: University of Hawai'i Press, 1999); Linda Tuhiwai Smith, *Decolonizing Methodologies: Research and Indigenous Peoples* (New York: Palgrave, 1999); Glen Sean Coulthard, *Red Skin, White Masks: Rejecting the Colonial Politics of Recognition* (Minneapolis: University of Minnesota Press, 2014); Dian Million, *Therapeutic Nations: Healing in an Age of Indigenous Human Rights* (Tucson: University of Arizona Press, 2013).

alike to declare the country "postracial."[2] The gay rights movement secured the ability to marry through the 2015 US Supreme Court case *Obergefell v. Hodges*, at which point mainstream gay-rights advocates celebrated the achievement of full equality.[3] Despite the recent claims to inclusion through civil and human rights protections, state violence and harm still continue, especially against marginalized communities at the intersections of race, class, gender, sexuality, religion and disability, among others.[4]

Scholarship in the burgeoning field of Critical Ethnic Studies has demonstrated that the hierarchies constructing racial, gender, sexual, and class-based differences are rooted in the systemic power relations of settler colonialism—white supremacy, capitalism, and heteropatriarchy. Standardized ideas about social relations constitute these systems by determining difference as a means to discipline. Determining difference as a marker for disciplining is foundational to how these power dynamics continue. Heteropatriarchy functions to discipline difference into a naturalized system of social relations through the imposition of a male/female gender binary, compulsory heterosexuality, and dyadic nuclear family relations.

This mode of relationality, foundational to settler colonialism, attempts to foreclose other understandings of gender, social relations, and kinship networks.[5] This power dynamic arose through a specific sociopolitical worldview that privileges whiteness, wealth, conformity with the gender binary, and compulsory heterosexuality as natural, rational, and civil.[6] These relations

2. Richard Delgado and Jean Stefancic, *Critical Race Theory: An Introduction* (New York: New York University Press, 2012), 26.

3. Obergefell v. Hodges, 135 S. Ct. 2584 (2015). For discussion of "full equality," see, for example, Ariane de Vogue and Jeremy Diamond, "Supreme Court Rules in Favor of Same-Sex Marriage Nationwide," *CNN*, June 27, 2015, accessed October 20, 2015, http://www.cnn.com/2015/06/26/politics/supreme-court-same-sex-marriage-ruling/

4. See: Dean Spade, *Normal Life: Administrative Violence, Critical Trans Politics, and the Limits of the Law* (New York: South End Press, 2011); Joey L. Mogul, Andrea J. Ritchie, and Kay Whitlock, *Queer (In)Justice: The Criminalization of LGBT People in the United States* (Boston: Beacon Press, 2011); and Eric A. Stanley and Nat Smith (eds.), *Captive Genders: Trans Embodiment and the Prison Industrial Complex*, 2nd ed. (Oakland, CA: AK Press, 2015).

5. Arvin, Tuck, and Morrill, "Decolonizing Feminism," 13.

6. Following Oyèrónké Oyewùmí, I use the term "worldview" to describe Eurocentric privileging of the visual to represent the cultural logic of European societies, as opposed to "worldsense," which Oyewùmí uses to describe non-Western cultures' world

are not predetermined or endemic to social relations. Rather, they are a product of a particular trajectory of organizing sociopolitical relations that we can trace to the rise of colonial-modernity.[7]

As an analytic, colonial-modernity reflects the ways in which colonialism has been foundational to modernity. The rise of colonialism instituted a massive shift in sociopolitical relations that cohered systemic power relations through hierarchies of difference. As anticolonial theorist Patrick Wolfe has articulated, colonialism is not an event, but a structure; its logics recur through systemic colonialism, settler colonialism, and neocolonialism. Using a genealogical methodology, I employ a rereading of the first legal legitimization of Spanish colonialism by sixteenth-century Spanish jurist Francisco de Vitoria in order to engage the relationship between universal rights and civility within colonialism. This article offers an alternative lens on the history and origin of universal rights to show how Vitoria's work determined the legitimate exercise of universal rights through heteropatriarchal standards of civility.[8] The concept of civility furthers heteropatriarchal disciplining of social relations into accordance with Western (European/Christian) norms and standards.[9] I therefore argue that Vitoria's work constructs a set of shared universal rights on implicitly exclusive terms by fundamentally limiting who is capable of exercising universal rights.

Given the historical construction of universal rights and civility, this essay considers what it means to still talk in terms of furthering universal rights today. Because the structure of settler colonialism is ongoing, Vitoria's legitimation of Spanish colonialism through universal rights are deeply embedded in

---

frames that privilege many senses other than the visual, or a combination of senses. [Oyèrónké Oyewùmí, *The Invention of Women: Making an African Sense of Western Gender Discourses* (Minneapolis: University of Minnesota Press), 2–3.

7. Though a contested term, for purposes of this article I place colonial-modernity as formations of modernity grounded in colonialism. See: Saurabh Dube, "Introduction: Colonialism, Modernity, Colonial Modernity," *Nepantla: Views from the South* 3, no. 2 (2002): 203; and, Maria Lugones, "Heterosexualism and the Colonial/Modern Gender System," *Hypatia* 22, no. 1 (Winter 2007): 192.

8. The position of this argument is also to constantly question and critically analyze concepts such as and similar to the notions of the universal, civility, and normalcy throughout this essay.

9. Arvin, Tuck, and Morrill, "Decolonizing Feminism," 8–34.

the ongoing ideology of colonial-modernity. Placing Vitoria's work alongside queer and trans scholarship and activist critiques of mainstream LGBT rights demonstrates the ongoing consolidation of heteropatriarchy through notions of civility as embedded in the law to condition privileged access to an inherently exclusionary universal. The notion of so-called universal rights operates to bring people into parity with one another, based on the determination of such standards as set by the West. However, examining the emergence of the notion of the Western-universal through Vitoria's construction of universal rights reveals the issues in our present as part of the long-standing power relations of colonial-modernity. Under this construction, how could universal rights fundamentally function as universal?

UNIVERSAL CIVILITY

The civilizing mission is entrenched within the project of colonialism.[10] The concept of civility, in its most basic definition, articulates a difference between those who demonstrate the proper elements of civilization, and those who are considered to be uncivil. Federal Indian Law scholar Robert Williams, Jr. argues that the link between civility and conquest is deeply embedded in Western society, going back to Greco worldviews.[11] Throughout Vitoria's argument, this distinction between civil and uncivil is constantly at work, most notably in his framing of all Native peoples as "barbarians" in violation of natural law. In today's terms, the discourse of civility extends into determinations of proper citizenship, respectability, and normalcy.

---

10. Anghie argues that the setup of Vitoria's "civilizing mission" of colonialism as a way to exclude non-Europeans and conquer the land, and also to examine how this civilizing mission operates in relation to jurisprudential paradigms regarded as radically different, as a part of the larger project that aims to address the relationship between colonialism and international law. Anghie, Antony. *Imperialism, Sovereignty, and the Makings of International Law.* Cambridge: Cambridge University Press, 2005.

11. Robert Williams Jr., *Savage Anxieties: The Invention of Western Civilization* (New York: Palgrave Macmillan, 2012).

The origins of modern universal rights

Spanish King Charles V called upon Vitoria in 1537 to legally justify the project of colonialism and its institutions.[12] Responding in part to the narratives of brutal conquest by the *conquistadores*, Vitoria needed to demonstrate that Spanish conquest was operating under the proper legal accordance.[13] In particular, Vitoria was called to demonstrate that the Spanish had appropriate "just title," or legal rights, to be in the New World. Delivered forty years after Columbus landed in the Americas, Vitoria's work reflects the terms of the massive shift in sociopolitical relations, which by that point had violently conjoined Europe, the Americas, West Africa, and spread into the Philippines and south Asia through the coherence of systemic racial chattel slavery, emergent capitalism, and the missionizing spread of Christian conquest.[14]

In answering the question of what title justified the Spanish colonial conquest, Vitoria was confined to the legal justification of the late Middle Ages. However, as Vitoria delineated throughout the lecture *On the American Indians*, none of the standard justifications worked in this instance.[15] Vitoria himself held that when the Spanish landed in the New World, they had no just title for conquest: "In conclusion, the Spaniards, when they first sailed to the land of the barbarians, carried with them no right at all to occupy their countries."[16] Because of earlier precedence he had to follow, Vitoria also dismisses legitimate title on the basis of "discovery," and spreading Christianity. Though these two concepts will surface again as determinants for *intra*-European colonial competition, they are not the foundational basis on which the origins of colonialism are legally legitimized.[17]

---

12. Lewis Hanke, "Pope Paul III and the American Indian," *The Harvard Theological Review* 30, no. 2 (April 1932): 65–102.

13. Francisco de Vitoria, "On the American Indians," in *Vitoria: Political Writings*, eds. Anthony Pagden and Jeremy Lawrence (New York: Cambridge University Press, 1991), 234, 238, 244.

14. Lisa Lowe, *The Intimacies of Four Continents* (Durham, NC: Duke University Press, 2015); Cedric Robinson, *Black Marxism: The Making of the Black Radical Tradition* (Chapel Hill: University of North Carolina Press, 2000).

15. Anghie, *Imperialism*, 15.

16. Vitoria, "On the American Indians," 264.

17. On the Doctrine of Discovery, see, for instance, Robert J. Miller, *Native America, Discovered and Conquered: Thomas Jefferson, Lewis and Clark, and Manifest Destiny*

Vitoria provided the legal justification for Spanish colonial expansion into the Americas as predicated on the denial of Native societies' exercise of universal rights through their relegation to the uncivil. Vitoria utilized the framework of a universal, which does not actually contemplate inclusion for all, but rather privileges inclusion only for the civil European. Vitoria could not rely on the traditional medieval frameworks of European law to justify the colonial project, because none of them actually work to justify Spanish conquest. It was of a new order. Vitoria had to articulate a legal standard that would allow the lucrative endeavor of Spanish colonialism to continue, so that Spain was not found in violation of legal doctrines and potentially forced to forfeit its expansive project to another European crown.[18] In order to solve this dilemma, Vitoria resorted to a reformulation of a millennia-old Roman legal concept: the law of nations, which enables all nations to exercise the universal rights to trade, travel, and preach.[19] Vitoria espoused that the law of nations serves as the authority to create binding rights under which all nations operate. He further legitimated this notion of rights by claiming it would create a "common good" for humanity.[20]

The law of nations is important because it allowed Vitoria to place European and Native societies into the same plane of legal jurisdiction.[21] Through the law of nations framework, Vitoria determined that the Spanish were legitimately occupying their New World holdings through the right of the Spanish to travel,[22]

(Lincoln: University of Nebraska Press, 2008).

18. James Muldoon, *Popes, Lawyers, and Infidels: The Church and the non-Christian World 1250–1550* (Philadelphia: University of Pennsylvania Press, 1979), 142.

19. Vitoria states, "My first conclusion on this point will be that *the Spaniards have the right to travel and dwell in those countries, so long as they do no harm to the barbarians, and cannot be prevented from doing so.* The first proof comes from the law of nations (*ius gentium*), which either is or derives from natural law, as defined by the jurist: 'What natural reason has established among all nations is called the law of nations.'" [Vitoria, "On the American Indians," 278.]

20. Vitoria states, "But even on the occasions when [the *law of nations*] is not derived from natural law, the consent of the greater part of the world is enough to make it binding, especially when it is for the common good of all men." [Vitoria, "On the American Indians," 281.]

21. Anghie, *Imperialism*, 20.

22. In addressing the first "just title" for Spanish occupation, "of natural partnership and communication, Vitoria states that "the Spaniards have the right to travel and

preach,[23] and right to trade.[24] This allowed him to justify the extension of European governance, sociopolitical relations, and law into the Americas. By establishing this jurisdictional framework, Vitoria argued that the Spanish were entitled to exercise these universal rights as the legitimate grounds for colonial expansion. Furthermore, under the medieval doctrine of Just War, the universal right to trade legally legitimate the enslavement of Black people kidnapped into enslavement from continental Africa.[25]

Once Vitoria configured the law of nations as the universal framework joining the vast sociopolitical orders of the new world and the old world, he determined that the exercise of universal rights were not applicable for societies that were considered uncivil.[26] He explained this through the grounding of the law of na-

---

dwell in those countries, and cannot be prevented by them for doing so," as a right derived from the law of nations. [Vitoria, "On the American Indians," 278.] In this section, Vitoria cites Augustine for the denial of right of passage as an *iniuria* [injury] sufficient for war. [See specifically: Vitoria, "On the American Indians," Question 3, Article 1, Section 1, 278n75.]

23. Vitoria addresses this point at length within the section titled "Just titles by which the barbarians of the New World passed under the rule of the Spanish." [See Vitoria, "On the American Indians," 278–284.] Additionally, in the discussion of the second possible just title, "for the spreading of the Christian religion," Vitoria states, "my first proposition in support of this is that Christians have the right to preach and announce the Gospel in the lands of the barbarians," citing biblical scripture for this basis, and continues: "Second, it is clear from the preceding article, since if they have the right to travel and trade among them, then they must be able to teach them the truth if they are willing to listen, especially about matters to do with salvation and beatitude, much more so than about anything to do with any other human subject." [Vitoria, "On the American Indians," Question 3, Article 2, Section 9, in *Vitoria: Political Writings*, 284.]

24. Within the first just title, "of natural partnership and communication," legitimated through the *law of nations*, Vitoria states as the second proposition that the Spaniards may lawfully trade: "In the first place, the law of nations (*jus gentium*) is clear that travellers may carry on trade so long as they do no harm to the citizens; and second, in the same way it can be proved that this is lawful to divine law. Therefore any human enactment (*lex*) that prohibited such trade would indubitably be unreasonable. Third, their princes are obliged by natural law to love the Spaniards, and therefore cannot prohibit them without due cause from furthering their own interests, so long as this can be done without harm to the barbarians." [Vitoria, "On the American Indians," 279–280]; On Vitoria's elevation of the right to trade to the status of a universal right, see Georg Cavallar, *The Rights of Strangers, Theories of International Hospitality, the Global Community, and Political Justice Since Vitoria* (Burlington: Ashgate, 2002).

25. See, for example, Robinson, *Black Marxism*, 110.

26. Anghie states that in Victoria's formulation, natural law is the new "universal" system, a "novel system of universal natural law." Anghie, *Imperialism*, 19.

tions in "natural law," which is governed through reason: "What natural reason has established among all nations is called the law of nations."[27] Reason is the demonstration of civility, which Vitoria argues Native peoples possess. Vitoria states, "The proof of this is that they are not in point of fact madmen, but have judgment like other men. This is self evident, because they have some order (*ordo*) in their affairs . . . which indicates the use of reason."[28] However, Vitoria determines that Native societies possess only the *capacity* for reason as demonstrated by their uncivil aberrant cultural practices, which in turn justifies disciplining them into conformity with civilized Christian standards.[29]

The determination of reason does not entitle Native people to legitimately govern their own land. Vitoria uses the formation of a universal jurisdiction that binds all societies in order to hold that European ideology should be the standard for global governance and social relations. Under the right to preach, Vitoria justifies the imposition of civility through spreading Christianity to correct

---

27. Vitoria, "On the American Indians," 278. Situated within the Roman concept of the law of nature, European relations and social order were naturalized through the "capacity for reason" as resting primarily with Christian-Europeans: Roman law was thought of as the common basis for legal criteria and procedures and facilitated the expansion of property rights, contracts, and commercial transactions needed for an expanding mercantile society. At the root of Roman law were the principles of the "law of nature," which Black states embodied both the ten commandments and the law of nations (*ius gentium*), which primarily referred to "property rights, the sanctity of promises and principles of justice to be observed in buying, selling, lending, borrowing, letting, and hiring." Antony Black, *Political Thought in Europe 1250–1450* (Cambridge: Cambridge University Press 1992), 89.

28. Vitoria, "On the American Indians," 250.

29. Fitzpatrick argues that Vitoria first includes the Indians in the "universal order" and then expels them for purposes of not matching the norms of European society and "natural reason." [Peter Fitzpatrick, "Terminal Legality: Imperialism and the (de)composition of Law," in *Law, History, Colonialism: The Reach of Empire*, eds. Diane Kirkby and Catherine Coleborne (Manchester: Manchester University Press, 2001), 11.] Additionally, Antony Anghie argues that while Vitoria acknowledged the Indigenous peoples had their own governance structures and thus were not "incapable of reason," this same ability for reason bound the Indigenous "other" to the system of natural law and the law of nations: "Consequently, it is almost inevitable that the Indians, by their very existence and their own unique identity and cultural practices, violate this law, which appears to deal equally with both the Spanish and the Indians, but which produces very different effects because of the asymmetries between the Spanish and the Indians." [Antony Anghie, "The Evolution of International Law," *Third World Quarterly* 27, no. 5 (2006): 743.]

those who are in a state of sin and violation of natural law as the duty of the Spanish: "Since all those peoples are not merely in a state of sin, but presently in a state beyond salvation, it is the business of Christians to correct and direct them. Indeed, they are clearly obliged to do so."[30] By constructing Native societies as in possession of universal reason and within the same universal jurisdiction, Vitoria could claim that because their sociopolitical practices differ from Europeans, they must be properly brought into accordance with true reason—as civility, justified under the law of nations.

Vitoria bases the determination of incivility upon "natural law violations," which included but was not limited to sodomy, lesbianism, polygamy, buggery, bestiality, and cannibalism.[31] Violations of natural law are categorically marked in opposition to proper comportment with Christian European standards. These violations of natural law that form the basis of Vitoria's justification of the civilizing project are the foundational premises of colonial heteropatriarchy.

Additionally, Vitoria stated that if Native people resist Spanish conquest they are in violation of the Spaniards' universal rights to trade, travel, and preach: "If the barbarians attempt to deny the Spaniards in these matters which I have described as belonging to the law of nations, that is to say from trading and the rest . . . and they insist on replying with violence, the Spaniards may defend themselves, and do everything needful for their own safety. It is lawful to meet force with force."[32] Vitoria argued that if the Spanish are doing no harm then Native societies are not legitimately entitled to resist Spanish occupation.[33] Any Native resistance, read as a violation of universal rights, then subjects Native societies to legitimate warfare, conquest, and enslavement under the doctrine of Just War: "But if the barbarians deny the Spaniards what is theirs by the law of nations, they commit an offense against them.

---

30. Vitoria, "On the American Indians," 284.

31. Vitoria, "On the American Indians," 273.

32. Vitoria, "On the American Indians," 282.

33. "It is an act of war to bar those considered as enemies from entering a city or country, or to expel them if they are already in it. But since the barbarians have no just war against the Spaniards, assuming they are doing no harm, it is not lawful for them to bar them from their homeland." Vitoria, "On the American Indians," 278.

Hence, if war is necessary to obtain their (Spanish) rights, they may lawfully go to war."[34]

Vitoria relied on the reconfiguration of the law of nations because there was no precedential legal doctrine that justified the large-scale development of the project of colonialism. As political theorist Duncan Ivison explains, rights are a reflection of social relations.[35] I argue that Vitoria's work reflects the profound shift in social relations that systemic colonialism instituted, which, in turn, is a distinct shift from the operation of medieval rights. Medieval rights did not cohere to a singular, stabilized definition in the same way we think of the modern individuated right.[36] Traditional theories of rights development place the emergence of modern rights during the 16th-17th centuries of the so-calledEnlightenment. While Enlightenment theory certainly had an important role in shaping the individuated right, I am interested in challenging this narrative to instead consider how Vitoria's universal rights of colonialism configured a transition to individuated rights centuries before the Enlightenment.

Vitoria grounded the emergence of the individuated right in civility by determining which groups of people were entitled to access using heteropatriarchal notions of civility. Positioning the origination of modern rights in this formative historical moment, as opposed to in the Enlightenment, recognizes the impact of the already-forming colonial conditions of racialization, gendering, and sexual disciplining as in fact determinative of the ontological construction of universal rights. By reflecting the shift in sociopolitical relations of colonial-modernity, Vitoria constructed a framework of universality that inherently excluded those marked as uncivil from accessing it. Vitoria was operating from a particular position of European colonial power. This position does not in fact account for the experiences of all people across the world, but rather frames the European framework as civil and superior, and therefore universal, against and above all other societies because they were marked as different, and therefore uncivil.

---

34. Vitoria, "On the American Indians," 282.

35. Duncan Ivison, *Rights* (Montreal: McGill-Queen's University Press, 2008), 10.

36. See Ivison, *Rights*.

Disciplining the universal

The universal rights of the law of nations, and specifically the right to preach, configured the disciplining of natural law violations through the violent heteropatriarchal ordering of compulsory dyadic heterosexuality, the gender binary, and the attempted eradication of all other possible sociopolitical-spiritual-relational frameworks. Implicit in this framing are the embedded dynamics of anti-Blackness, anti-Indigeneity, the persecution of pagans, and Islamophobia that cohere within the colonizing fervor of Spain and other European countries in the late middle ages leading up to the moment of 1492.

The disciplining and criminalization of gender non-normativity and sexual acts between people not in compliance with the gender binary is well documented throughout the colonial register.[37] For example, in 1519, Hernan Cortez sent a letter to Spanish King Charles V asking for permission to punish Native peoples on the basis of claiming that all Native peoples were sodomites engaging in "abominable sin."[38] The Spanish historians that published the *General History of the Indies* beginning in 1526 detailed many firsthand reports claiming homosexuality and gender transgressions as common in Native societies, which continued to fuel justifications for conquest prior to Vitoria's legal examination.[39] People who presented outside the gender binary were often the first to be targeted for violence and death. Native Studies scholar Scott Morgenson argues that as the precursor to establishing colonial rule, people who did not conform to the gender binary were explicitly targeted within structures of colonial conquest.[40]

Settler colonialism functioned through this dynamic to produce a universally regulated social order that enforced certain types of social relations as primary and natural. These constructions of gender and sexual identity formation operated to *condition* the power

---

37. Frederico Garza Carvajal, *Butterflies Will Burn: Prosecuting Sodomites in Early Modern Spain and Mexico* (Austin: University of Texas Press, 2003).

38. Richard C. Trexler, *Sex and Conquest: Gendered Violence, Political Order, and the European Conquest of the Americas* (Ithaca: Cornell University Press, 1995), 1.

39. Trexler, *Sex and Conquest*, 1–2.

40. Scott Morgenson, "Theorising Gender, Sexuality, and Settler Colonialism–An Introduction," *Settler Colonial Studies* 2, no. 2 (2012): 14.

relations of settler colonialism.[41] Morgenson argues that western law worked to uphold heteropatriarchy as a social structure that was "universalized whenever settler societies come to be structured by a heteropatriarchal binary sex/gender system."[42] This phenomenon then became normalized not just to settlers or the Indigenous nations they occupy but to the whole world, which attempted to force the totality of *all* societies to conform to the western universal. Heteropatriarchy worked to undergird universal rights as the social and legal constructs that cohered, as both objective and legal, the violent incoherence of settler colonial governance.

In the narrative of Western development, gender is often framed as a binary that all cultures have, while gender nonconformity is an allegedly new development arising in the west. Colonial Studies scholar Maria Lugones emphasizes the importance of not naturalizing gender within critiques of colonialism so as to see the imposition of the gender binary not just as normative but as tied to the violent domination at work in differentiating notions of freedom through colonialism.[43] Some social structures had an understanding of three genders, more than three genders, and some did not determine relations on a gendered relation at all.[44] For example, African Gender Studies scholar Oyéronké Oyewùmí argues that the construct of gender itself is a colonial imposition, showing how in Yoruba society, gender was not an organizing principle prior to Western colonization.[45] Native Studies scholar Qwo-Li Driskill argues that "Two-Spirit" is a term that signifies resistance to definitions of sexuality and gender of colonialism, as reflective of other forms of relationality outside of heteropatriarchy.[46] Native feminist work has articulated the differing relations of Indigenous kinship as opposed to nuclear

---

41. Morgenson, "Theorizing Gender," 14–15.

42. Morgenson, "Theorizing Gender," 13.

43. Lugones, "Heterosexualism," 186–187.

44. Maria Lugones, "The Coloniality of Gender," *Worlds & Knowledges Otherwise* (Spring 2008): 8–11; see also Oyèrónké Oyewùmí (ed.), *African Gender Studies: A Reader* (New York: Palgrave Macmillan, 2005).

45. Oyewùmí, Oyèrónké. *The Invention of Women: Making an African Sense of Western Gender Discourses*, 31. Minneapolis: University of Minnesota Press, 1997.

46. Qwo-Li Driskill, "Stolen From Our Bodies: First Nations Two-Spirits/Queers and the Journey to a Sovereign Erotic," *Sail* 16, no. 2 (Summer 2004): 52.

families, which in turn are not dependent on heteropatriarchal formations of power relations.[47] My intent here is not to position all Indigenous societies as holding the same relationships to gender and sexuality, or that those varied relations were not without their own complications. Instead, I am focused on the imposition of a *singular*, universal structure for social relations that position the gender binary and heteropatriarchy as the standard form of relationality within colonial-modernity.

The construction of the universal in Vitoria's work is a false one. On its face it is objective and all encompassing, but in effect only operates to bring Indigenous societies into the universal so as to be disciplined, justifiably killed, enslaved, and fundamentally constructed as the "other" to the European settler. Through this framework, Indigenous societies writ large—across the globe—are legally differentiated from the European as inferior. This positions non-Europeans, including enslaved Africans, as conscripted to status of almost human and never achievably human, as already racialized in distinction to the superior, civil European.[48] This is not to elide the differentiated treatment and experience of how the racializing logics of anti-Blackness and Native erasure develop and function differently within colonial-modernity, alongside other racialized hierarchies.[49] Rather, positioning the formation of the European as civil *through* the demarcation of Indigeneity as uncivil, via logics of anti-Blackness and Native erasure, determines a white subjecthood, framed as a civil human, who is then entitled to accessing such 'universal rights' over and against those positioned as uncivil. Through this reading, we can locate how logics of racialization functioned to construct civility under colonialism as European supremacy, and its subsequent outgrowth of white supremacy.

47. Arvin, Tuck, and Morrill, "Decolonizing Feminism," 14–15; see also, for example, Mark Rifkin, *When Did Indians Become Straight? Kinship, the History of Sexuality, and Native Sovereignty* (New York: Oxford University Press, 2011).

48. See Sylvia Wynter, "Unsettling the Coloniality of being/power/truth/freedom: Towards the Human, after Man, its Overrepresentation—An argument," *CR: The New Centennial Review* 3, no. 3 (2003): 257–337; as well as Alexander Weheliye, *Habeas Viscus: Racializing Assemblages, Biopolitics, and Black Feminist Theories of the Human* (Durham, NC: Duke University Press, 2014). For a discussion of enslaved Africans as incorporated through the logic of just war, see Robinson, *Black Marxism*, 111.

49. For a discussion of racialized hierarchies under colonialism, see also Lowe, *Intimacies of Four Continents*.

From within the framework of colonial-modernity then, white supremacy, heteropatriarchy, and capitalism cohere as foundational systemic power relations that condition differentiated racialized and gendered treatment and access within our present institutions.

The disciplining of peoples into civility is well embedded in western societies, both in external and internal conquest. Within the trajectory of western society, incivility has been characterized as a myriad of practices and acts—paganism, polygamy, mysticism, witchcraft, and gender transgressions, among many others.[50] The quest to discipline social relations into civility continued to develop through the expansion of Roman-Christian Europe, in the persecution of the mystics, deviant formations of Christianity, the witch trials, the disciplining of paganism, the courtrooms of the Spanish Inquisition, the reification of a natural state of social relations, and in the construction of gender as a stable and determinate category predicated on a binary.

These narratives produce harmful standards of respectability as a prerequisite for state sanctioned inclusion, reinforcing rather than undermining heteropatriarchal and white supremacist standards of civility. To position Vitoria's work as a point of origin for the trajectory into our present demonstrates that the law has always disciplined deviance. Under this framework, the law cannot confer universal rights in a restorative way but will instead continue to reify and recondition the hierarchies at work within colonial-modernity.

REFORMATIONS OF POWER

What does reflecting on the concept of Vitoria's universal rights offer our present moment? The state condones and privileges practices that conform to Western standards of what is considered to be normal gender presentations, sexual relations, and household configurations. As such, the determinations of what is civilized continues to function in part through legal codifications of comportment to heteropatriarchal social norms.

---

50. See Silvia Federici, *Caliban and the Witch: Women, the Body and Primitive Accumulation* (New York: Autonomedia, 2014); Muldoon, *Popes, Lawyers, and Infidels*, 76–88; Williams, Jr., *Savage Anxieties*.

In situating civility as the formative determination for inclusion in the universal, we can trace connections to calls for inclusion today. Universal rights have been touted as a means of relieving disenfranchisement and harm. However, despite recent gains in the mainstream gay rights agenda, violence continues to devastatingly impact queer and trans communities, especially for people living at the intersections of disability, undocumented status, low income, street economy survival, and as targets of racialized state violence. By engaging contemporary queer and trans critiques of calls for incorporation, this final section addresses the stakes of inclusion and focuses on the question of who is left out and at what costs. The implication of this inquiry is that we must rethink standardized notions of gender, sexuality, and social relations as stable categories and instead consider that their enforcement functions as a key aspect of how western power is continually consolidated. Foregrounding how constructs of gender and sexuality are foundational to western power demonstrates that racial heteropatriarchy is a deeply rooted systemic power relation, and that because the colonial construct of universal rights remains predicated on conformity, increased inclusion will not ultimately alter this dynamic.

Universal inclusion

The recent gains of the mainstream LGBT rights agenda, such as the passage of gay marriage, contestations over trans inclusion in the military, and the repeal of Don't Ask, Don't Tell, position homonormativity—a striving to be "just like you"—as the desired state for queer and trans people. But this narrative is harmful, especially for people who cannot or do not want to comply with determinations of "normal" sexuality and gender. For instance, issues concerning gender conformity are receiving a lot of attention in our current moment. With the rise of transgender celebrities, the general increase in transgender visibility, debates centering access for transinclusive bathrooms and healthcare, and contestations over raising transgender children, we are seeing more mainstream media engagement with gender nonconformity than ever before. Alongside increased visibility, however, the notion of acceptable adherence to the gender binary still persists, leaving gender nonconforming people more susceptible to violence. Projects that seek inclusion into the heteropatriarchal mainstream universal are incentivized based on proximities to normal and acceptable constructions of gender as it reaffirms the gender binary. Trans, genderqueer, and gender nonconforming people who do not fit within the heteropatriarchal expectations of the gender binary are further displaced through systems of power that read nonnormative bodies as threats or impossibilities.[51]

Trans activist and poet Alok Vaid-Menon argues that greater transgender visibility and acceptance has not worked to alleviate harm for nonbinary people:

> The rest of us—whose identities are more fluid, more difficult for strangers to comprehend and relate to—may not be visible in media but are more noticeable on the streets. As it stands, according to a nationwide survey by the National Center for Transgender Equality, nonbinary people, especially those of us who are people of color, are more likely than binary trans people to attempt suicide, be harassed by the police, live in abject poverty and be sexually and physically assaulted. What has become evident is that so many of us who do not pass as male or female are still regarded as disposable by both cis and trans communities. Too often, efforts to gain acceptance and rights for trans men and trans women has meant ignoring those of us who are not as easily categorized.[52]

Although political gains have produced changes that encourage wider acceptance of trans people, this often operates through a focus on trans people who are read on one side of the gender binary. Heteropatriarchy compels people toward conforming to conceptions of gender framed as biological and understood primarily through scientific facts about distinct and separate "male" and "female" categorizations that correlate to expected behaviors, presentations, and social roles. As Vaid-Menon shows, when we

---

51. Spade, *Normal Life*, 41.

52. Alok Vaid-Menon, "Greater Transgender Visibility Hasn't Helped Non-Binary People—Like Me," *Guardian*, October 13, 2015, http://www.theguardian.com/commentisfree/2015/oct/13/greater-transgender-visibility-hasnt-helped-nonbinary-people-like-me.

understand the ways that heteropatriarchy works to construct trans, genderqueer, and many other formations of gender nonconformity as problematic divergences from this binary, we can work to focus less on inclusion into spaces that reaffirm those power relations and instead focus on other formations of social relationality that not only work to dismantle those systems but also center nonnormative ways of being that people are already practicing.

Creating new categories for inclusion through the law will not lead to the acceptance of gender nonconformity, because the standards for inclusion are rooted in notions of civility and conformity with the gender binary. Trans activist and legal scholar Dean Spade states that legibility under the law will not resolve the fundamental misrecognition of gender nonconformity for trans identified people.[53] Spade's *Normal Life* articulates how the law incorporates bodies under notions of legibility. This work demonstrates that to create more medical or administrative categories that resolidify which trans bodies demonstrate acceptable gender conformity is to fundamentally misrecognize possibilities outside the gender binary. The proliferation of further categorization operates on the terms of the law, and is therefore already determined by heteropatriarchal relations. Under systemic heteropatriarchy, the law disciplines people into legibility so that the state can determine access and benefits on the basis of deservedness, conformity, and criminality.

Given that systemic social relations are rooted in heteropatriarchy, rights-based inclusion is limited because it cannot work to undo heteropatriarchy as the system of power that continuously produces the construction of acceptable formations of sexuality and gender. Our very notions of what gender *is* have been conditioned through a regulation toward a rigid male-female binary that is enforced through the state-based practices of gender marking on IDs and birth certificates, in schools, in placement in prisons and gender segregated facilities, through access to benefits, healthcare, and a myriad of other mechanisms of demarcation. An analytic centering the power relation of heteropatriarchy understands that it is not better access to rights or "proper" placements

---

53. Spade, *Normal Life*.

in institutions like prisons that should be the aim of queer and trans resistance work, but rather a focus on dismantling the systems of power that produce notions of deviance as threats to a white supremacist and heteropatriarchal social order.

Narratives of state incorporation through access to rights frame only certain issues such as marriage and military participation as "gay issues," eliding the larger systems such as immigration detention, regulatory youth services, imprisonment, and difficulty in accessing state benefits and services that affect *all* people, including queer and trans people. Hate crimes legislation, under its stated goal of protection against racially and sexually motivated violence, has not decreased the likelihood of violence against queer and trans people. Instead, it has expanded policing and prisons as sites that violently affect queer and trans people, especially those who are low income and of color. Hawaiian scholar and trans activist Kalaniopua Young details how the dynamics of heteropatriarchy and settler colonial rule enforce legal and juridical apparatuses to justify the encapsulation of Indigenous peoples into the carceral space of prisons and policing: "The legal system has long been a site for legitimizing this process of land and cultural dispossession and ongoing indigenous alterity. According to this logic, at any point one can be silenced and forcibly pushed into camps and reserves and be labeled threatening to a liberal sensibility that sees itself as progressive, civil, modern, and multicultural."[54] Queer and trans people of color have always been fighting from a politics of struggle and survival against state violence working from the intersections of race, class, gender, and sexuality.[55] The rise of the movement for mainstream gay rights co-opted these liberation politics into mainstream rights-inclusionary campaigns to uphold heteronormative values of class ascendancy, marriage, and military participation that nonmainstream movements continue to counter.

---

54. Kalaniopua Young, "From a Native *Trans* Daughter: Carceral Refusal, Settler Colonialism, Re-routing the roots on an Indigenous Abolitionist Imaginary," in *Captive Genders*, 88.

55. Che Gossett, Tourmaline, and A.J. Lewis, "Reclaiming Our Lineage: Organized Queer, Gender-nonconforming, and Transgender Resistance to Police Violence," *S&F Online* 10.1–10.2 (2011/2012), http://sfonline.barnard.edu/a-new-queer-agenda/reclaiming-our-lineage-organized-queer-gender-nonconforming-and-transgender-resistance-to-police-violence/.

The specificity of the formation of colonial relations is important for framing calls to enter into the space of the universal through rights-based redress. Native Studies scholars Maile Arvin, Eve Tuck, and Angie Morrill argue that incorporation through civil rights functions as a project of expansion into a "multicultural universal" to maintain settler colonialism. By incorporating more people into the project of the United States, settler colonial governance is routinely secured and expanded to elide the ongoing conditions of occupation and genocide that maintain it. Arvin, Tuck, and Morrill argue against this type of multicultural inclusionist project because it works to naturalize settler colonialism, heteropatriarchy, and capitalism: "The prevalence of liberal multicultural discourses today effectively works to maintain settler colonialism because they make it easy to assume that all minorities and ethnic groups are different though working toward inclusion and equality, each in its own similar and parallel way."[56] Flattening the conditions of oppression for different categories of people through multicultural inclusionary laws and policies works to reaffirm the notion that these issues can be overcome if groups conform to standards of white life and achieve recognition through rights. Multiculturalism assumes not only that all groups of people fighting for rights have equal concerns, but that the universal will be able to account for all of them. A relational analysis instead allows us to understand that different groups of people experience different proximities to the systems of settler colonialism, white supremacy and heteropatriarchy, and receive different access to their privileges and benefits. This framework then allows for a rearticulation of concerns based not on formal inclusion into the universal through the flattened positionality of "diverse" groups, but rather through a focus on the dismantlement of the very systems that produce such privileges and inequalities in the first place.

These important critiques have demonstrated that gaining rights and protection under the law does not fundamentally shift the conditions of violence that continue to most impact low-income, trans and gender nonconforming people, people with

---

56. Arvin, Tuck, and Morrill, "Decolonizing Feminism," 10.

disabilities, Native people, immigrants, and people of color. An abolitionist politics formulates an analysis of why inclusion and equality into a universal predicated on unequal distributions of wealth through racial capitalism and state violence founded on settler colonialism will not deter the harm facing queer and trans people but rather recondition the continued expansion of the systemic violence of the universal.

Trans activist and filmmaker Tourmaline frames the importance of what is at stake when inclusion into the protected realm of the state is the primary goal of movement work. Tourmaline articulates that the contemporary moment has produced an increased visibility for trans people both in the media and in the eyes of the state, but that this is happening alongside increasing and extremely high rates of violence affecting the trans and queer community. Tourmaline ultimately argues that increasing visibility and inclusion does not equate to increasing safety:

> So often, visibility uses the lens of respectability to determine who, even in the most vulnerable communities, should be seen and heard. I believe that, through the filter of visibility, those of us most at risk to state violence become even more vulnerable to that violence. When we're trying to be normal, when we're trying to be included in a culture that never wanted us to be in the first place, we don't get to talk about our lives. We don't get to talk about sex work, we don't get to talk about being disabled, we don't get to talk about prison, or homelessness, or living with HIV. And if we can't talk about those parts of our lives, we can't come up with the strategies we need to survive, the strategies that give us the power to defend all parts of ourselves and our communities. And I'm saying that those least respectable ways of being, those most undesirable ways of being, are some of our communities' most profound ways of living against the state. . . .
> I think about the profound relationships and structures for care that were created by people being deeply and utterly disrespectful to and disloyal to the state and its morals. What I'm saying is that we don't need to be in a formal organization to do this profound antistate work. Just by hanging out and being social, just by taking care of each other, we are already doing the work that state doesn't want us to do. So when the state invites us in, we have to ask what ways of being the state will demand that we

stop doing, as a condition for inclusion? What ways of being,
that help us survive and thrive, do normalcy, respectability, and
visibility never allow for?[57]

Tourmaline articulates how the production of visibility for queer
and trans people forecloses discussion about aspects of people's
lives that are not deemed acceptable for inclusion into the universal, exemplifying how seeking state-based inclusion into a so-called
multicultural and diverse universal functions through narrativizing
queer and trans people as normal and deserving of incorporation
at the expense of those who do not fit those narratives. Following
Tourmaline's inquiry, when we seek inclusion into the white supremacist and heteropatriarchal universal, what do we risk losing
from our lives that is in fact essential to a celebration of nonnormative understandings of social relationality? What might be at stake
in passing over the very aspects of our lives that formulate different
relationality outside of incorporation into the intensive regulation
and violence of the state? An abolitionist framework must consider
the inherent limitations of rights-based inclusion into the universal because of the colonial construction of modern rights based on
notions of civility. Through framing universal rights as originating
in the attempt to legitimize colonial-modernity, we can move away
from rights and toward fighting for something more.

Beyond the universal

Under the violent conditions dictated by the systemic power relations of white supremacy, heteropatriarchy, and capitalism, rights
operate as a form of self-defense, one that is necessary to engage
in supporting everyday survival and resistance.[58] That work is immensely important, and happens every day in the most material
of circumstances—getting people out of prison or out of immigration detention, fighting for trans-inclusive healthcare, and getting people back on state benefits when they have been kicked off,

---

57. Tourmaline, "What Are We Defending?" *Reina Gossett*, April 6, 2015, http://www.
reinagossett.com/what-are-we-defending-reinas-talk-at-the-incite-cov4-conference/.
58. Kimberlé Crenshaw, "Race, Reform, and Retrenchment," in *Critical Race Theory:
The Key Writings that Formed the Movement*, eds. Kimberlé Crenshaw, Neil Gotanda,
Gary Peller, and Kendal Thomas (New York: The New Press, 1995), 117.

among many other instances. The position of this argument is not that those things are not vitally important or urgently necessary. Rather, calls for inclusion through universal rights positioned as solving harm and exclusion are ultimately unable to deliver fundamental and material change of systemic power relations and state violence. For queer and trans people most affected by these conditions, legal recognition has not worked to undo the underlying systemic power relations mediating violence and harm.

The concept of the universal is one borne out of inherently limited access—of those who are considered civil within a system that predetermines which bodies will have an easier time accessing the protections, privileges, and benefits of the state. I have argued that the concept of inclusion into the universal is always already limited by its colonial construction—its framework is conditioned by white supremacy, heteropatriarchy, and capitalism. This affects all people, but queer and trans people of color occupy a pronounced positionality within the intersectional spaces between these three systems of power. If the goal of resistance work is to abolish systems of power, and in turn to abolish colonialism, then as long as colonialism and its ongoing instantiations of settler colonialism and neocolonialism continue, rights will never bring about the change queer and trans people are seeking. So we must ask ourselves, when we seek justice, is it rights that we seek? Or is it the "something more" we have always already inhabited? Mainstream LGBT people, white people, and people with access to wealth must all disengage from the benefits of these systemic power relations to consider something different, something that will not bring more people further up in the hierarchy so that the structure grows, but rather something that will seek to dismantle it altogether. For, in the words of Audre Lorde, the master's tools will never dismantle the master's house.[59]

We already practice this critical work within our everyday lives. Our communities are invested in practices of care; in resisting the confines of "expected" behavior; questioning logics of heteropatriarchy in our lives; working through our own understandings of gender outside a strict gender binary; offering support, healing,

---

59. Lorde, "The Master's Tools," 111.

and harm reduction practices outside what the state condones; working through our own constructions of conflict resolution and community accountability; creating chosen families, practicing polyamorous relations, engaging in friendships that center love, and working beyond heteronormative constructions of jealousy and property-based relations that undergird heteronormative dyadic expectations. From the moment colonialism extended its violent reaches through projects of Western imperial expansion, Indigenous people and people living under colonialism world-wide have been resisting colonial heteropatriarchy. We are engaging in everyday practices of building and rebuilding, practicing, learning, and relearning how to live and love in the face of these systems, resisting calls for conscription into the interrelated and violent disciplinary projects of heteropatriarchy, capitalism, white supremacy, and colonialism. This work demonstrates that in these practices, we are already something more than what we are told the universal space of inclusion will offer.

Ongoing histories and practices of struggle and resistance have demonstrated what is at stake when our focus is solely on inclusion into the universal. Moving from a space that questions universal inclusion while fighting for a redistribution of resources through many tactics allows for a consideration of what possibilities for relationality are foreclosed when engaging primarily in rights-based redress, as well as what other possibilities exist for offering other ways of being in the world. In order to fully account for the realm of the universal, framing the development of universality as occurring within the rise of colonial-modernity can expose the dynamic between rights and the legitimations for colonialism as based on heteropatriarchy. To see these power relations not as separate, but in fact as constitutive of the formation of the "universal" of modernity, exposes the limitations of rights-based incorporation as a fundamental reaffirmation of settler colonial state power used to negotiate the freedom and legitimacy for some as constantly conditioned on the unfreedom and illegitimacy of others.

As critical queer and trans movement work has articulated, resistance to these power relations is the work that involves everyone, which must include leaving behind our investments in inclusion under the façade of universal equality and open our eyes to the ongoing work that is already happening through engaging with communities in resistance. The lives we live are complicated lives, with complex and intertwined relationships to colonial heteropatriarchal logics. Our histories are multifaceted, and live through us in our ongoing struggles. Let us remember to tell these histories as they are—with their complications, difficulties, and in the hope of what it means when we work through and against them in building together.

And in holding this, we must also hold the awareness that the institutions and projects of the universal will always seek to co-opt us, to bring us in so that we may have the privileges to fight their wars, marry in their churches, extract their profits, and expand their diversity; so that we might have a coveted set of rights promised to all deserving citizenry, the right to carry on the neocolonial and imperial violence that is the project of the United States, the right to settle and perpetuate investment in this stolen land, the right to the pursuit of multicultural white supremacist happiness. And so we must also carry with us the knowledge that their prisons will never make us safer, that their laws will never fully include all of us, and that the ability for only some to climb over that wall and blend into cookie-cutter models at the expense of those continually pushed out, murdered, and ignored will never be enough.

Part of this ongoing work, built through the resistance and struggle over the past five hundred years as methodologies of abolitionism, is to look for those convergences, to seek the layers upon layers of consolidation, the concentric genealogies, not necessarily as purely linear or chronological but through a framework that can support the move to resist inclusion into a universal that has always maintained a limited access into its exclusive realm. May we hold within us the understanding that these logics run deep, but so too, do we. And in turn, may we move toward a sense, deep and across many realms, that there is always something more. In our resistance, in our survival, and in our remembered names, we are already something more.

'WE CAN BE HERE ANOTHER FIVE HUNDRED YEARS'

A CRITICAL REFLECTION ON SHIRI PASTERNAK'S *GROUNDED AUTHORITY*

Nick Estes

Every year our family and relatives climb what is now called Black Elk Peak to welcome back the thunders. We are among, perhaps, thousands of Lakotas, Dakotas, and dozens of different Indigenous nations who make the annual pilgrimage to He Sapa, the Black Hills. Since time immemorial, they say, Indigenous peoples have made this journey back to the center of our universe, *the heart of everything that is,* to welcome home the Wakinyans, the thunder beings. The ceremony welcomes back our relatives from the West, who bring the rain, lightning, and hail. It marks the beginning of the summer ceremonial season. There is an esoteric knowledge and history of this particular place that has taken us countless generations as a people to understand. It was here that Lakota visionary and holy man Nicholas Black Elk received his prophetic visions when he was just nine years old. John Neihardt has famously, or infamously—depending on how you look at it—transcribed that vision in the national bestseller *Black Elk Speaks.*[1] Here Black Elk envisioned the horrific trials of the Lakotas under US colonialism and the coming of the seventh generation—our current generation—who will cleanse the earth and bring the Red Nations back from the edge of the abyss.

---

1. See John G. Neihardt, *Black Elks Speaks: Being the Life Story of a Holy Man of the Oglala Sioux* (Lincoln: University of Nebraska Press, 2004).

THE IMAGE ABOVE IS FROM THE VIDEO, "NO MINING –ALGONQUINS OF BARRIERE LAKE LAND DEFENDERS CAMP – GROUNDWIRE NEWS" VIA ORGANIZING FOR JUSTICE, HTTPS://ORGANIZINGFORJUSTICE.CA/?P=941]

As much as it is a place tied to the continual renewal of life, it is also a site of ongoing contestation. Black Elk Peak was only recently renamed from Harney Peak, a name many found offensive. On September 5, 1855, US Army General William Harney commanded the slaughter of eighty-six Lakotas—half of them women and children—at Blue Water Creek. For his atrocities, the Lakotas named Harney "Woman Killer." In 2015, a South Dakota board contested changing the peak's name. Some proposed calling the peak by its true Lakota name, Hinhan Kaga Paha. Settlers found the name too difficult to pronounce because it wasn't English. After much pressure, a federal board renamed the peak after Black Elk, in honor of his powerful vision and contributions to Lakota philosophy. Regardless of the peak's name, Indigenous peoples still maintain a direct connection to this place and make annual pilgrimages.

Every year, state park officials stop our long line of cars. We are asked to pull over to the side of the road so as not to hold up the steady stream of tourists entering the park for hiking, biking, and climbing over the Memorial Day weekend. This year I was given the honor and privilege of talking to the park rangers. I've seen this scenario play out time and time again, and have memorized the script. I roll down the window and the ranger cautiously approaches my vehicle, the way highway patrolmen do.

"What's your business?"

"This is 1868 treaty lands, which were never legally ceded according to the 1980 Supreme Court decision. We're visiting our land. Thanks for taking care of it, but we can handle it from here."

I smile trying to disarm her with humor. The ranger's face turns red. She is either scared or angry or both. I can never tell. She leaves to talk to what looks like her supervisor, an older woman. The older woman approaches the car before checking my license plates. She scribbles something on a pad and then pops her head in my window.

"How many cars?" She asks.

"A dozen."

"Okay."

And she walks away. I get out of the car and wave through the caravan.

"Sir, get back in your car."

I don't comply. She's not a *real* cop, she doesn't have a gun, I tell myself.

"We're going through," I say.

Now she's angry because of the commotion we are causing. Curious tourists pop their head out their windows. She's standing there with a firm look on her face, holding our day passes to put in our front windows so the rangers won't tow our cars. She holds the passes like a stern parent holding car keys, reluctant to hand them over to a teenager on a Friday night. I get the lecture.

"You know, you have to call in ahead of time before we can issue passes."

Reminding me she's "bending" the rules before she "allows" us to enter.

"This is treaty land," I remind her.

"But this isn't a federal park," she shoots back. "It's a state park."

Meaning: it's land that "belongs" to the state of South Dakota, unlike the rest of Black Hills Forest, which are under federal management.

"It's still treaty land," I remind her, "and we didn't sign treaties with your state."

"Well, next time, let us know in advance."

"Okay," I say. "Next year, just like the last tens of thousands of years before that, we are coming here on this date like we always have. Mark your calendar so you're not surprised. It will save both of us time." She scowls and shoves the passes in my hand and walks away. We move through the barricade.

This is a routine encounter, bound to repeat itself so long as our "sacred site" remains under state management and jurisdiction. Most of our caravan had been to various frontline protests against the Dakota Access Pipeline or against the police murders of young Lakota men in Rapid City, South Dakota. The crossing of these barricades, however, was not an overtly political act of opposition. Or so we think. We are simply returning home to our origins but in the process are treated as trespassers.

Nevertheless, the encounter with the park rangers is loaded with meaning and history. The question posed to *us* is: what legal authority do we have to enter these lands without first paying for permission? The question we are taught to pose to *them* isn't quite as simple: what gives you the authority to question our authority to do so? This is the premise of Shiri Pasternak's *Grounded Authority: The Algonquins of Barriere Lake Against the State*.[2] The historical and political circumstances are different but similar between Black Elk Peak and the Algonquin's struggle against the colonial state at Barriere Lake, the topic of the book. In the long list of historic clashes between Algonquins on one side and the long list of federal, territorial, and law enforcement authorities on the other, each is not, Pasternak argues, "only a moment of conflict" but they are also instances of "how legal authority is established—far from the courts, detached from constitutional frameworks, shaping the borders of settler law."[3] In other words, each event shows jurisdiction and legal authority are literally built from the ground up through everyday encounters or everyday forms of state-making.

To best illustrate her convincing analysis of actually existing jurisdiction, Pasternak asks us to sharpen our metaphorical guillotines—or our skinning knives—to lop off the head of the king, the sovereign, the head of state. What authority proliferates in the

2. Shiri Pasternak, *Grounded Authority: The Algonquins of Barriere Lake Against the State* (Minneapolis: University of Minnesota Press, 2017).

3. Pasternak, *Grounded Authority*, 1.

absence of this false symbol of power? Surely, in Turtle Island what remains and grows in the absence of the long shadow cast by colonialism are the robust forms of Indigenous legal authority: the enduring, preexisting, and co-developed authorities existing alongside imperial and colonial legalities. But from where does Indigenous authority derive? It certainly does not come from a divine ruler, the sovereign, or the most powerful political and territorial imaginary in history: the nation-state. These realms of "civilization" categorically consign Indigenous peoples to that lawless space where life is, to quote Hobbes, "solitary, poor, nasty, brutish and short." A place we can call death. On the other hand, Algonquin political authority, Pasternak powerfully demonstrates, derives from a multiplicity of institutions, individuals, and other-than-human agents that encompass the resilience of Indigenous life in the face of constant erasure, disappearance, and elimination.

It is from the decapitated body of the king that Pasternak begins her careful autopsy of the corpse of settler sovereignty. In some ways, *Grounded Authority* is the *Gray's Anatomy* of actually existing settler jurisdiction. The idea of a centralized state ignores the function of its organs—the various instruments, institutions, and techniques of rule that often work in tandem with each other (and sometimes against each other). The complex, and oftentimes, contradictory and overlapping regimes of law reveal settlement as an incomplete and, in the case of Barriere Lake, a failed project. Yet, zombie-like, its headless corpse relentlessly assaults the Indigenous political authority that intimately manages, protects, consumes, and replenishes the life forces of other-than-human agents embedded in the land. For instance, Barriere Lake Algonquins have been, until relatively recently, under customary Indigenous governance systems. Governing authority, in this instance, is derived from an intricate kinship system and land practice.

Customary governments pose a problem precisely because the Canadian federal government possesses no power over the governing practices of Indigenous-derived leadership, and therefore no control over the social order of the communities. The solution is to cast customary governments as "lawless." On this front, the law sanctions its own nonexistence and calls for the continual violation and subduing of Natives, especially those who appear to possess the ability of calling attention to the tenuous and precarious claims of a settler legal authority. Pasternak documents this practice of imagining lawlessness through the very material practices of jurisdiction, such as the rampant imprisonment, profiling, harassing, and criminalization of traditional band leadership. In contrast to settler legal authority, Indigenous customary leadership derives its political authority from the very earth upon which it walks, talks, and lives. Traditional leadership makes decisions about how the elaborate community trapline system prevents over-harvesting and enables the just and equitable distribution of wild game. The only way to keep this complex trapping system running is to have intimate knowledge of the land—and to know when, and when not, to harvest. It also requires knowing the animal relatives and respecting their gifts to the community. Such knowledge is not just about taking life but also about observing how it survives, sometimes for the benefit of humans or just pure interest in all its mysteries—like how a bear shits in the woods. Pasternak observes that in one Indigenous knowledge report on the Barriere Lake:

> One also learns. . . about the use of moose, beaver, and bears, especially for medicinal purposes—an area that is vastly under researched and poorly understood in the scientific community but is suspected to be of extreme importance to the long-term health of wildlife populations, and represents only a fraction of Algonquin knowledge on the subject. For example, the Algonquins have observed that the beaver uses yellow pond lily (*cikitebak, akidimô*) for its lungs, the moose uses balsam fir (*aninâdik*) for wounds and sickness and black spruce (*sesegâdik*) to help females before giving birth, bears use trembling aspen (*azâdi*) for a spring tonic, laxative, and dewormer, and the black bear uses multiple kinds of bark (such as the white spruce, the mountain ash, and eastern white cedar) to help with hibernation.[4]

The intimate knowledge of the land isn't just about innocent curiosity but profoundly relates to how a people survive and

---

4. Pasternak, *Grounded Authority*, 87.

reproduce themselves on that land. That is why Indigenous political authority is such a threat—it is literally embedded in the land.

Highly adaptable, Barriere Lake Algonquins have over time developed a mixed economy, supplementing cash income where complete dependence on the land is impossible. The ability of the community to continue to physically reproduce itself relatively unaided by the outside world is testament to its grounded authority in the land. The taking of territory often coincides with attacks on Indigenous economies first and foremost. Indigenous subsistence hunting, gathering, and agriculture initially provided the means to effectively resist settler encroachment. By destroying subsistence economies, by separating Indigenous producers from the land and attempting to make them totally dependent on federal annuities or cash economies, the accumulation process is relaunched (again and again and again) by waging total war on the whole of Indigenous life. In the case of Barriere Lake, the attacks are primarily upon its jurisdictional authority. Perhaps severely weakened in some periods more so than others, that authority, however, has never been entirely vanquished.

Snatching away jurisdictional authority is literally about snatching the food from the mouths of Algonquins. Lack of jurisdictional power can literally be felt through the pangs of hunger. It has a real material consequence. During the mid-1990s, the Department of Indian Affairs attempted to usurp customary governance by installing a dissident faction, or an Interim Band Council, into power through—by both Canadian and Barriere Lake measures of the law—illegal means. To force Barriere Lake into submission, Canadian officials created the conditions of what journalist Charlie Angus called a "starve or submit scenario" to force the surrender of the customary government.[5] Federal money and programming was cut. For more than a year, children didn't go to school, the community lived without power, electricity, medical services, and adequate phone services. What effectively amounted to an economic embargo—which in other circumstances would be considered an act of war against a sovereign nation—denied Algonquins' basic human rights and the ability to hunt. Their will, however, did not

---

5. Pasternak, Grounded Authority, 179.

bend and they continued to barricade a logging road to force territorial and federal governments to honor their agreements for the co-
management of forests and wildlife.

Not until the imposition of the band council system, which
failed, and then a third party management system—which has
also failed or is currently failing—did Barriere Lake have its autonomy thrown into crisis. In protest of these attempts to overthrow
its long-held self-governance practices kept intact by a council of
Algonquin Elders, the entire community engaged in brave and high-
risk acts of resistance. In other contexts, removing self-determined
leadership structures would be considered bald imperialism—
such as "regime change"—for the purposes of gaining access to
a country's wealth and resources. (This, too, could be seen as an
act of war.) The brave courage to stand up to arbitrary and violent
state power inspired other acts of resistance, such as the standoff
at Oka.

We are taught to view settler colonialism as a structure and
not as an event. Yet, there is an eventfulness to the ways in which
jurisdiction is enacted on the ground. One could say neither the
multiple blockades of logging roads by the Algonquins nor the
multiple attempts by territorial and federal officials to overthrow
the Mitchikanibikok Anishnabe Onakinakewin system of land
use and governance were stand-alone events. Rather, each instantiation of either settler jurisdiction or Algonquin jurisdiction is a
concentration of key elements of longer historical processes and
claims to authority. The former has historically sought to eliminate the latter, while Algonquin customary governance has, despite all odds and the callous aggressiveness of an invading society, sought peaceful coexistence and even co-management of its
hunting lands with territorial and federal authorities through the
Trilateral Agreement system.

Grounded Authority is a rare book that you can judge by its
cover. As its cover photo, Barriere Lake Algonquin youth sit with
handmade placards facing a police line about a dozen yards (or
meters) away. There is tension between the two lines of children
and the armed white men, the physical manifestations of the colonial state. Between them is a stretch of highway: so-called no
man's land, a fabricated *terra nullius* under armed guard. It's a

timeless scene that occurred relatively recently—but there is no more stereotypical colonial encounter than that of the police facing down Indigenous peoples. Clearly pictured, the "threat" the police are there to manage—the Indian Problem that is out of control—are children who have been thrown into a life and death fight to have a future life on the land. How did this come to be?

The rise of counterinsurgency tactics by law enforcement to crush Indigenous land defense movements under the powers of the Emergency Management Assistance Program (or EMAP) in Canada is eerily reminiscent of the language and intent of the Emergency Management Assistance Compact (or EMAC) in the United States. While EMAP was created to monitor and manage "civil unrest," its powers were expanded to include the monitoring of fires and floods, or natural disasters. In the US, EMAC granted states the powers to solicit support from emergency services from different law enforcement jurisdictions around the nation to monitor and manage natural disasters, such as floods and fires. Yet, EMAC powers were used by the city of Baltimore to crush the Black uprising after the police murder of Freddie Gray and more recently the movement at Standing Rock to stop the Dakota Access Pipeline. What is revealed in both contexts of the US and Canada is that emergency management monies have become the new modes of Indigenous expropriation by deploying heavily militarized police forces against the whole of Indigenous societies, in order to protect "critical infrastructure," such as pipelines and highways systems. In other words, to protect the international flow of capital. These tactics are nothing short of counterinsurgency: waging war against civilian populations. To mask and hide the illegality of the trespass of pipelines, roads or capital through Indigenous territories, it is settler law that criminalizes Indigenous peoples. As a result, mainstream media, liberal "allies"—and sometimes even our own—uncritically divide communities and camps into the "good Indians" versus the "bad Indians." This also applies to questions of tactics, such as "legitimate" or "illegitimate" forms of protest, or "nonviolent" or "violent"—as if someone wakes up one day and decides they are going to engage in a violent protest. Such speculations ignore crucial questions. Such as, when we examine the cover of *Grounded Authority*, we should be asking, what makes Algonquin children legitimate targets for police violence? What makes any Indigenous person a legitimate target for police violence? What authorizes that violence? Who pays for it?

We can think of settler colonialism, and therefore settler jurisdiction, as targeting Indigenous peoples and their political authority for elimination. But what is clear, in Pasternak's account of things, is that the everyday enactment of jurisdiction is a form of low-level warfare—or lawfare—that targets not just humans for elimination but also nonhumans. Unlike other forms of genocide such as the Holocaust, which targeted solely humans and had a beginning and an end, settler colonialism has not ended and it targets other-than-human Indigenous kinship relations for destruction. This war is asymmetric that includes theories of collective punishment, the taking of children, the forcing of Indigenous communities to choose between their lives or surrendering or ceding their nonhuman kin, the use of native scouts and auxiliaries that are coopted by colonial governance systems, the use of reserves as spaces of containment and the concentration (or sometimes removal) of Indigenous leadership, the targeting of socioeconomic institutions as the bases for Indigenous autonomy, and the impulse to "civilize" in order to pacify. It is this force, this power, that some seek or are sometimes forced to enter into relations with—which is their prerogative and authority to do so. But it begs the question, how does one reconcile its everyday relations with a highly militaristic, white supremacist empire? Can there ever be reconciliation with the other-than-human worlds as well—the other targets of this colonial machinery?

These are questions that Indigenous peoples elsewhere on Turtle Island are looking to First Nations for answers as we watch their state-led reconciliation process unfold—for better or worse. Regardless of that process, I am deeply inspired by the Barriere Lake struggle and the profound knowledge they have imparted to help us understand Indigenous jurisdiction struggles; and maybe there is something else to be learned about possible pathways to Indigenous freedom and peaceful coexistence other than further ensnaring Indigenous peoples in the traplines of state power. What Pasternak calls the "steady accretion of restrictions" to Indigenous self-determination, which is simultaneous to the layering of colonial authority that governs the land by carving out spatial patterns of land use and population control, should be, in my view, contrasted against another kind of accretion that makes the confinement and the endgame of elimination an impossibility.[6]

The selection of Algonquin customary leadership is for life, since it takes a lifetime of accumulated knowledge about the land to be a successful leader. This pushes against the temporal framings of liberal democracies and the instantaneous election processes and the overthrow of Indigenous leadership by settler decree. The slow—and sometimes frustrating—nature of Indigenous political processes is, too, a steady accumulation of ways of knowing, experiencing, and practicing relationality to humans and other-than-humans. This accretion is a radical consciousness, deeply embedded in history and place and cannot be measured or simply overturned by colonial fiat. This accretion is a centuries-old practice, and carries with it the memories of past, present, and already forthcoming struggles against the state. It pushes back not only against the spatial order of settler jurisdiction but also its self-possessed temporality as an enduring feature of the land. While never perfect but always perfecting, it provides the approximation of peace and freedom, inspiring others to continue the fight. And it cannot be jailed, beaten, pepper-sprayed, or slandered into submission.

The words of Marylynn Poucachiche best illustrate the waiting game Algonquins have won against settler jurisdiction. In October 2009, Poucachiche faced off with riot police in one of the many struggles at the small reserve at Barriere Lake. Her words speak to the farsightedness, long memories, and deep connections to the lands—*the grounded authority*—that most settlers (and sometimes even ourselves) are conditioned to forget: "Look at how much money they spend on you guys. . . . You want to keep us on this reserve? Tiny little reserve? Well, we're not going to stay here. You guys, you can stand here for maybe twelve hours. Us, we can be here another five hundred years."[7]

---

6. Pasternak, *Grounded Authority*, 64.

7. Pasternak, *Grounded Authority*, 221.

'HOW DOES STATE SOVEREIGNTY MATTER?'

Shiri Pasternak's response to Nick Estes

My book poses a question that was raised for me by the Algonquins of Barriere Lake. One that I think is both basic and profound: what does the sovereignty of the modern state matter without the power to exercise jurisdiction on the ground?

The fact that the Algonquins were not at all troubled by the idea of Canada or its central government, or its claims to sovereignty, upset some assumption I didn't even realize I held. Namely, that somehow Canada's claim to be *their* country mattered to the Algonquins somehow. But it really didn't. Because they saw Canada as *my* government and not theirs. So, as a matter of fact, Canada and the province of Quebec just didn't have the authority to govern their lands.

I had somehow got the idea that the power to exercise jurisdiction was an outgrowth of sovereignty. Those are the scales of power we are taught. But on the blockades at Barriere Lake I realized that jurisdiction was the organizing principle of sovereignty: if you couldn't control the people on their lands, you could not exercise your sovereignty as a state. This leads of course to an incredible degree of violence of different kinds to bring recalcitrant Indians into compliance.

What does the sovereignty of the modern state really matter? I think about this all the time now, maybe more than ever before. In June 2018, I became a co-founder of the first Indigenous-focused think tank in Canada. The Yellowhead Institute launched at Ryerson University, Toronto, and we shot into the world with a report on the Liberal government's record on Indigenous rights.

We put the Prime Minister's claim that, "No relationship is more important to Canada than the relationship with Indigenous People" to the test of jurisdiction. What is the Liberal vision for its relationship to Indigenous peoples? Turns out, more of the same: power remains paramount to the state, though the administration of this power becomes increasingly decentralized and redistributed through the Indian Band Council system designed and closely managed by ever-expanding, highly specialized ministries of Indian Affairs.

The following year, we put out "Land Back" in 2019, a Red Paper report on the strategies of ongoing dispossession of Indigenous lands and the ways Indigenous peoples are fighting back to assert their jurisdiction. One of the key pieces of research we did for this report was examining the success rates of injunctions served against First Nations, mostly in the case of resource extraction. While 76 percent of injunctions filed against First Nations by corporations were granted, 81 percent of injunctions filed against corporations by First Nations were denied. The late Secwepmec leader Arthur Manuel called injunctions the "legal billy club" of the settler state for good reason.

One of the key tests for injunctions is proving "irreparable harm." Here, the courts have bent over backward to protect the economic status quo of provincial resource extraction in the face of Indigenous opposition. Most recently, for example, in January 2020, the courts ruled on an injunction served by Coastal Gaslink regarding their right to pursue construction for a liquified natural gas pipeline through the unceded territory of the Wet'suwet'en Nation. Justice Church in the BC Court of Appeal found that the economic loss to the company far outweighed the losses the nation would suffer as a result of severely restricted access to their lands and the destruction of habitat and waters. Illegible and irrelevant to the court is the Wet'suwet'en Nation's jurisdiction. As Sleydo', the Gidimt'en Checkpoint spokesperson, has stated: "We have never ceded or surrendered our lands. This is an issue of rights and title with our sovereign nation, and the RCMP [Royal Canadian Mounted Police] are acting as mercenaries for industry."[1]

---

1. Charlie Smith, "Gidimt'en spokesperson Sleydo', aka Molly Wickham, accuses

To me, this formulation of the problem brings into focus exactly the kind of encounter Nick Estes begins his book review with: the Black Elk Peak climb he does with his family to welcome back the thunders. The intrusion and harassment of state park officials is founded on the ranger's belief that they have the authority to regulate the conduct, mobility, cultural practices, and governance systems of the Lakotas and Dakotas and others who travel to the Black Hills to do their work. Here is a confrontation soaked in the dredges of genocide, where state authority presumes to disrupt inherent Indigenous jurisdiction through the bureaucratic arm of conservation authorities, and the pushback by Nick and his family refusing state sovereignty through the exercise of Lakota jurisdiction.

In *Our History Is the Future*, Nick's history of Standing Rock and the NODAPL struggle, he demonstrates that rebuilding the Oceti Sakowin nation is a deep and ongoing struggle to undo the violent disorders of settler colonialism and set the crooked path straight.[2] The struggle, as he sees it, is to reshape the nation back from its curvatures to serve settlers infrastructures around water supply at the cost of sacrifice zones of Lakota lands; reshape the value of the Black Hills away from its extractive value in gold to a sacred place; strike out in solidarity between Indigenous peoples and working classes to wage revolution against the accumulative imperative of a capitalist society in constant crisis. And ground the authority of Indigenous peoples in the care of land, waters, and women, in the face of an economic system constantly looking to fix capital through expansion and intensification of resource markets, such as hydrocarbons, that burn up the planet.

Nick gives us an Oceti Sakowin picture of what it means to be against the state in relation to the Indigenous lands upon which we live. Barriere Lake give us another. Our task as settlers is to seek out Indigenous visions of the future against which we live and let them frame our own principles, actions, and political commitments.

RCMP of acting as mercenaries for industry," *The Georgia Straight*, December 21, 2019, https://www.straight.com/news/1339641/gidimten-spokesperson-sleydo-aka-molly-wickham-accuses-rcmp-acting-mercenaries-industry.

2. Nick Estes, *Our History Is the Future* (New York: Verso Books, 2019).

It wasn't until I met Russell Diabo—the Mohawk policy analyst who also introduced me to Barriere Lake—that I understood that a critique of the state that was not rooted in Indigenous law was not worth the cost of fabric to wave a black flag. I committed myself to learning what it meant to live in relation to Indigenous law rather than settler law because recognizing the illegitimacy of the Canadian state is not enough. Upholding the authority of Indigenous nations is the beginning of this meaningful revolution.

ART

O WIND, TAKE ME TO MY COUNTRY /
O LOVE, TAKE ME TO MY COUNTRY

Jess X. Snow

Migration is time travel fueled by wind, and the love songs of our motherlands are carried across oceans in the voice boxes of migrant mothers and daughters.

A portrait of brown Sudanese-Migrant poet, Safia Elhillo and a visual meditation of her poem "Vocabulary" which notes "the arabic word هواء (hawa) means wind / the arabic word هوى (hawa) means love." The title, "O wind, take me to my country / O love, take me to my country" are lyrics from Fairouz's songs, a celebrated Lebanese singer.

This piece was exhibited in a group show called Brown Don't Drown, curated by Savage Habbit, at 17 Frost Gallery, in Brooklyn. (9"x12" | Gouache on Paper | 2016)

ZIONISM AND NATIVE
AMERICAN STUDIES

Steven Salaita

It was only a matter of time before Zionism and Native American Studies (NAS) came into conflict—or, to be more precise, before Zionists began targeting the field for acrimony and recrimination, as they have long done to various humanities and social science disciplines.[1] With an increasingly global focus (in concert with emphasis on local concerns), a commitment to material transformation, a disdain for US imperialism and militarism, a rejection of state power in nearly all its manifestations, and a plethora of young artists and scholar-activists interested in Palestine, it's unsurprising that Israeli colonization would become a topic in the field.[2] And because most people in the field don't have nice things to say about Israel, some of the state's apologists have forced themselves into Indigenous spaces with a singular purpose: to intimidate its practitioners into obedience. As usual, those undertaking the intimidation know nothing about the people they endeavor to subdue. Over five centuries of history prove that Indigenous peoples are not given to submission.

The Zionist assaults on NAS rely on well-worn tactics and narratives, but they also entail some new strategies. Pro-Israel operatives

---

1. See, for example: Joseph Massad, "Joseph Massad Responds to the Intimidation of Columbia University," *The Electronic Intifada*, November 3, 2004, https://electronicintifada.net/content/joseph-massad-responds-intimidation-columbia-university/5289; John Gravois, "A New Fact on the Ground: Nadia Abu El-Haj Wins Tenure at Barnard College," *The Chronicle of Higher Education*, November 2, 2007, https://www.chronicle.com/article/A-New-Fact-on-the-Ground-/39883; Colleen Flaherty, "Seek and Hide," *Inside Higher Ed*, May 31, 2017, https://www.insidehighered.com/news/2017/05/31/why-did-fresno-state-cancel-search-professorship-named-after-late-edward-said.

2. See, for example: Erica Violet Lee, "Our Revolution: First Nations Women in Solidarity with Palestine," *Moontime Warrior*, August 19, 2014, https://moontimewarrior.com/2014/08/19/our-revolution-first-nations-women-in-solidarity-with-palestine/; Nadia Ben-Youssef, Nick Estes, and Melanie Yazzie, "Reclaiming Native History, from New Mexico to Palestine," *The Nakba Files*, July 20, 2016, http://nakbafiles.org/2016/07/20/reclaiming-native-history-from-new-mexico-to-palestine/.

have never limited themselves to specific disciplines, targeting Palestinians wherever they were located within the university—concurrently deploying a secondary but no less confrontational focus on Black radical scholars—but these days the pro-Israel punishment industry is expanding its target zone through a combination of relaxed standards and increased anguish. Recent events at Dartmouth College, discussed below, clarify the nature of that expansion.

In examining the relationship between Zionism and NAS, it's critical to think past obvious explanations. It's easy to say that because Palestine exists in NAS the pro-Israel punishment industry now targets it, but we elide lots of important possibilities by repeating that formulation, which has the potential to instrumentalize NAS as an adjunct to overseas geographies and thus to minimize, if only unwittingly, the ongoing dispossession of Native nations in North America. Zionist displeasure with NAS is best situated in the context of US and Canadian colonization, with which the Israeli variety is symbiotic.

Zionist interference in NAS hasn't merely sought to regulate Palestine. It is paradigmatic of the so-called "special relationship" between the US and Israel and therefore vigorously opposes North American decolonization. This dual concern with Israel's reputation and America's moral standing, so easily conflated, illuminates crucial features of Palestine as a global presence while highlighting the difficult conditions attending to Native scholarship. Most iterations of Zionism include devotion to US colonization. It's no longer enough to conceptualize Israel merely as an appendage of US foreign policy interests. Too many concrete alliances, mutual training programs, concerted policing strategies, weapon exchanges, and synchronized acts of oppression exist for that metric to capture the intensity of the alliance, which is mutually constitutive (economically, militarily, culturally, and discursively).

If we explore the discourses of those who decry (or merely chide) Native scholars for opposing Israeli policies, or for supporting Palestinian freedom, five features emerge:

1. Outrage or befuddlement that a people as noble as Native Americans could possibly reject Israelis, their natural allies.

2. An impulse to police the scope and content of NAS.

3. Profound misunderstanding (or ignorance) of the field's methodologies, ethical and philosophical commitments, and intellectual traditions.

4. A belief, often tacit, that the US should retain its claim as steward of Native populations.

5. Deep anxiety about a perceived loss of authority in academe.

These discursive norms aren't identical to the ones that exist vis-à-vis repression of Palestine Studies, though there's overlap. Identifying that overlap is useful, but here I want to assess the broadened focus of the pro-Israel punishment industry and then consider the implications of the encounter between Zionism and NAS.

THE DUTHU DARTMOUTH DEANSHIP

In March, 2017, Bruce Duthu accepted a position as dean of the College of Arts and Sciences at Dartmouth College. Duthu is a prominent figure in NAS and the occupant of an endowed chair in a prestigious department. Few Natives become upper administrators, so the ascension of Duthu at an Ivy League university, whatever one thinks of the utility of managerial aspirations, was a noteworthy achievement. The appointment got processed and Duthu received the usual congratulations when, two months later, somebody discovered that Duthu once signed a statement favoring the boycott of Israeli academic institutions, a popular position in the Southern Hemisphere.

But common sense in the South is often taboo in the North and so even though he inhabits a field that rejects US nationalism, Duthu was doomed by nationalistic sentiment. No indication exists that Duthu harbors any special animus for Israel or affinity for Palestine; in fact, he walked back his endorsement of the Boycott, Divestment and Sanctions movement (BDS), as initiated in limited form by the NAISA Council,[3] without disavowing his empathy for Palestinians. That his endorsement of the statement appears to

---

3. Native American and Indigenous Studies Association, "Declaration of Support for the Boycott of Israeli Academic Institutions," *Palestinian Campaign for the Academic & Cultural Boycott of Israel*, December 18, 2013, http://pacbi.org/pacbi140812/?p=2305.

have been a function of his position as a NAISA officer rather than an ideological commitment did little to assuage his detractors.

The chatter around Duthu's resignation exposes the mentality of the pro-Israel punishment industry. Dartmouth economist Alan L. Gustman offered a dose of comic paranoia unbefitting a person presumably devoted to the rigor of social science: "The chant of the BDS movement, from the river to the sea, is anti-Israel, anti-Zionist and profoundly anti-Jewish. . . . Again, this movement has become a cover for many anti-Semites who like nothing better than to once again be free to exercise their prejudices."[4] He helpfully noted that he has "no reason to believe that Duthu is anti-Semitic." Speculation about Gustman's attitude toward Native Americans and Arabs is thus far unavailable.

Venerable saboteur Cary Nelson played moderate Zionist to Gustman's extremist, appearing to back Duthu's appointment. "[Duthu] is hardly a hardcore boycott advocate," Nelson observed. "Some people can sign a BDS petition without imposing that agenda on the rest of their professional life, while others cannot."[5]

Let's compare this observation with Gustman's claim that "[it's] not appropriate to appoint an advocate of BDS, thereby providing the BDS movement with a foothold at the highest levels of our administration."[6]

Here we have two Zionist fanatics, one in favor of Duthu's appointment, the other against. A close reading of their quotes, however, indicates that both say essentially the same thing: a litmus test on Palestine enforceable by dilettantes with no qualifications beyond an irrational devotion to Israel must exist before Native scholars can be allowed career promotions. Apropos of the field's general relationship with US academe, familiarity isn't necessary to have an expert opinion about NAS.

The pro-Israel punishment industry relies on the settler's prerogative to freely grant authority as required to maintain colonial hierarchies. Zionist academics anoint themselves arbiters of NAS,

---

4. Alan L. Gustman, quoted in Colleen Flaherty, "Blacklisted for BDS?," *Inside Higher Ed*, May 23, 2017, https://www.insidehighered.com/news/2017/05/23/popular-native-american-studies-scholar-declines-deanship-dartmouth-amid-concerns.

5. Cary Nelson, quoted in Colleen Flaherty, "Blacklisted for BDS?"

6. Gustman, quoted in Colleen Flaherty, "Blacklisted for BDS?"

something we saw repeatedly in the past few years, thanks largely to Nelson's efforts, vis-à-vis the Zionist destruction of American Indian Studies at the University of Illinois at Urbana-Champaign (though the problem has existed alongside the field since its inception). Not content merely to obliterate academic freedom, Nelson set out to discredit the entire field by conceptualizing it as given to demagoguery, incompetence, dereliction, and irrationality.[7]

This self-granted authority vis-à-vis NAS is possible only because of a long history of entitlement on campus in general. Many Zionist scholars consider themselves uniquely fit to judge which viewpoints are acceptable and thereby interject themselves as indispensable arbiters of the reward economy. The culture of US academe gives them latitude to act on those judgments. For instance, Dartmouth Jewish Studies director Susannah Heschel, in an apparent display of support for Duthu, noted that "he is not promoting or facilitating the boycotting [of Israeli institutions] . . . on the contrary, he is doing the opposite of boycotting," adding that BDS is "very dangerous, wrong and nasty."[8] These are the words of somebody accustomed to being consulted.

Like Nelson, Heschel implies that certain views on Israel constitute grounds for punishment. In her mind Duthu doesn't descend into anti-Zionism, an affliction about which the wrong kind of people need to be "educated."[9] He is salvageable as an ethnic subject. This sort of magnanimity reinforces conditions that harm Indigenous scholars. In the articles reporting Duthu's resignation, we see this theme repeated with slight rhetorical variations. Duthu is one of the good Natives who, while given to lapses of judgment, isn't very hard on Israel. He is therefore qualified to be a dean. None of these articles quote a Native or Palestinian, or even an anti-Zionist Jew, only people

---

7. Vicente M. Diaz, "The Salaita Case and Cary Nelson's Use of "Academic Freedom" to Silence Dissent," *The Electronic Intifada*, August 14, 2014, https://electronicintifada.net/content/salaita-case-and-cary-nelsons-use-academic-freedom-silence-dissent/13756.

8. Susannah Heschel, quoted in Mika Jehoon Lee, "Concerns Arise Over Duthu's Appointment as Dean of Faculty," *The Dartmouth*, May 12, 2017, https://www.thedartmouth.com/article/2017/05/concerns-arise-over-duthus-appointment-as-dean-of-faculty.

9. Susannah Heschel, quoted in Rachel Frommer, "Newly-Appointed Dartmouth Dean Steps Down After Facing Barrage of Criticism Over BDS Ties," *The Algemeiner*, May 22, 2017, https://www.algemeiner.com/2017/05/22/newly-appointed-dartmouth-dean-steps-down-after-facing-barrage-of-criticism-over-bds-ties/.

opposed to BDS. Such exclusions are a journalistic custom that validates pro-Israel normativity and reinforces the impression that Palestine is exclusively the concern of those who identify as Jewish. In this case, Indian Country also suffers discursive erasures. It is unwise to imagine Israel as inconsequential to Natives.

Israel's participation in the dispossession of Indigenous peoples is inscribed in the narrative dynamics of the Duthu controversy. Gustman, for example, worries about extant Palestinian influence, and hints at the dangers of unchecked Native influence, in ways that are rightly considered anti-Semitic when the subject is one of Jewish influence. Only because Natives and Palestinians inhabit a wretched position in academe are they so casually subject to racist suppositions. Academic racism both precedes and validates the supervisory role Zionists confer to themselves in relation to colonized demographics.

This racism produces material consequences for its perpetrators and victims. Many observers assume that targets of recrimination are worthy of recrimination merely because they were targeted, as against the timeless authority of the perpetrator. Relations of power can define notions of probity. Take Cary Nelson, for example. He damaged his reputation as a stalwart of academic freedom by leading the assault on his colleagues in American Indian Studies at UIUC, including partnership with far-right demagogues and complicity with the Israeli security state.[10] These actions weren't a basis for punishment, however.

Now Nelson is again everywhere, organizing against human rights in the MLA, interjecting himself in Native American Studies, providing quotes on topical matters for industry publications.[11] That institutions and individuals in academe continue

---

10. Ali Abunimah, "Zionist Groups Planned to Lobby University of Illinois Trustees Over Salaita Appointment," The Electronic Intifada, August 11, 2014, https://electronicintifada. net/blogs/ali-abunimah/zionist-groups-planned-lobby-univ-illinois-trustees-over-salaita-appointment. An example of Cary Nelson's complicity with the Israeli security state is seen in how Tel Aviv University's Institute for National Security Studies (INSS) and the Israel Action Network held a book release event for Nelson's co-edited book, The Case Against Academic Boycotts of Israel, on December 22, 2014 at the INSS in Tel Aviv.

11. Cary Nelson, "The BDS Disinformation Campaign in the Modern Language Association," Fathom, Winter 2016, http://fathomjournal.org/the-bds-disinformation-campaign-in-the-modern-language-association/.

to entertain him as an expert on anything other than dishonesty, snitching, and duplicity illustrates how uninviting academe is for those positioned against state power.

Nelson isn't exceptional. Ringleaders of campus repression rarely lose their rarified positions; in fact, they are often rewarded. This inveterate feature of US academe both reflects and reproduces the institutional norms of settler colonization, which treat the violence of modernity as a civilizational imperative. Authoritarianism is the currency of American redemption, made available for study but studiously ignored during presidential elections, faculty searches, geostrategic fads, and every other moment when the populace is expected to lionize personalities. Linear history, feted as insuperable progress, is actually a series of regressions to colonial authority. Academe has been so easily corporatized because its elites prevent it from developing in ways that value (or tolerate) unorthodoxy.

Consider that Gustman will suffer no repercussions for his crusade against Duthu. (If anything, he has burnished his own administrative credentials.) Heschel will continue to be lauded as a voice of compassion and reason.[12] The off-campus groups that interfered will be further emboldened. Duthu, on the other hand, has to face down a permanent demotion. Victims of the pro-Israel punishment industry earn lifetime sentences.

While Gustman and Heschel intervene in ways that should cause any discerning observer to object, Nelson, despite his hopeless attempt to sound open-minded, offers the most objectionable intervention. Allow me to speak more plainly: it's not Cary Nelson's business what happens at Dartmouth. It's not Cary Nelson's business what happens in Native American Studies. It's not Cary Nelson's business who does and doesn't support BDS. It's not Cary Nelson's business to sort the good people of color from the bad people of color. And yet in the structures within which he functions it actually is his business. He exemplifies a specific class of white senior scholar who exercise the responsibility of managing political standards on campus. Administration

---

12. "Great Professor Series: Susannah Heschel," *The Dartmouth Review*, February 17, 2016, http://dartreview.com/great-professor-series-susannah-heschel/.

forever summons men of that class to the task. It is their duty, their pleasure, their passion, their birthright, their burden. That's why men like Nelson never offer "no comment."

We can return to one of his comments to recognize the settler's indomitable subject position: "Some people can sign a BDS petition without imposing that agenda on the rest of their professional life, while others cannot." Neither the *Chronicle of Higher Education* nor *Inside Higher Ed*, where this passage appears, has ever considered the question in the inverse. Can people be devoted to Israel without imposing that agenda on the rest of their professional lives? Given the unabated growth of the pro-Israel punishment industry and Nelson's own obsession with safeguarding Israel's reputation, it's a question worth raising if we're going to be in the business of implicating professionalism based on political opinions. (It's worth noting that there's no known instance in the history of US academe where a professor has been fired for supporting Israel or for unethical practices vis-à-vis Indigenous communities.) That only the dark thoughts of subalternity are marked for surgical restriction indicates that enlightenment often does little more than project onto the subaltern its most incriminating anxieties.

Despite Duthu's ambiguous response to the controversy, it's important for observers to condemn the behavior of his adversaries (and ostensible supporters). We can remain mindful of Duthu's personal circumstances while simultaneously assessing the broader implications of the imbroglio for NAS and the various scholarly and activist communities with which it is in conversation. Zionists didn't merely interfere with Duthu's career; their actions are deleterious to the field Duthu represents. Are its practitioners now obliged to appease Zionists before seeking promotion? Must they check with the local supporters of settler colonization before they undertake transnational organizing? Is their self-governance contingent on the magnanimity of their oppressor? After all, they have just been warned that their criticism of colonization must remain confined to points of view that please the settler.

CIVILIZING AGGRESSION

Dialogue between Natives and Palestinians goes back at least half a century. The first substantive interchange occurred during the heyday of the American Indian Movement [AIM], when Native activists, like their Black Panther peers, looked to global liberation struggles for inspiration and solidarity, proffering both to anticolonial movements in return. The radical politics of the time put numerous armed groups across the globe into communication.

In turn, many efforts to chronicle Native activism engage on some level with Palestine, Algeria, Zimbabwe, South Africa, Cuba, Northern Ireland, and other contemporaneous struggles. NAS has numerous antecedents, but in important ways it is derivative of that moment, helped along by campus organizing that demanded representation of underserved ethnic, racial, and national groups. Its presence in US academe, then, ranges from tenuous to unwelcome. It sometimes acts as a repository of managerial grandstanding about diversity and at others as a productive link between colleges and Native nations. We cannot ascribe a specific function to NAS that universally captures its place on campus, but we can observe that it regularly encounters, or creates, a tension between cultures of resistance and sites of state power.

Some Zionist agitators see in that tension an opportunity to shame NAS away from the spaces of academe hostile to settler colonization—spaces long derided as radical or unrigorous. Their vision of NAS is quaintly anthropological. It exists to decode culture, to vitalize American diversity, to celebrate resilience, to unearth civilizational origins, to transmit ancient wisdom to a modern world always in need of redemption. All that decolonization stuff? It degrades the field's integrity. Any suggestion of complicating rather than perfecting modernity inhibits the purpose of higher education.

This vision of higher education as guardian of responsible inquiry—absent, of course, the omnipresent dynamics of colonial power—underlies the pro-Israel punishment industry's justifications for disciplining wayward individuals. That the industry would come into conflict with NAS, especially as Palestine is invigorated through movements for North American decolonization, seems inevitable, but linking Zionism to NAS only through Palestine misses important elements of the story.

NAS's commitment to decolonization is incongruous with the type of academy regulated by Zionist agitators, from progressives like Heschel to extremists like William Jacobson of *Legal Insurrection*. We have seen that liberal Zionists are happy to join reactionary forces when the protection of Israel is at stake. We have scant evidence of those liberals entering into alliance with movements and individuals perceived as radical. These are strategic decisions, yes, but they also speak to people's structural positions in relation to their professional aspirations. The Zionist cannot accept being implicated in Israeli colonization and is even less prepared to be identified with the settlement of the United States. By flagging Natives for recrimination, the Zionist doesn't merely save Israel from scrutiny, but also protects a system of neoliberal commerce to which Israel is indispensable.

Israel's indispensability to American militarism is regularly evident. During the movement in Standing Rock to preserve ancestral land from the environmental devastation of oil pipelines, US authorities availed themselves of security firm G4S, a long-time stalwart in Palestine before the BDS movement pushed it out.[13] The US government likewise approached the Standing Rock protests as a counterterrorism operation, a move that coheres with its treatment of radical activism around Palestinian, Puerto Rican, Hawaiian, and Black liberation.[14] Israel is an American talisman in matters of terror. And Israeli authorities work with US police departments across the country.[15]

Counterterrorism isn't merely a legal tactic, but a frame of reference, a defensive posture, and an ideology, a result of the

---

13. teleSUR, "G4S Admits It Guards Dakota Pipeline as Protesters Get Attacked," *teleSUR*, September 6, 2016, https://www.telesurenglish.net/news/G4S-Admits-it-Guards-Dakota-Pipeline-as-Protesters-Get-Attacked-20160906-0036.html.

14. Alleen Brown, Will Parrish, and Alice Speri, "Leaked Documents Reveal Counterterrorism Tactics Used at Standing Rock to 'Defeat Pipeline Insurgencies,'" *The Intercept*, May, 27, 2017, https://theintercept.com/2017/05/27/leaked-documents-reveal-security-firms-counterterrorism-tactics-at-standing-rock-to-defeat-pipeline-insurgencies/.

15. Jewish Virtual Library, "US-Israel Strategic Cooperation: Joint Police & Law Enforcement Training," *Jewish Virtual Library*, no date, https://www.jewishvirtuallibrary.org/joint-us-israel-police-and-law-enforcement-training.

hardboiled belief that Native sovereignty (much less liberation) imperils the United States. Terrorism is the requisite antithesis to the imaginary of a stable, exalted nation-state. If it is an act of terror for Natives to assert basic rights, then Indigeneity becomes foreign, an unsettling departure from its traditional role as a pastoral validation of the body politic. Native assertions of self-determination represent an unpacified history, the source of deep settler anxiety, where landscapes conquered into docility threaten to become animate and rebel against their corporate steward.

It is easy to frame anti-Zionism as a rejection of the US polity, something that happens regularly, albeit with variegated iterations, in Native scholarship. Anti-Zionism and anti-Americanism needn't be articulated together to generate settler anxiety and the rancor that often follows. The pro-Israel punishment industry is concerned with a particular order of the world, one in which their glamorized nation-state maintains a rarified presence. More than anything it is interested in protecting that world from the unglamorous crudeness of condemnation. Even without mentioning Palestine, certain features of NAS are a nightmare for Zionism.

Just as continuous returns to authority restrict political vision in the US, regressions to normativity in North American academe hamper intellectual creativity. Such is the design of universities that reproduce neoliberal imperatives, a structure campus Zionists adamantly enforce. I recall, for example, the time on a Facebook NAISA thread when Sergei Kan, an anthropologist of Tlingit cultures and an Israeli apologist of spectacular pettiness, invoked a viral essay I had written about the problems with the phrase "support our troops" as a way to discredit my participation in NAS on the grounds of inadequate patriotism.[16] Khan has likewise targeted Kahnawake scholar Audra Simpson, whose book *Mohawk Interruptus* proffers a sophisticated reading of Indigenous liberation, a prospect Kan appears to find highly troublesome.[17]

The pro-Israel punishment industry makes heavy use of Metis goon Ryan Bellerose to purify NAS of its decolonial tendencies.

---

16. Steven Salaita, "No, Thanks: Stop Saying 'Support the Troops,'" *Salon*, August 25, 2013, https://www.salon.com/2013/08/25/no_thanks_i_wont_support_the_troops/.

17. Audra Simpson, *Mohawk Interruptus: Political Life Across the Borders of Settler States* (Durham, NC: Duke University Press, 2014).

Bellerose prowls the Internet to find Indigenes nefarious enough to criticize Israel and then lavishes the offenders with vitriol. He has attacked J. Kehaulani Kauanui and Robert Warrior, among others, calling them "idiots" and "asshats" and questioning their ethnic authenticity.[18] (A few years ago, Bellerose showed up to a talk I gave in Alberta and got himself removed, physically threatening Native women in the audience on his way out.)

Bellerose is an extreme example—Hillel Montreal once cancelled an event with him because of his belligerent behavior—but still he represents the sanctified rendition of a phenomenon that Indigenous scholars regularly endure: aggressive men demanding compliance by deploying tactics of shame and intimidation.[19] However eagerly the genteel and urbane pro-Israel observers of NAS may want to distance themselves from people like Bellerose, we must point out that liberal Zionists evince more tolerance for reactionary hacks than for the targets of their opprobrium.

NATIVE AMERICAN STUDIES WITHOUT ZIONISM

As somebody with a history of conflict with the pro-Israel punishment industry and an investment in the fields of American Indian and Indigenous Studies, I can offer a few pragmatic observations that I hope readers might find useful.

We should treat the pro-Israel punishment industry as a nuisance and not an interlocutor. We can conceptualize it as a nuisance without minimizing the harmful outcomes it is capable of producing. It is crucial to develop strategies for surviving recrimination, or for eliminating it altogether. It is likewise crucial to expose and analyze the industry's detrimental presence in academe. Treating that industry as a nuisance is a way of taking it seriously without accommodating its unsolicited interventions. We cannot

18. See Ryan Bellerose, "Don't Mix Indigenous Fight with Palestinian Rights," *Indian Country Today*, January 11, 2014, https://newsmaven.io/indiancountrytoday/archive/don-t-mix-indigenous-fight-with-palestinian-rights-ZW7cD8KF9kWxOkWNjsnRlQ; and, Ryan Bellerose, "Dances with Idiots," *Israellycool*, April 1, 2014, http://www.israellycool.com/2014/04/01/dances-with-idiots/.

19. Janice Arnold, "Hillel Cancels Talk by Controversial Aboriginal Zionist," *The Canadian Jewish News*, March 23, 2015, https://www.cjnews.com/news/canada/hillel-cancels-talk-controversial-aboriginal-zionist.

allow it to have a voice within Native American Studies despite the difficulty of ignoring the noise it makes from the outside.

I suggest treating Zionist displeasure with our work as a site of productive inquiry: what does this reactionary interest in NAS tell us about the field? In inoculating ourselves against recrimination, how are we developing intellectual spaces that bypass or evade the traditional strictures of academe? In what ways can those spaces be meaningful to the communities we represent?

The pro-Israel punishment industry isn't an aberration; it makes manifest an implicit feature of American higher education: that Indigenous peoples are unwelcome whenever they supersede the safe romance of mascotry. Aspiring to liberation is inherently hostile. Decolonization is anathema to norms of responsibility. The field's leading scholars attempt to *undermine private ownership* and *land-grant mythologies,* narrative bellwethers of US higher education.[20] If the goal of Zionist meddling is to destroy affiliation with radical geographies, then it unwittingly facilitates one of the discipline's basic needs—to disaffiliate from the institutions that house it.

Conflict with pro-Israel zealots is a professional detriment, but also a philosophical affirmation. Few political formations make the corporate, colonial marrow of campus more obvious. In this sense, Zionist recrimination is useful in that it forces onlookers to profess their real affinities. Those who allow flaccid ideals of diversity to colonize the real work of antiracism must either stay silent, a damning ethical choice, or align with the unenlightened conservatives they pretend to abhor.

For those in NAS and related fields, the appearance of Zionist martinets and their tacit enablers can be something of a clarifying ritual. The kinds of responses those martinets generate (or don't) help advocates of decolonization determine whether US academe even deserves to survive. This formula is neither flippant nor facetious. To the contrary, it is a statement of principle. Native American Studies doesn't exist to marshal Indigenous peoples into the service of redeeming the colonial university, but to ensure that they outlast it.

---

20. Glen Coulthard, *Red Skin, White Masks: Rejecting the Colonial Politics of Recognition* (Minneapolis: University of Minnesota Press, 2014). Jodi A. Byrd, *The Transit of Empire: Indigenous Critiques of Colonialism* (Minneapolis: University of Minnesota Press, 2011).

EMBODIED REFUSALS

ON THE COLLECTIVE POSSIBILITIES
OF HUNGER STRIKING

Michelle Velasquez-Potts

In January 2002, hunger strikes began at Guantánamo Bay detention camp. Released prisoners reported to the Center for Constitutional Rights that the first Guantánamo hunger strike began "in response to the mistreatment of the Qur'an by a military police officer (MP) in Camp X-Ray."[1] Incidents leading up to the strike included officers stomping, kicking, and throwing Qur'ans belonging to detainees. After eight days, a senior officer apologized, assuring that the Qur'an would not be disrespected or touched again. In the following month, another hunger strike began after an officer "removed a homemade turban from a prisoner during his prayer."[2] Over the coming months, the strike grew to include the participation of 194 prisoners. It would be articulated as a protest prompted by prisoners' indefinite detention, harsh living conditions at the site, and religious intolerance. Military officials acknowledged at this point that the detainees were protesting "their murky future."[3]

Although the camp spokesperson refused to release the identities of the men striking, the *Miami Herald* reported that the "Justice Department did notify the attorneys of captives who became so malnourished that they required military medical forced-feedings."[4] New procedures for force-feeding were introduced in 2006, which included "strapping detainees to a chair,

---

1. Barbara Olshansky and Gitanjali Gutierrez, "The Guantánamo Prisoner Hunger Strikes and Protests: February 2002–August 2005," *The Center for Constitutional Rights*, 2005, http://www.ccr-ny.org, 6.

2. Olshansky and Gutierrez, "The Guantánamo Prisoner Hunger Strikes and Protests," 6.

3. Olshansky and Gutierrez, "The Guantánamo Prisoner Hunger Strikes and Protests," 7.

4. "Twenty-Four Force Fed Captives," *Miami Herald,* July 17, 2013, http://www.miamiherald.com/news/nation-world/world/americas/guantanamo/article1950931.html.

forcing a tube down their throats, feeding them large quantities of liquid nutrients and water, and leaving them in the chair for as long as two hours to keep them from purging the food, according to detainee accounts and military officials."[5] These procedural shifts point to how the medical clinic at Guantánamo Bay became a site of punitive suffering, blurring the line between life and non-life, inducing a state of what I call "suspended animation."

Suspended animation, I've noted elsewhere, is itself a medical term for the temporary cessation of the body's vital functions. In my theorization, it characterizes modes of brutality, such as forced-feeding, practiced by the state that are life-sustaining rather than merely repressive and/or pain inducing.[6] Suspended animation offers a framework for understanding how the state manages and regulates its captives, and how it induces medicalized control over bodies. As a technique of governance, suspended animation develops beyond past regimes of managing/controlling prison populations in that it does not simply "make live" but incapacitates the prisoner's refusal to the demand to live, forcing incapacitated forms of life in its wake.[7] The deployment of the feeding tube highlights how life and death are central components to the choreography of not only torture but the practice of hunger striking as well.

Hunger striking—the refusal of food as an act of political protest—is most commonly associated with prison struggles of the twentieth and twenty-first centuries. The refusal to eat is often the only recourse those imprisoned have to protest the conditions of not only the prison but also the sociopolitical circumstances surrounding one's incarceration. If the prison both symbolically and materially manages and controls the life of the prisoner, then the threat of self-starvation directly challenges the institution's grasp

5. Josh White, "Police End Probe into Moroccan Ex-Guantanamo Detainees' Case," in "Press Release," Algeria Watch, February 27, 2006, https://algeria-watch.org/pdf/pdf_en/campaign_guantanamo/press_270206_050306.pdf.

6. See Michelle C. Velasquez-Potts, "Staging Incapacitation: The Corporeal Politics of Hunger Striking," Women and Performance: A Journal of Feminist Theory 29, no. 1 (2019): 25–40; and Velasquez-Potts, "Carceral Oversight: Force-Feeding and Visuality at Guantánamo Bay Detention Camp," Public Culture 31, no. 3 (2019): 581–600.

7. See Michel Foucault, The History of Sexuality: Volume 1: An Introduction, trans. Robert Hurley (New York: Vintage, 1990).

on life, biological and otherwise. Below I offer a brief sketch of several hunger strikes waged between the early 2000s and our immediate present that occurred in diverse settings such as Turkey and California. These examples are in no way exhaustive. They do, however speak to the continued rise in the use of solitary confinement as the preferred mode of punishment inside of prisons, as well as the deployment of forced-feeding to delimit prisoner-led protests. Honing in on the relationship between these two technologies calls our attention to the terror of the prison, to its social death, but also its ever-emergent forms of punishment. Ultimately, hunger striking is a practice that asks those of us on the outside to listen, look, and be in solidarity with those on the inside refusing the bourgeoning technologies of the prison-industrial complex. It's also a practice that asks us to imagine prison abolition as an expansive transnational project; one predicated upon, what we might call, embodied acts of refusal.

HUNGER STRIKING AS REFUSAL

Hunger striking is an embodied articulation of the struggle between life and death waged inside the prison. It emerges as a form of refusal predicated upon inaction, for example: the subject refuses to comply with prison protocol, refuses to nourish the body, and even refuses to invest in the idea of the future. The striker lives for the now while also challenging forms of management, such as force-feeding, that insist upon life. Performance theorist Tina Campt defines refusal as "a rejection of the status quo as livable and the creation of possibility in the face of negation i.e., a refusal to recognize a system that renders you fundamentally illegible and unintelligible; the decision to reject the terms of diminished subjecthood with which one is presented, using negation as a generative and creative source of disorderly power to embrace the possibility of living otherwise."[8] Following Campt, it is precisely hunger striking's negation that gives it its power, protesting the pain, suffering, boredom, and unrest inherent to life in prison.

---

8. Tina Marie Campt, "Black Visuality and the Practice of Refusal," *Women and Performance* 29, no. 1 (2019): 79–87, 83.

In the contemporary moment, there has been a resurgence of hunger strikes inside of prisons and detention camps around the world. Scholar-activist Angela Davis argues that bridging policing and punishment across the globe is "capitalism and the spread of U.S.-style prisons throughout the world."[9] Davis goes on to write that the "global prison economy is indisputably dominated by the United States. This economy not only consists of the products, services, and ideas that are directly marketed to other governments, but it also exercises an enormous influence over the development of the style of state punishment throughout the world."[10] A prime example of this connection, one Davis also notes, is between the hunger strikes waged in both Turkey and California's Pelican Bay State Prison, which was designed with long-term confinement and isolation in mind. In 2000, Turkish prisoners began protesting high-security prisons known as "F Types." These prisons replaced collective confinement wards with solitary confinement cells, cells that were modeled off of US Supermax prisons. Over eight hundred prisoners would go on to participate in a mass hunger strike in opposition to solitary confinement. The strike would escalate to eventually include death fasts and self-immolation.[11]

Four hundred prisoners in Pelican Bay's Security Housing Unit (SHU) went on hunger strike on July 1, 2011, to protest the restrictive conditions and length of confinement in the SHU. Over the next three weeks, at least 6,600 prisoners across California participated in the strike in solidarity with Pelican Bay. The majority had been in solitary anywhere from five to twenty years, exposed to extreme sensory deprivation.

What tethers hunger striking across political and geographical bounds is that its central function is to draw attention to violent state practices that seek to subjugate minoritized persons across gender, race, sexuality, and religious lines. The practice serves as a powerful critique of not only the institution of the prison itself but also the proliferation of forms of state-authorized violence too often times

9. Angela Y. Davis, *Are Prisons Obsolete?* (New York: Seven Stories Press, 2003), 100.
10. Davis, *Are Prisons Obsolete?*, 100.
11. For a comprehensive study of the Turkish death fasts see Banu Bargu, *Starve and Immolate: The Politics of Human Weapons* (New York: Columbia University Press, 2014).

normalized and hidden from public view. Indeed, hunger striking produces forms of solidarity that extend outside of the prison. From Guantánamo Bay to Turkey to Pelican Bay, hunger striking is an embodied mode of refusal whereby protesters demand sovereignty of land and body, an end to indefinite detention, torture, and the use of carceral technologies such as solitary confinement. The power of hunger striking is in its ability to draw attention to how prisons and punishment dominate the global landscape. Thinking these struggles in relation to each other while also paying attention to increasingly medicalized forms of punishment, such as force-feeding, shows the need for our abolitionist imaginaries to explore the terrain of hunger striking, as collective struggle, but also the technologies deployed in opposition to hunger striking, such as the feeding tube. For example, the Pelican Bay hunger strikes is one example of the implementation of force-feeding in US domestic prisons with what California Corrections names "refeeding."

Although it remains unclear whether any Pelican Bay strikers were force-fed during this strike, what is clear is that the state's rhetoric of "preserving life" at any costs isn't limited solely to Guantánamo Bay, but to US domestic prisons and most recently US detention centers as well.[12] In the remainder of this essay, I attempt to conceptualize what role the self-directed violence of hunger striking plays in forging life out of spaces of unfreedom such as the Supermax prison, where the torture and isolation that ensue produce, or attempt to produce, a non-sentient existence in subjects. Drawing on the important ethnographic research of Keramet Reiter and Lisa Guenther, I return to the Pelican Bay

---

12. As of September 2019, three Indian political refugees have been forcibly fed in an Immigration and Customs Enforcement Facility (ICE) in El Paso, Texas. The men began hunger striking July 8, 2019, but initial hunger strikes began in January of 2019 when at least nine Indian men went on strike demanding immediate release and asylum from political persecution. *The Guardian* reports that ICE forcibly fed at least six of the nine hunger strikers using naso-gastric tubes. This is the first-time advocates have documented the use of force-feeding in US immigrant detention centers. See Eric Galatas, "Asylum Seekers' Hunger Strike Reaches 60th Day," *Public News Service*, September 6, 2019, https://www.epbusinessjournal.com/2019/09/asylum-seekers-hunger-strike-reaches-60th-day; and Amanda Holpuch, "Revealed: Man Force-Fed in ICE Custody at Risk Due to 'Substandard Care,' Doctor Says," *The Guardian*, August 30, 2019, https://www.theguardian.com/us-news/2019/aug/30/ajay-kumar-hunger-strike-asylum-seeker-us-detention.

strikes to think through how hunger striking functions as a form
of abolitionist solidarity and world-making practice inside the
prison while also attending to how the forced-feeding of prisoners
aims to suppress communal practices of refusal. In the case of
Pelican Bay, prison officials were unable to completely manage
the political dissent that hunger striking and litigation helped facilitate. This inability to adequately discipline the prisoner's body
through solitary confinement resulted in authorizing force-feeding as an alternative means of containment.

PELICAN BAY AND SOLITARY CONFINEMENT

Solitary confinement, as a normalized mode of punishment in
contemporary US prisons, was conceived as a response to the
Black Power Movement. In the 1970s, political organizing was
gaining momentum both inside and outside of prisons. For
example, in 1972 at Marion Penitentiary in Illinois, a group of
prisoners organized, across racial and ethnic lines, a labor strike
protesting the unlivable conditions of their incarceration. In her
phenomenological study of solitary confinement, philosopher
Lisa Guenther writes that at Marion Penitentiary "inmates were
tear-gassed and left naked in their cells for three days. All prisoners were forced to participate in a behavior modification program
called CARE (Control and Rehabilitation Effort), and 149 prisoners were kept in solitary confinement and sensory deprivation for
eighteen months."[13] Programs such as CARE emerged out of another 1970s behavioral science experiment, the Special Treatment
and Rehabilitation Training Program (START). START was used
as a baseline for prison programs that targeted individuals considered politically radical. Particularly vulnerable to these increasingly standardized technologies of isolation were Black activists
associated with organizations such as the Black Panthers. Indeed,
the focus of these behavioral programs was to implement practices such as solitary confinement that would debilitate the political
organizing associated with radical politics.[14]

13. Lisa Guenther, *Solitary Confinement: Social Death and its Afterlives* (Minneapolis:
University of Minnesota Press, 2013), 130.
14. For more on this history see Guenther, *Solitary Confinement*, 91–93; and Emily

From the late seventies to mid-eighties, litigation and judicial oversight began to emerge on behalf of prisoners contesting
the conditions of solitary confinement. Brutality on the part of
guards, unsanitary living conditions, lack of nutritional food, over-
crowded cells, and lack of educational programs would all be at
the forefront of prisoners arguing that their Eighth Amendment
rights were being violated: their conditions were "cruel and unusual."[15] This moment is generally considered the second wave
of solitary confinement, a moment concerned with rehabilitation
and reformation of the subject vis-à-vis behavioral programs. Our
current moment is solitary confinement's third wave: the era of
the control prison, neoliberal economic and social policies concerned with risk management, privatization of punishment, and
increased overall surveillance.[16] It's currently estimated that between twenty-five and eighty thousand prisoners are in Supermax
confinement across forty-four states.[17]

Opened in 1989, Pelican Bay is located in Crescent City,
California, and was one of the world's first Supermax prisons. It
was designed as the best of the best in corrections technology, with
long-term confinement and isolation in mind. It serves as both a
traditional maximum-security prison, with a 2,000-prisoner capacity, and a Supermax security complex with 1,056 windowless isolation cells: 132 pods of eight cells each.[18] The Security Housing Unit
(SHU) cells, where the majority of hunger strikers were held, meas-
ure eleven by seven feet and have no windows. The cells are painted

---

Thuma, *All Our Trials: Prisons, Policing, and the Feminist Fight to End Violence*
(Champaign, IL: University of Illinois Press, 2019). On this period Thuma writes,
"'[The] cultural and political discourses about racial protest were imprinted on medical
diagnoses of mental illness in the 1960s and 1970s, and "new 'psychochemical' technologies of control merged with concerns about the 'uncontrollable' nature of urban
unrest.' As activists involved with the black liberation, Puerto Rican independence,
anti-war, and Red Power and Brown Power movements were sent to jails or prisons
on charges linked to their political activities, prison administrators registered an acute
sense of concern that prisoner dissent was aided and abetted by imprisoned radicals
and the larger social movements with which they were affiliated" (58).

15. See Reiter, *23/7*, 10–13.

16. For more on the neoliberalization of punishment see Guenther, *Solitary
Confinement*; and Stephen Dillon, *Fugitive Life: The Queer Politics of the Prison State*
(Durham, NC: Duke University Press, 2018).

17. Guenther, *Solitary Confinement*, 131.

18. See Reiter, *23/7*, 19, for more on the architecture of Pelican Bay.

white or grey to reduce visual stimulation and are furnished with a bed, table, seat, toilet, and sink. There are no windows, or a very small one high enough to allow only a bit of light and no view of the outside. Fluorescent lights and surveillance cameras are kept on twenty-four hours a day. Prisoners are permitted a television, a radio, books, magazines, and a legal pad.[19]

By 2010, more than five hundred prisoners had lived in continuous isolation for more than ten years. By the mid-1990s, it was standard practice to place prisoners with alleged gang status into solitary. The stated purpose of the SHU is to segregate those perceived to pose a high-security risk. Prisoners are isolated for twenty-two to twenty-four hours a day, and florescent lights are used in the cell all day and night. There is a "cuffport" in the door: a slot where the prisoner's hands are cuffed and uncuffed. Meals are delivered through the cuffport twice a day. The cuffports can be bolted to prevent "bombing," which is where prisoners throw their feces and urine at guards. When such acts of resistance happen, prisoners can be "forcibly extracted from their cells by an emergency response team in riot gear. They may be pepper-sprayed or tasered and put in four- or five-point restraints (with wrists and ankles fastened to the ground, with or without a helmet fastened to the ground) or in a restraint chair. Officers are entitled to perform strip searches of inmates—including cavity searches—if they suspect the inmate of possessing contraband items."[20]

The debilitation inherent to isolation is precisely why four hundred prisoners in Pelican Bay's Security Housing Unit (SHU) went on hunger strike on July 1, 2011, to protest the restrictive conditions and length of confinement in the SHU. Over the next three weeks, at least 6,600 prisoners across California participated in the strike in solidarity with Pelican Bay. The majority had been in solitary anywhere from five to twenty years, exposed to extreme sensory deprivation. On July 20, 2011, some of the strike demands were met: prisoners could take one picture of themselves a year to send to their families; they could have colored pencils, wall

---

19. See Reiter, 23/7, 10, and Guenther, *Solitary Confinement* for more on the general architectural landscape of SHUs.

20. Guenther, "A Critical Phenomenology of Solidarity and Resistance in the 2013 California Prison Hunger Strikes," 51.

calendars, and warm caps for outdoor exercise during winter; they could access exercise equipment; and, more food options were offered.[21] Undoubtedly the tactic of hunger striking was useful in drawing awareness to the prisoners' cause, yet it was also short-lived due to the legal authorization to force-feed strikers, or what California Corrections refers to as "refeeding."

CRUEL AND UNUSUAL

Prisoner-rights litigation continue to contest the practices described above at Pelican Bay, highlighting the power struggle inherent to the space of prison. In the 1995 Eighth Amendment case *Madrid v. Gomez*, upon hearing that prisoners were being chained to toilets and beds with their hands and feet bound together or left outside in cages the size of telephone booths, half naked and exposed to other prisoners and harsh weather, Judge Thelton Henderson stated that "leaving inmates in outdoor cages for any significant period—as if animals in a zoo—offends even the most elementary notions of common decency and dignity."[22] Henderson sought to protect the "human dignity" of prisoners in SHU at Pelican Bay but ended up reproducing prolonged solitary confinement.[23] He never found solitary confinement cruel and unusual as a practice, only the conditions of the prison—and thus wanted to ensure that institutions met constitutional standards. Such logic prioritizes the corporeal body and draws a line of distinction between what conditions the mind but not the body can withstand. "Loneliness, frustration, depression, or extreme boredom," for Henderson, are manageable, while the "animalizing" treatment described above crosses a legal and moral line.[24]

Legal scholar Colin Dayan notes that the emphasis placed on corporeality in Eighth Amendment cases is striking: "courts attend to the body, not the intangible qualities of the person (e.g.,

---

21. Reiter, 23/7, 196.

22. Quoted in Guenther, *Solitary Confinement*, 134. See *Madrid*, 889, F. Supp., at 1146.

23. Guenther, *Solitary Confinement*, 95.

24. Quoted in Colin Dayan, "With Law at the Edge of Life," *South Atlantic Quarterly* 113, no. 3 (2014): 629–639, 633. See Guenther, *Solitary Confinement* for a posthumanist critique of solitary confinement, what she terms a "violation of (human and nonhuman) animal ontology" (127).

psychological pain or fear) or the deadly social components of indefinite solitary confinement."[25] Contemporary solitary confinement, as demonstrated by Henderson, aims to disappear the mind while managing the body. Henderson concluded that cruel and unusual punishment was applicable for prisoners in isolation who "are at a particularly high risk for suffering very serious or severe injury to their mental health . . . such inmates consist of the already mentally ill, as well as persons with borderline personality disorders, brain damage or mental retardation, impulse-ridden personalities, or a history of prior psychiatric problems or chronic depression."[26] The state predictably evades any responsibility for its role in reproducing such psychic ailments. A Cold War logic lingers on here, in that mind and body are deemed separate entities with the material body taking precedence in these Eighth Amendment cases.

Another reason that the SHU has not been successfully challenged on Eighth Amendment grounds as "cruel and unusual" is that it is not considered a "punishment" but a disciplinary practice executed by prison administrators, keeping it within legal bounds.[27] The distinction here is between a "sentence" issued by a court, which is a form of punishment, and a penological discretionary decision by prison staff to preserve the "security" of staff and prisoners. This would include secluding alleged gang leaders and prisoners who attempt to escape, refuse to work, are caught in possession of contraband, self-harm, or express suicidal ideation.[28] But as journalists Josh Harkinson and Maggie Cladwell report, "Prisoners can be thrown into the SHU indefinitely without any due process, meaning that they never get a chance to review or contest the

---

25. Dayan, "With Law at the Edge of Life," 633.

26. Colin (Joan) Dayan, "Legal Slaves and Civil Bodies," *Nepantla: Views from the South* 2, no. 1 (2001): 3–39, 24–25.

27. Reiter, 23/7.

28. Although beyond the scope of this essay, it is also important to note the overwhelming numbers of queer and trans prisoners placed in SHU. This can be because queer and, in particular, trans prisoners seek protective custody from general population due to gender-based violence—though more often than not, trans prisoners face more violence, including sexual violence by guards, while in solitary confinement. For more on trans incarceration and the gendered logics of the prison-industrial complex, see Eric A. Stanley and Nat Smith, *Captive Genders: Trans Embodiment and the Prison Industrial Complex* (Oakland: AK Press, 2011).

evidence that they've done something wrong."[29] This emphasis on the intent of punishment dates back to *Wilson v. Seiter* (1991), where Justice Antonin Scalia found that, regardless of how much a prisoner suffers at the hands of a guard or any other official, if the intent to cause severe harm, physical or otherwise, is not proven, then the ramifications on the prisoner's mental and physical health is not enough to warrant judicial review.[30] "The Court's logic," writes Dayan, "thus strips the victim of the right to experience suffering, to know fear and anguish. Legally, the plaintiff has become a nonreactive body, a defenseless object."[31]

Dayan's point is particularly apt regarding the Pelican Bay strike. As the strike escalated, with more and more men hospitalized, it became clear that prison officials held a monopoly on the suffering of prisoners. The social death produced through solitary confinement was deemed acceptable but the self-induced suffering of starvation was seen as coercive and manipulative. Such biopolitical entanglements cannot simply be reduced to who gets to live and who gets to die. Life, in both instances, is leveraged against individual subjects and collectives, pitting self-determination against life and retribution. Ultimately, the state's desire to preserve biological life is bound up with its interest in punishment.[32] The state decides the health of the mind, the integrity of the body, and when living death is allowed to become natural death, making force-feeding an excellent mask for such control over life. Prison authorities make distinctions between social death and biological death. The feeding tube is a torture instrument of life that disallows natural death but also disallows the practice of hunger striking, which seeks to make visible the unlivability of solitary confinement and the isolationist practices of the prison.

---

29. Josh Harkinson and Maggie Caldwell, "50 Days without Food: The California Prison Hunger Strike Explained," *Mother Jones*, August 27, 2013, https://www.motherjones.com/politics/2013/08/50-days-california-prisons-hunger-strike-explainer/.

30. See *Wilson v. Seiter*, 501 U.S. 294 (1991).

31. Dayan, "Legal Slaves and Civil Bodies," 26–27.

32. For more on this point see Mara Silver, "Testing *Cruzan*: Prisoners and the Constitutional Question of Self-Starvation," *Stanford Law Review* 58, (2005): 631–662. Silver writes, "retributive-based punishment requires no action by the offender demonstrating personal accountability other than serving out the required sentence. Therefore, 'doing the time' is critical" (643).

"REFEEDING" AS MEDICALIZED PUNISHMENT

Two years after the first hunger strike at Pelican Bay, on July 8, 2013, thirty thousand prisoners across California penitentiaries refused their state-issued meals, resuming the largest hunger strike in the state's history. The strike committee, known as the Pelican Bay SHU–Short Corridor Collective, listed five demands:

> 1) to end group punishment for individual rule violations, 2) to reform gang validation procedures, 3) to comply with the recommendations of a national commission on long-term solitary confinement, 4) to provide adequate and healthy food, and 5) to expand rehabilitation, education, and recreation programs.[33]

To draft the demands, "prisoners had shouted at one another through plumbing pipes in their cells and drain pipes in the exercise yards, passed notes under cell doors ('kites'), and communicated through advocates in San Francisco, sending letters back and forth, seeking help in amplifying their demands."[34] The stakes would indeed prove higher for the 2013 strike. Dozens of prisoners were hospitalized, and one died by hanging himself in his cell.[35] This suicide highlights the utter untruth of the argument that isolation manages mental health and disability inside the prison. The practice not only exacerbates mental illness but reproduces it in such a way that it's impossible to know which comes first for most imprisoned people.

As Emily Thuma argues in her study on feminist responses to prisons and policing throughout the 1970s and 1980s, what prisons and mental hospitals deem appropriate behavior "rende[r] any expressions of independence or autonomy as nonnormative and dangerous," making behaviors such as "political activism or organizing activity, refusal to accept medication, refusal to accept arbitrary orders, or refusal to do prison work" constitutive of serious mental health issues that must be treated.[36] Yet, as Thuma counters, so-called "'crazy' behaviors [a]re strategies for navigating and surviving the conditions

33. Guenther, "A Critical Phenomenology of Solidarity and Resistance in the 2013 California Prison Hunger Strikes," 47.
34. Reiter, 23/7, 30.
35. Reiter, 23/7, 30.
36. Thuma, *All Our Trials*, 78.

of prisons and mental health institutions."[37] Hunger striking, then, is one such response to the literal space of death that the prison so often becomes.[38] Following Thuma's provocations, hunger striking tests the limits of the biomedicalization of punishment and its long history inside of prisons and psychiatric facilities. And this is not to ignore the very real psychiatric concerns that prisoner's experience, and indeed seek help for. Rather we must resist the ableist logic that contends that all psychic differences are indicative of a bodymind in need of state-mandated cures and medicalization. My invocation of suspended animation, from which I began this essay, is meant, then, as a framework to better understand the relationship between medicalization and technologies of punishment, as well as the complexities of embodied resistance to these carceral practices.

Even as carceral technologies such as solitary confinement seek to diminish sociality, the reality is more complicated. Forms of relationality can ensue and with them defiance. So successful was the prisoners' collective refusal that in August 2013, with 129 prisoners refusing meals at Pelican Bay, state officials requested authorization to "refeed" hunger strikers—the process of reintroducing food after significant malnourishment or starvation. As Keramet Reiter's ethnography of the hunger strikes recounts, at this point, a "handful" of participants had been hospitalized. Since many of the men had signed "do not resuscitate" directives, their lawyers conceded and began to negotiate with the prison. Judge Henderson ruled that California prison doctors could "refeed" inmates if the prison's chief medical executive decides that a hunger striker is at risk of "near-term death or great bodily injury."[39]

37. Thuma, *All Our Trials*, 78.
38. Importantly, here Thuma is writing about women's incarceration and the ways that protest so often is masculinized, and as such, constructed as more pathological in relation to women. While I only gesture toward the gender politics of hunger striking in this essay's conclusion there is much more to be said, much of which is unfortunately, beyond the scope of this essay. However, Thuma's argument also resonates with the pathologization of the strikers at Guantánamo Bay. The military's use of diagnostic discourse frames the men held captive, the majority of whom are Arab and/or Muslim, as irrational and unstable. This framing relies on a categorization of Muslims and Islam predicated upon a racialized discourse positioning the East as backward and fanatical, and the West as modern, civilized, and rational. For more on this construction in US counterterrorism, see Raphael Patai, *The Arab Mind* (Tucson, AZ: Recovery Resources Press, 1973).
39. See *Plata v. Brown*, Case No. C01-1351, TEH, "Joint Request for Order Authorizing

Further, the court stated that a large-scale prison hunger strike "poses significant challenges in the prison setting and presents difficult, sometimes conflicting, policy questions concerning institutional safety and security, inmate-patient autonomy over their person and the receipt of medical treatment, the ability of medical staff to monitor and provide adequate care to striking inmates and medical ethical requirements pertaining to the protection of patients from harm while respecting patient autonomy."[40] Throughout the 2013 strike, prison officials framed their response to the strikes through the framework of care. California Corrections spokespeople, such as Elizabeth Gransee, made clear that hunger strikers' caloric intake would be carefully monitored and that vitamins, electrolytes, and liquid nutritional supplements were offered regularly to prisoners.[41] Beds and the "highest levels of care" would be available at the prison's healthcare facilities.[42] The message was clear: prison doctors would not only monitor the health of prisoners but also take all measures to "preserve life," even if that meant resorting to the feeding tube. The force-feeding of prisoners at Pelican Bay demonstrates a technological way of rupturing the political defiance of the hunger striker and underscores the power of self-harm to expose what the prison seeks to hide.

In the years since the strike at Pelican Bay, California Correctional Health Care Services has created a "CCHCS Hunger Strike, Fasting, and Refeeding Care Guide," which includes the risks involved in refeeding. California Correctional Health Care Services dedicates an entire page to the risks involved in refeeding, apparently as a deterrent to hunger striking.[43] Reiter notes the vagueness of the term *refeeding*, asking, "Did it mean prison

---

Refeeding under Specified Conditions of Hunger Striking Inmate-Patients and Order Thereon," 4, solitarywatch.com/wp-content/uploads/2013/08/Plata-Hunger-Strike-Stipulation.pdf.

40. See *Plata v. Brown*, 2.

41. Joe Johnson, "Inmate Strike Sparks Health Risks, Concerns," *Sentinel*, August 16, 2013, https://hanfordsentinel.com/news/local/crime-and-courts/inmate-strike-sparks-health-risks-concerns/article_b3e9108e-06bf-11e3-96ad-0019bb2963f4.html.

42. Johnson, "Inmate Strike Sparks Health Risks."

43. California Correctional Health Care Services, "CCHCS Hunger Strike, Fasting, and Refeeding Care Guide," July 2013, https://cchcs.ca.gov/wp-content/uploads/sites/60/2017/08/MassHungerStrikeCareGuide.pdf.

officials could provide intravenous fluids and nutrients to prisoners who lost consciousness? Or did it authorize forcing a tube down a wide-awake prisoner's nose against his will?"[44] I argue, however, that "refeeding," in this context, is nothing short of force-feeding.[45] The threat of force-feeding at Pelican Bay, then, is indicative of what Nicolas Rose calls *ethnopolitics*—that which shapes the conduct of human beings by acting upon their sentiments, beliefs, and values.[46] The ethnopolitics of California Corrections' stance on hunger striking emphasizes the preservation of life while drawing from the rhetoric of patient autonomy to argue that the strikers aren't mentally competent enough to make their own medical decisions. The tension between patient autonomy and the state boils down to what is deemed care by institutions such as hospitals and prisons, and how asserting one's right to die by refusing palliative care or choosing to starve necessitates refusing legible practices of care. Hunger striking, then, is that which points out how the prison is a place of unfreedom that draws from the vocabulary of autonomy to uphold a liberal fiction of rehabilitative justice. A place of utter unfreedom such as the prison cannot negotiate autonomy. Here, the supposed autonomous patient is replaced by the inactive subject, who refuses medical intervention, food, or the rehabilitation of the prison in place of a political defiance that places them at what Dayan so aptly names the "edge of life."[47]

Less than a month after the refeeding authorization, the strike officially came to an end. On September 5, 2013, after a core group of forty prisoners had refused meals continuously for sixty days and hundreds more had participated for days or weeks on end, the hunger strike was suspended after state assembly member Tom

44. Reiter, 23/7, 60.

45. It is important to note that refeeding as the introduction of food back into one's system isn't always coercive. According to Azadeh Zohrabi, a member of the Prisoner's Mediation Team, there were prisoners who underwent the process voluntarily. My interest here is how the term "refeeding" is deployed strategically by CCHCS as a way to delegitimize the hunger strikes, but also to mask the medicalized violence of prison protocol. See "Exclusive: As Judge Oks Force-Feeding, California Prisoner on 47-Day Hunger Strike Speaks Out," *Democracy Now*, August 23, 2013, https://www.democracynow.org/2013/8/23/exclusive_as_judge_oks_force_feeding.

46. Nikolas Rose, *The Politics of Life Itself: Biomedicine, Power, and Subjectivity in the Twenty-First Century* (Princeton: Princeton University Press, 2006), 27.

47. Dayan, "With Law at the Edge of Life," 634.

Ammiano and state senator Loni Hancock committed to holding a legislative hearing before a joint Public Safety Committee. In response to these hearings, the California Department of Corrections and Rehabilitation conducted an internal policy review and a case-by-case audit of SHU prisoners. Further, a class-action lawsuit initiated by hunger-strike organizers and the Center for Constitutional Rights, *Ashker v. Brown*, was advancing in the courts. The lawsuit set out to challenge long-term solitary confinement in California as unconstitutional.

During the Department of Corrections and Rehabilitation audit, 528 case files of SHU prisoners were reviewed, 343 were approved to be moved into the general population, and an additional 150 were placed in programs to get them ready to "step down" to the general population. In June 2014, an additional 214 prisoners were transferred to the general population and another 180 to the step-down program. However, it soon became apparent that many of the prisoners being transferred were being placed right back into SHU—and were also plaintiffs in the lawsuit *Ashker v. Brown*. In September 2015, prison officials agreed to settle *Ashker*. The agreement "prohibited the assignment of prisoners to the SHU based solely on their status as gang members, capped all stays in the SHU at five years, made the provisions retroactive, and required prison officials to provide prisoners' lawyers monthly data reports for two years about the characteristics of the SHU populations." Other state prison systems have since adopted similar reforms.[48]

Although the Pelican Bay strikes led to significant reform to isolation practices, we shouldn't ignore the ease with which refeeding or force-feeding was weaponized against the solidarity forged across racial and ethnic lines. Indeed, every federal court tasked with addressing the issue has sanctioned force-feeding, and the Federal Bureau of Prisons has clear guidelines detailing protocol for handling prisoners who participate in a hunger strike.[49] Here the feeding tube at first glance has the same ef-

48. Reiter, 23/7, 202.
49. See the case of William Coleman, a prisoner in Connecticut who was force-fed from 2008–2013. Coleman understood being force-fed as a way for the prison to "let him slide," feeding him only when absolutely necessary. Coleman calls this the "torture gap." See Ann Neumann, "The Longest Hunger Strike," *Guernica*, January 15, 2013,

fect as solitary confinement. Dayan writes, "solitary confinement and execution both mark the continuum between unnatural (civil or spiritual) death and natural (actual and physical) death."[50] But, it might be that this isn't the case with force-feeding, that force-feeding is precisely that which disrupts the continuum between life and death. Perhaps, here, the strange and elusive "refeeding" takes new significance, acting as a grammar for the act of making live again and again.

ABOLITION/REFUSAL

The Pelican Bay hunger strikes quickly led to negotiations and, as such, force-feeding remained a short-lived threat. The hunger strikes at Guantánamo Bay, from which I started, however, have played out very differently over the past two decades. Their refusal to eat, which is to say their embodied refusal to comply with the unlivability of indefinite detention, was met almost immediately by the feeding tube and continues to the present day. The maintenance of life by way of force-feeding occupies a paradoxical position insofar as it is both life-affirming and life-denying, an application of torture and infliction of pain in the name of biological life. But, this emphasis on mere biology isn't where I'd like to end this essay. I want to conclude on the political and collective life forged at both Guantánamo Bay and Pelican Bay, respectively. Indeed, forged in prisons and detention camps across the world. There are many more stories to tell, such as the hunger strikes waged by trans women of color in a California detention center in 2015, or Irom Chanu Sharmila, an Indian women's rights activist who was on hunger strike for sixteen years protesting the Indian government's Armed Forces (Special Powers) Act.[51] These collective acts

http://www.guernicamag. com/features/the-longest-hunger-strike; and Jacob Appel, "Rethinking Force-Feeding: Legal and Ethical Aspects of Physician Participation in the Termination of Hunger Strikes in American Prisons," *Public Affairs Quarterly* 26, no. 4 (2012): 313–335.

50. Dayan, "Legal Slaves and Civil Bodies," 17.

51. With the exception to literature on the British Suffragette movement of the early 1900s there hasn't been significant attention paid to hunger strikes inside of women's prisons. One notable exception is *Begoña Aretxaga, Shattering Silence: Women, Nationalism, and Political Subjectivity in Northern Ireland* (Princeton, NJ: Princeton University Press, 1997).

of refusal speak to a feminist abolitionist politic that Eric Stanley writes "is not simply a reaction to the PIC [prison-industrial complex] but a political commitment that makes the PIC impossible. . . . In other words, while we hold on to abolition as a politics for doing anti-PIC work, we also acknowledge there are countless ways that abolition has been and continues to be here now."[52]

Hunger striking, and being in solidarity with strikers, is one of countless ways that we see abolition being imagined in our unfolding present.[53] Indeed, hunger striking necessitates a different conception of time, where one acts in the present for a future beyond them. The hunger striker's reconceptualization of time strikes me as ultimately what shapes most, if not all, political activism and acts of state defiance. The work of prison abolition is to build a world without prisons and punishment, even as the abolitionist knows they may not see the material manifestation of their work. To this end, any anti-state terror praxis, such as hunger striking and prison abolition, is about imagining a different world and building towards it.[54] Abolition time isn't linear, with the world one builds towards awaiting to be grasped. Rather, abolition is a practice that's lived and experienced in the day to day. It's to live in the world yet to be made. To think hunger striking in this way, it seems to me, is a powerful instantiation of living in the face of the prison and making a life anyway—a life that ironically deprioritizes one's own biological life and corporeal integrity in favor of the political life of collective struggle.

Aretxaga's text is one of the few feminist ethnographies of the female Irish nationalists held at Armagh prison, where they also participated in the hunger strikes of 1981.

52. Stanley, *Captive Genders*, 8.

53. For more on how solidarity has been enacted see the "Prisoner Hunger Strike Solidarity Coalition." The coalition started in 2011 in San Francisco and is "made up of grassroots organizations, family members, formerly incarcerated people, lawyers, and individuals... to work in solidarity with California prisoners on the long-standing issues that gave rise to the 2011 and 2013 strikes... and the struggle against the ongoing human and civil rights failures connected to California's torture legacy of solitary confinement." https://prisonerhungerstrikesolidarity.wordpress.com/about/.

54. For more on what this work looks like see Critical Resistance; INCITE! Women of Color Against Violence; Survived and Punished; Sylvia Rivera Law Project; The Audre Lorde Project; FIERCE!; Bay Area Transformative Justice Collective; and Gay Shame, among many others.

NOTES ON PHOTOGRAPHY, POWER, AND INSURGENT LOOKS

Stefanie Fock

On July 8, 2015, twenty-eight-year-old Çilem Doğan got arrested in Adana, Turkey, after she shot her ex-husband, who had repeatedly abused her and tried to force her into prostitution. For their coverage of this case, Turkish and international media repeatedly reproduced a photograph in which Çilem Doğan is handcuffed between two police officers, but giving two thumbs up to the camera. While there is contradictory information about the date and incident of this shot,[1] there seems to be a general agreement on the message communicated through it—Çilem Doğan does not regret her actions. The meaning of this conclusion, however, has been interpreted in at least two ways. While the photograph has been used to highlight the image of the unrepentant female murderer, it has also been appropriated and widely spread as a symbol of feminist empowerment.

When I first looked at this photograph, my eyes confronted it in the latter sense. A feeling of satisfaction occurs every time I look at this picture, in which I neither see a victim nor a perpetrator but an empowered survivor. This feeling immediately overwhelms my body. Even though—or exactly because—it implicates pain, grief and rage, this photo is encouraging. In Turkey and beyond it has caused a noisy echo of people demanding Çilem Doğan's release, and speaking up against gender violence, femicide, and

---

1. Several sources say that the photograph was taken when Çilem Doğan got arrested at her father's house in Adana. The *Hürriet Daily News*, however, explains that the shot shows the moment when the detainee was carried to the courthouse for medical checks the day after her arrest. See *Hürriet Daily News* 2015. [incomplete cit; fix]

FIGURE 1: ÇILEM DOĞAN GETS ARRESTED BY POLICE.
SCREENSHOT TAKEN FROM TWITTER (ORIGINAL PHOTO BY DHA).

the criminalization of women's self-defensive actions. For me, the photograph has also been inspiring to reconsider the power inherent to photography, to think through the political relations that characterize photographs, and to deliberate about the transformative potential of insurgent ways of looking.

In the following I will neither undertake an in-depth engagement with the history that made Çilem Doğan kill nor make the claim to abolish murder charges for survivors of gender violence. Instead of focusing on the event the photographer sought to register, I intend to use the photograph to approach a political understanding of photography itself. For this purpose I refer to Ariella Azoulay's writings on the question of what photography is.[2]

Azoulay deals with photography as an event that is triggered by the camera but does not necessarily lead to the existence of a photographic image.[3] Producing, distributing, and consuming photos are parts of a sequence of diverse actions encompassed by the term photography. A camera always influences a given situation, but there is not always a visual outcome of the event of photography, or at least not for everybody. Often the photographed persons are not the ones to see the photo. And, even if the camera is actually switched off and no pictures taken, people still experience photography.

---

2. It is important to clarify that the kind of photography Ariella Azoulay is concerned with is one "in which photographs [of people] are taken on the verge of catastrophe." Ariella Azoulay, *The Civil Contract of Photography*, trans. Rela Mazali and Ruvik Danieli, 2nd ed. (New Tork: Zone Books 2014), 85.

3. See, in particular: Ariella Azoulay, "What is a photograph? What is photography?" *Philosophy of Photography* 1, no. 1 (2010): 9–13; Azoulay, "On Photography," *Maf'teakh. Lexical Review of Political Thought*, issue 2e (Winter 2011): 65–80; Azoulay, *The Civil Contract of Photography*, 2nd ed. (New York: Zone Books, 2014).

"Photography is an apparatus of power that cannot be reduced to any of its components: a camera, a photographer, a photographed environment, person, or spectator."[4] The event of photography takes place as an encounter between people, between people and the camera, and between people and the photograph. The third is a testimony to the moment when photographer, photographed person, and camera encounter one another: a moment in which no one participant holds the absolute power to determine the meaning of the visual outcome. The aim of this understanding of photography is neither to downplay the privileged position commonly occupied by photographers nor to minimize their responsibility of defining the boundary of the photograph. Nevertheless, "s/he alone does not determine what will be inscribed in the frame and what might be reconstructed from it regarding the situation photographed."[5]

To unsettle the long-standing notion that the photographer is the only individual author of a photograph means to open up possibilities to consider and use photography as an instrument that employs power to photographed persons and spectators. "Photography is a form of relation that exists and becomes valid only within and between the plurality of individuals who take part in it."[6] Consider the agency of the photographed persons who often participate actively, even if they did not give their consent to be photographed in the first place. In addition, it points to the chance and the responsibility of the spectator to transform photography "from a simple, convenient, efficient, (relatively) inexpensive and easily operable tool for the production of pictures into a social, cultural, and political instrument of immense power."[7]

In order to make photography practical for political intervention, it is imperative to understand that the reality supposedly captured by the photographer and authentically *reproduced* by the camera is, in practice, *produced* through the event of photography. The idea that a photograph contains meaning *in itself* has to be abolished Pictures neither speak for themselves, nor do they hold

---

4. Azoulay, *The Civil Contract of Photography*, 85.
5. Azoulay, "On Photography," 12.
6. Azoulay, *The Civil Contract of Photography*, 85.
7. Azoulay, *The Civil Contract of Photography*, 129.

a single or stable point of view. They allow negotiations about the matter they indicate, because what is visible is not innate to the picture but projected into it. This is why Azoulay requests not to treat photographs as the final product of a finite photographic act, but as a practice: "[A photo] is in fact a new beginning that lacks any predictable end. . . . It acts, thus making others act. The ways in which its action yields others' action, however, is unpredictable."[8] Such a vantage point enables imagining that change can be achieved through an insurgent way of looking that resists subordination under a dominant regime of perception.[9]

According to Azoulay,[10] a first step toward change consists in altering the question of what I am looking at when regarding a photograph. This allows me to foreground why the photographed persons are looking at me. With this objective in mind, I look again at the photo of Çilem Doğan. My look fades out the background and concentrates on the three women at the forefront. The two at the outside wear police uniforms, while Çilem Doğan appears handcuffed in the middle. The officer at the left links arms with her, a presumably cozy gesture, which seems strange due to the arrest. All three women actively participated in the photographic act when they refused to look at the camera. All three decided to look at the ground, but the detainee kept her head erect, while the

---

8. Azoulay, *The Civil Contract of Photography*, 129.

9. Ariella Azoulay's civil imagination has influenced my thoughts on the transformative potential of insurgent looks. The theory Azoulay lays out in writings like *The Civil Contract of Photography* deals with the relation of photography and citizenship in disaster contexts, and is hence far more complex than my reference to her definition of photography as an event. Based on the Israeli-Palestinian context the author is coming from, her idea of a civil contract of photography creates the possibility to overcome a concept of citizenship that is limited by the nation-state. She introduces a "new [deterritorialized] conceptualization of citizenship as a framework of partnership and solidarity among those who are governed [citizens and noncitizens], a framework that is neither constituted nor circumscribed by the sovereign." [Azoulay, *The Civil Contract of Photography*, 23.] For her approach to the ethics of the spectator as a crucial component of the civil contract of photography, she presents the notion of the civic space of the gaze and underlines the importance of rethinking our interrelation with it. In this article I will not go into her particular idea of the photographic citizenry in detail, however it could certainly be an enriching task to broaden the discussion of the photograph of Çilem Doğan in terms of the civil contract of photography. Especially, because of Azoulay's concern over the vulnerable citizenship and sexual abandonment of women that leads her to question if the lack of visibility of the event of rape precludes the possibility to see and treat it as a human disaster.

10. Azoulay, *The Civil Contract of Photography*, 18.

police officers (incidentally or deliberately) dropped theirs with the strange visual effect of delegating prominence to Çilem Doğan. The latter especially highlighted her active participation in the creation of her picture when she lifted up her two thumbs.

This gesture illustrates Azoulay's assertion that the production of a photograph "is created and inspired by a relation of an external eye." [11] By giving two thumbs to the camera Çilem Doğan addressed a hypothetical community of spectators whose interest in the picture could lead to responsibility toward her and, at best, to action against the ongoing violence many women are experiencing. Even without her directly looking at me, her consent to be transformed into a picture becomes visible through her interaction with the camera. With her upraised thumbs she seems to say, "Yes, take my picture," and furthermore, "Yes, I did it, everything is okay." She transformed the photographic event into a moment of recognition of her actions, desiring to be seen as a lawbreaker who did not resist the arrest but rather refused the possibility that her agency could remain unnoticed. By means of her re-action—facing the arrest and the photoshoot—she foreclosed the risk of being (visually) victimized.

Çilem Doğan reinforced her publicly performed self-assurance when telling police, "Will women always die? Let some men die too. I killed him for my honor." [12] Through her performance in front of the camera, she translated this powerful exclamation into a use of photography as a political instrument. As if she consciously prepared for her photographic staging before she actually encountered the photographer and the camera, the T-shirt she is wearing in the photo underlines her corporal resolve: *Dear past, thanks for all the lessons. Dear future, I am ready!* The recent past: resisting the violent acts of her husband. The immediate future: prison. For the court, the photo contains the potential to use it as visual evidence in order to criminalize the detainee because of her lack of regret, which is often an aggravating argument with regard to charges. In many cases, the textual embedding of the picture in mass media can be read as the attempt to strengthen such an image of the unrepentant female murderer who,

11. Azoulay, *The Civil Contract of Photography*, 129.

12. This statement has been quoted in each and every article about the case of Çilem Doğan, as well as used by feminist approaches to her acts on Twitter and other social networks.

on top of everything, became "an Internet sensation."[13]

For *Don't Let Your Eyelash Fall to Ground: Women Look For Their Lives*, Feminist Group Istanbul collected reports of "women who had to kill/injure man in order to not get killed."[14] As they explain, the big problem has been the inability to include those stories of women who have not made it into the news, although they come up every day. The stories of women who kill their husbands to stay alive, raise the question "of whether they would have killed if they had received effective protection from authorities after seeking help against their abusers."[15] It has been reported that Çilem Doğan sought institutional help several times. During her closing statement at the trial she declared, "I never wanted this to happen, but I had no other option." She refused to be seen as a murderer, claiming her right to self-defense.[16]

This is why she is "looking" at me. She saw both the photographer facing her and the participation in the photographic act "as a framework that offer[ed] an alternative—weak though it may be—to the institutional structures that have abandoned and injured [her]."[17] The clear link between self-defense, breach of law, and conscious participation in the photographic act shows that Çilem Doğan assumed the existence of a community of spectators who claims "to enact photography free of governmental power and even against it, if it inflicts injury on others."[18]

Obviously, the unequal relation of Çilem Doğan to the power that governs her cannot easily be overcome beyond the event of photography. Ultimately, an insurgent way of looking cannot

---

13. Rashell Habib, "Turkish Woman Kills her Abusive Husband, Becomes an Internet Sensation," July 15, 2015, http://www.news.com.au/lifestyle/real-life/news-life/turkish-woman-kills-her-abusive-husband-becomes-an-internet-sensation/news-story/50ba3fb43216e0cf3b8e75e1093idoed. Nevertheless, by reproducing Çilem Doğan's words and pictures, mass media have seen themselves forced to write about the possible apprehension of the killing of an abusive husband as a legitimate form of self-defense, although they usually reported on it in an ambivalent way.

14. ÇT/DG, "Women Kill 2 Men, Injure 2 Others Inflicting Violence on Them in March," *Bianet*, May 9, 2016, https://m.bianet.org/bianet/women/174570-women-kill-2-men-injure-2-others-inflicting-violence-on-them-in-march.

15. Sibel Hurtas, "Why Turkish Women Are Rallying Behind this Killer," *Al Monitor*, June 23, 2016, http://www.al-monitor.com/pulse/originals/2016/06/turkey-women-rights-violence-abusive-husband.html.

16. Hurtas, "Why Turkish Women are Rallying Behind this Killer."

17. Azoulay, *The Civil Contract of Photography*, 18.

18. Azoulay, *The Civil Contract of Photography*, 105.

prevent her incarceration, because it neither takes the sovereign patriarchal power off the state and its legal institutions nor directly changes the realities of gender-based violence. Still, ever since Çilem Doğan participated in the photographic act, her picture has been acting and yielding the action of others:

> Women's rights activists have rallied behind Doğan, calling for her acquittal and insisting that self-defense is a legitimate right. Every hearing during her trial was accompanied by demonstrations; letters of support flooded in to Doğan while she was in jail. A petition campaign calling for her acquittal has gathered more than 130,000 signatures. The T-shirt Doğan happened to be wearing on the day of her arrest has become a symbol in the struggle for women's rights. According to Doğan's lawyers, the T-shirt . . . will be put on display at the Women's Library in Adana.[19]

The T-shirt, and the photograph in which Çilem Doğan is wearing it, have become powerful symbols for Turkish feminist movements. This represents an important example of empowering modes of visually representing women who experience and resist gender violence. To deconstruct normative images of women's social roles by creating nonvictimized representations of survivors of gender violence forms a powerful part of transforming insurgent looks into action.

Photography can play an important role in this process, not because of the false assumption that photographs can be in themselves insurgent, but because the event of photography is not dictated by the ruling power, even if the ruling power attempts to control it. The woman in the picture I used to generate a political understanding of the event of photography is sentenced for murder but (visually) refuses to recognize this verdict's legitimacy. Paraphrasing Azoulay, against the potential use of such a photo to criminalize Çilem Doğan, the insurgent look should keep it open as a photographic event that might criminalize the current laws as illegitimate state tools regarding the situation of women who resist gender-based violence.[20]

---

19. Hurtas, "Why Turkish Women are Rallying Behind this Killer."
20. Ariella Azoulay, "What is photography," *Philosophy of Photography*, Vol. 1, No 1, 2010. Available at http://cargocollective.com/AriellaAzoulay/What-is-photography.

ART

WE ARE NOT IN THE LEAST AFRAID OF RUINS
Amanda Priebe

IT HAS TO BURN
BEFORE IT CAN GROW

An Interview with Amanda Priebe by Brooke Lober

Brooke Lober: *I'm excited to hear more about your art, which inspired the guiding theme for this issue. Can we start by talking about your recent work, "We Are Not in the Least Afraid of Ruins"?*

Amanda Priebe: That was a piece I did at a residency in Estonia. I was in a really tiny village and former Soviet collective farm next to the Russian border. It actually reminded me a lot of Alberta somehow, where I'm from: the landscape was very similar and the cold, the isolation. I took a lot of inspiration from the land there. I found these old tractor windows in the barns that they had on the property and I started painting on them, this smoke that's for me sort of ever present with the forest fires in Alberta, with the tear gas at the demonstrations I've been to. It's always this ambivalent symbol of transformation for me somehow. So I just started painting the smoke onto these old tractor windows using oil paint. On some of the windows I drew images from my grandparents' farm, and on others I wrote this famous quote from [the Spanish anarchist] Durruti.[1] The whole old collective farm which used to be a flaxseed production center was actually in various degrees

---

1. "It is we [the workers] who built these palaces and cities, here in Spain and in America and everywhere. We, the workers. We can build others to take their place. And better ones! We are not in the least afraid of ruins. We are going to inherit the earth. There is not the slightest doubt about that. The bourgeoisie might blast and ruin its own world before it leaves the stage of history. We carry a new world here, in our hearts. . . .That world is growing in this minute." Van Pessen, Pierre. "Buenaventura Durruti Interview - Pierre Van Paasen." Libcom.org. August 5, 2016. Accessed March 17, 2020. https://libcom.org/history/buenaventura-durruti-interview-pierre-van-paasen.

of ruin, so I took these big glass panels and put them around in the buildings and photographed them. This was more personal for me, being in a moment where I also needed to believe in that transformation myself, that one day we really will inherit the earth and be prepared to build. It's about destruction, but more importantly, about what comes after.

BL: *Maybe that's a good place to talk about the pinecone from "Proposal for a World on Fire."*

AP: Yeah, the pinecone is definitely from that same place. I've been drawing these smoke clouds for years. In northern Alberta, forest fires are a natural part of the ecosystem, but because of climate change they've become more intense and more frequent. My grandparents' farm was always a really important place for me growing up, and I watched as it was almost destroyed by a forest fire in 2008. The surrounding forests burned, but the house itself was saved, although it has since been sold and entirely destroyed so the province can widen the main highway to the Athabasca tar sands projects.

The pinecone came after when I was thinking more about symbols for transformation. I think artists need to be good storytellers and to give people not only resources for transformation, but also symbols, ciphers, and new narratives; ways of looking at the world differently than what we currently have access to, which are very limited stories. I go back to nature for that a lot. The lodgepole pine needs really extreme conditions to germinate, and it has to burn before it can grow. For me this is kind of a personal symbol. I also use the fireweed (*Chamaenerion angustifolium*) in a similar way. It's the first plant to germinate at a burn site and prepares the ground for other species to take hold. When they're inevitably crowded out by the new species, the seeds stay dormant in the soil waiting for the next fire or disturbance to come to life.

We're now in a situation where the world is quite literally on fire, and if we're going to respond effectively to the lifeboat ethics and quickly spreading eco-fascism of the right, we need to think about what kind of narratives and stories counter that. It isn't facts that change minds; it's the stories we tell ourselves. So what stories do we need to be able to grow, even when the world is on fire?

BL: *You talk about art as a tool for transformation. How did you come to that?*

AP: I think my use of art as a tool began as an extremely personal thing. I don't come from an artistic family, nobody else spoke this language, and so it was something I could sort of escape to and use for play, or to work through issues and cope with life at my own pace. That really saved me over and over again.

In 2013 I was teaching English in Istanbul when Gezi Park happened. This really sharply brought into focus a lot of feelings I had been struggling with that nothing that I was making was connecting in the way I wanted it to. It was so obvious to me when I went to these demonstrations, seeing the way that art was used as so embodied, powerful, and genuine. Art was really part of the social fabric; it was really part of the movements.

Performance artist Erdem Gündüz started this *duran adam* movement, which means "standing man." People would spontaneously do these massive performance art pieces, standing motionless and silent in the squares, against police violence. There was this incredibly surreal moment at Beşiktaş stadium I witnessed where leftist football club Çarşı hijacked a construction excavator and rode it into battle against the police water cannon trucks, called TOMAs or *Toplu msal Olaylara Müdahale Araci* [Intervention Vehicle to Social Events]. After that, the symbol of the comically dubbed "POMA" excavator, or *Polis Olaylarina Müdahale Aracı* [Intervention Vehicle to Police Events] vs. TOMA was incorporated in protest posters and installations in the squares. In addition,he image of the penguin popped up everywhere too as a resistance symbol because the day the protests began, rather than covering the demonstrations, state-controlled media continued their broadcast of a documentary on penguins.

Afterwards, I went to the 2013 Istanbul Biennale, which tried to speak to the Gezi Park experience in different ways, but I found the event to be cold, dead, and emotionless. It was like visiting a museum exhibit of artifacts—everything was removed from the context that gave it life. So, for me, this was really a moment of "I'm just rejecting the gallery scene. I'm rejecting all of this." [Art] needs to have real impact on people's lives somehow. Art needs to be part of a lived experience.

Right now the projects I'm hoping to work on in the future are somewhat parallel to these ideas, using the art itself, or the place art occupies in capitalist society as a tool for social transformation. Another [Abolition] collective member, Max Haiven's book *Art After Money, Money After Art*,[2] has really inspired me to think much more broadly about that.

BL: *So Max is talking about more of a process-oriented way of understanding the relationship between art and social movements?*

AP: His work in this book brings together a lot of different examples of artists who use art in a socially transformative way, but go beyond the liberal imaginary of, as he says, art that "stakes its success on a moment of democratic revelation." He rejects this idea that what a political artist does is make these enlightening poetic experiences or objects for the gallery, and people go to see them and "upon seeing the art, will have the scales fall from their eyes, become radicalized and participate in some vehicle of democratic change."[3] I always felt that this doesn't work in the gallery context, which is why I've looked to movements, and recently art therapy, for other ways to use art. People don't go to galleries and look at art, have a moment of transcendence and then get involved in politics, do they? It's never worked for me like that.

Instead, there is a cynical view of the social construct that art exists within, and attempt to use that special place art occupies against this system. As Haiven writes, "there is little hope here in the liberatory or enlightening potential of art itself, but rather a post-cynical, radical utilitarian approach to art as a platform for other projects of mass creativity and the militant imagination."[4] For example, in Núria Güell and Levi Orta's *Degenerated Political Art Ethical Protocol*,[5] they actually set up a company in a tax haven and then donated it to radical cooperatives and anticapitalist groups so that they could get around state tax controls and things

2. Max Haiven, *Art After Money, Money After Art: Creative Strategies Against Financialization* (London: Pluto Press, 2018).

3. Haiven, *Art After Money, Money After Art*, 106.

4. Haiven, *Art After Money, Money After Art*, 107.

5. "Archive / Degenerated Political Art. Ethical Protocol," Arte Útil, https://www.arte-util.org/projects/degenerated-political-art-ethical-protocol/.

of that nature. What is the space that art occupies in capitalist society, and how can we use that space to further open the crack of
what we imagine to be possible and really give material support
to individuals and projects, not just "point to" issues or "expose
injustice" in a more abstract way?

BL: *Using the realities of the art world and the place of art in society to
do something radically subversive.*

AP: Exactly. Several years ago Peter von Tiesenhausen, who is a
landscape artist from my province, copyrighted his entire farm
as an artwork to stop a pipeline expansion through his property.[6] The oil company negotiators were always showing up trying
to talk to him, and he finally decided, "I'll just copyright the entire farm as an artwork and charge the oil companies who come
through $500/hour to speak with me." That both stopped the oil
companies from speaking with him and protected the land from
development. This was several years ago, and it really impacted
my thinking, so when I read Max's book and learned about other artists using similar techniques, I found the idea really powerful. There are so many radical implications of using the strange,
ambiguous space art occupies under capitalism in this way.
At the same time, I think it's important to contrast this case with
the struggle of the Beaver Lake Cree who are fighting the government of Canada and Alberta to uphold their treaty rights in
the same region, recognizing the cumulative effects of industrial
development on their territories. While legally defining land as
privileged 'art' might protect it from resource extraction projects,
Indigenous people—whose land Von Tiesenhausen's farm is actually on—are not granted the same rights.

In "Accomplices not Allies: Abolishing the Ally Industrial
Complex," the Indigenous Action media collective writes:

You wouldn't find an accomplice resigning their agency, or capabilities as an act of 'support.' They would find creative ways to weaponize

6. Stephen Keefe, "This Canadian Artist Halted Pipeline Development by Copyrighting
His Land as a Work of Art," *Vice*, November 6, 2014, https://www.vice.com/en_us/
article/5gk4jz/this-canadian-artist-halted-pipeline-development-by-copyrighting-his-
land-as-a-work-of-art-983.

their privilege (or more clearly, their rewards of being part of an oppressor class) as an expression of social war. Otherwise we end up with a bunch of anti-civ/primitivist appropriators or anarcho-hipsters, when saboteurs would be preferred. [7]

It is possible and necessary for artists, especially white artists, to use their privilege–and their art–as a weapon, in radically subversive ways, but we have to take the lead from and be accountable to the folks who are most directly impacted.

Recently I've been doing a lot more reading by Indigenous scholars: Leanne Betasamosake Simpson, Vine Deloria Jr., Glen Coulthard, Susan B Hill, Robin Wall Kimmerer, and it's pushing me to think a lot more about what it means for artists and an art practice to be in relation and how decolonization might be practiced by settler artists. I think that's an important piece of the needed transformation for me.

BL: *That action of using art as a weapon—it can happen through the acts of subversion you've been talking about, but can it also happen through public art? This feels like talking about a kind of mirror image of the art-world subversion. Like the embodied performance in Gezi Park. That's something that is apparently completely outside of the art market. It's participatory. It's doing something totally different. It's not subverting the art world, it is art.*

AP: I felt that for sure. However, I don't know that the people that were in those protests necessarily thought of it like that. Certainly some did but I think there was a huge variety of experience there. For me, I was going and taking tons of photos every day and it was always: "that's an installation, and that's an installation, and that's a performance piece, with stakes, with real implications." You're not just going to think and have an enlightening or moving experience; there were real, dangerous risks and real potential rewards. Movements are powerful art in a way that I never experienced with the constructed experiences of the art world.

It wasn't the fact that people made political art about the

---

7. "Accomplices Not Allies: Abolishing the Ally Industrial Complex," *Indigenous Action*, May 4, 2014, http://www.indigenousaction.org/accomplices-not-allies-abolishing-the-ally-industrial-complex/.

movement and their experiences in it that was so powerful; it was that they did it in the square, on the square, on the walls, together. They totally upended what public space meant, how it was normally used, and as a result also upended what it meant to be a person living in that space. A lot of artists do this kind of performance art in the public space outside of social movements, but the context is not the same, and I always feel it's missing that weight. I made a lot of prints after Gezi, using the photos I took, and was really unsatisfied with the results. They are just shadows of an experience, not transformational at all, except in whatever I derived from making them. I felt like what I was doing was an imitation of the movement. They go on the wall as objects of contemplation and they don't have that essence of what made the movement such a powerful experience.

BL: *Maybe art about the protest lacks the aura, the vibration, of art as protest. You've been talking about artistic practice as prefiguration. Can you talk about what you mean by that?*

AP: In 2012, Creative Time put out a book based on one of their exhibitions called *Living as Form.*[8] The book combines work by more typical performance artists working on political themes with interventions like the work done by Women on Waves who have a ship they sail around the world, providing abortion services to people where the procedure is illegal. If, as I believe, politics is located not primarily at the ballot box but in everyday life, then I tend to see all of my actions as composing the form of my work.

I think what artists do in general is we simultaneously see the world how it exists and how it *could* exist. That's just kind of the mindset you always have to occupy when you're making art. So, as a default, you're cultivating these resources for transformation. But under capitalism we've been really conditioned and directed into this ethic of productivity. As we all have to exist under capitalism, most artists are forced to use that way of looking at the world to make things or make experiences that we individually profit from, but this is of course capitalist recuperation. We don't have to think of art making like that. We can use those resources

---

8. Nato Thompson (ed.), *Living as Form* (Cambridge, MA: MIT Press, 2012).

for transformation as collective knowledge and employ them in a collective way.

I think in general, that's what movements do when we make art together, when we experience things together; it prefigures social relationships outside of this capitalist logic. There were great examples of this at Standing Rock, for example, of artists like Christi Belcourt and Isaac Murdoch mobilizing and shaping powerful stories, working at camp and creating this amazing visual culture, shifting the narrative from *protestors* to *protectors*.

There's a quote from Murray Bookchin that I really like, where he argues that social revolutions occur "not merely because the masses find the existing society intolerable (as Trotsky argued) but also because of the tension between the actual and the possible, between what is and what could be."[9] I think that's where art can come in to really tip the scales and push that crack open, increase the tension. I've become really frustrated with dystopia and this kind of nihilistic, dark, ironic aesthetic. We don't need more work that catalogues our despair, we all know how intolerable the situation is—what we need is more imagining, more prefiguring better futures, more weight on the "what could be."

BL: *You've made propaganda art, like the work you have available on Justseeds, but it doesn't feel didactic—like, it kind of departs from a certain kind of Shepard Fairey didacticism that is so common for political art.*

AP: I also really like doing guillotines and stuff! The Left has a pretty recognizable art aesthetic: bold, graphic, lots of black and red. For my political graphics I am really taking inspiration from historical leftist political art: the Parisian May '68 posters, Emory Douglas' bold graphics, and the extremely rich tradition of Mexican printmaking. I'm always thinking about symbols and thinking about how the symbols that we use actually shape our ideas of what's possible and our ideas of who is included in those symbols.

Like, if I'm just going to be making graphics of guillotines and Molotov cocktails, that's fun, I like it, but who is that actually talking to? I think in a weird way it's kind of the same problem

---

9. Murray Bookchin, *The Murray Bookchin Reader* (Montreal: Black Rose Books, 1999), 132.

as these very conceptual gallery artists. Who is that actually talking to? You make some very abstract cerebral thing that goes in a
white cube, and who is your audience?

BL: *Do you think that that kind of favoring of a certain kind of really
simplistic version of street rebellion as the aesthetic of leftist protest is
also gendered?*

AP: Definitely, yes. In 2018 I was lucky to be invited to show some
work at the Chouftouhonna Feminist Art Festival in Tunis, and
the piece I made addressed exactly that. I made an installation
of hundreds of hand-printed linocut Saskatoon berries. This
was from a memory and experience I had of always picking wild
Saskatoon berries with my mother and my grandmother. It's a
powerful thing. You're collecting food, you're then freezing it for
the winter and it was the food my mom would bake with when I
was sick. I started this project going through a really hard personal
crisis and having this overwhelming craving for saskatoons to try
and heal from that, but of course they don't grow here in Berlin so
I started to draw them instead.

I actually think the most revolutionary work is going on in
the process of building community through nurturing and caring
and feeding, which is work mostly done by women. So how do
we represent this as actually revolutionary? How do we start to
put that care work in the same category as throwing the Molotov?
Making sure people are fed, cared for, nurtured is what sustains
movements, and I think that ethic actually is the most revolutionary and anticapitalist. Who are the people that are doing this community building every day? It's very often the women. In my own
life, I've really gotten into cooking because it's really much more
powerful to me than a Molotov—making food for people. What
are the symbols and visual metaphors we can use for that kind
of revolutionary work? How could identifying with those symbols
change our perspectives and our priorities?

BL: *I had a very similar experience seeing how the uprising played out
in Oaxaca. In the wake of the uprising, I began to understand the way
that rebellions were happening in Mexico at that time. So much of the
representation of the movement, especially the way it was represented*

in the US, was like, throwing a Molotov onto a bus. Literally, a young man throwing a Molotov at a burning bus was a very popular image. But when you're actually there, it is really collectivities of women—but not just women, women and families—being able to feed masses of people, producing participatory creative projects, and also elders being very present, bringing a certain kind of wisdom and practicality to those sorts of movements—that's what has the potential to sustain. I was reading Silvia Federici at the time and began to understand repro-ductive labor in new ways. That experience also resulted in me doing more cooking!

AP: Yeah! I really went through this evolution growing up. My family is very traditional. My mom was a stay-at-home mom; she did the cooking, the cleaning, all the typical women's work. As a result of this, I totally rejected it for a really long time: "That isn't what I want. I'm a feminist. I don't want any of that shit. I'm not cooking. I'm not learning to cook. Fuck any man who thinks I'm going to be a good cook for him!" That was my knee-jerk reaction for a long time. Several years ago I really started realizing that this is internalized misogyny that devalues this powerful work. So I've really chosen to take that back, to cook for people. I want to cook for people. I go out of my way because it really brings people to-gether and this is really something material that you can provide.

I think with the art I'm also really interested in that kind of nourishment. What is the material thing you can provide to peo-ple? What does it do? Who is it for? This is very important, not just in an abstract, "well, it exposes an injustice, it gives people ideas," kind of way. I want the work to actually physically put resources in our hands that feed us.

BL: *And also putting it into a different realm of value that's not about value on a market, but another kind of nourishment.*

AP: Definitely. Imagination is one of the many major casualties of capitalist realism—so much energy and resources go into keep-ing us from even imagining how things could be different. Artists know how to imagine different worlds so why are we not doing that more socially? I think we're actually failing people a lot in this way. How can we do better?

I did a little graphic for the 2017 *Certain Days: Freedom for Political Prisoners* calendar which uses a quote from Subcomandante Galeano that I really like: "In contrast to traditional stories that begin with 'once upon a time,' Zapatista stories begin with 'there will be a time.'" The Zapatistas call their struggle "the war against oblivion" and understand deeply the role imagination plays in that fight. We need to learn from that. As Jeff Conant writes, "The assault on imagination is the first front of violence in the war against everything."[10] Really taking seriously what we are fighting for— not just against—and what we imagine in its place, is vital.

BL: *I'm curious if you have a way of describing abolition politics in relation to the imagination, or in relation to art making?*

AP: In *Are Prisons Obsolete?*, Angela Davis calls prisons "a key ingredient of our common sense."[11] As Davis writes, common sense for the ancestors of today's liberals included slavery, lynching, and segregation. I think the process of art making itself makes you inevitably hostile to these kinds of incurious platitudes. The art making process is conjuring, holding multiple realities simultaneously, balancing uncertainty and discomfort with action, making the impossible a reality—it's inherently at odds with common sense and naturally on the side of imagination. This could be radical knowledge, if wielded in the right way.

It's also about whose stories get told. In the collective imagination, the criminal evildoer is always "the other," the already marginalized. How can changing whose stories get told through art challenge this kind of classification?

In their work *The Undercommons: Fugitive Planning and Black Study*, Fred Moten and Stefano Harney write the abolitionist project should be seen as "not so much the abolition of prisons but the abolition of a society that could have prisons, that could have slavery, that could have the wage, and therefore not abolition as the elimination of anything but abolition as the founding of a

10. Jeff Conant, *A Poetics of Resistance: The Revolutionary Public Relations of the Zapatista Insurgency* (Oakland: AK Press, 2010), 48.

11. Angela Y. Davis, *Are Prisons Obsolete?* (New York: Seven Stories Press, 2003), 18.

new society."12 I think this reframing is really important, and is also what I'm trying to capture with these symbols like the smoke and the pinecone: I'm not thinking about abolition as destruction, I'm thinking about it as creation.

I think an abolitionist art practice would, like Davis suggests, imagine multiple alternatives to radically challenge and transform not only the existing carceral system, but all aspects of society. I see an abolitionist ethic as challenging current power structures and working towards an art that's integral to our collective social life, available to or practiced by everyone.

BL: *Artists know how to imagine. That's kind of a different imaginary than the imagination needed to create a socialist program, right? Both are crucial, but does art have something different to bring about?*

AP: I actually really want art to be in service in a very material way and a very practical way. On the one hand, yes, you need this space to be impractical and only be in the moment, be free to just experiment. Artists always talk about this as "flow," to just be in the moment, totally lost in the work. It's the most amazing feeling and it is necessary—that feeling does feed you. Occupy Wall Street said "we don't have any leaders, we don't have any program, we don't have any demands—that's the point." At the time, my own political thought process resonated with this kind of artistic flow orientation and I really thought, "Yes! That's awesome!" But now I want the demands, actually. I want the program. I think this has come from being influenced more recently by labor and tenant organizing struggles where campaigns are specific, goal-oriented, and about building power to win.

BL: *Art can contribute to or sustain a more utopian imaginary and more practical projects. Like, I think about the role of art in universities— I'm an adjunct—at this point I think contingent faculty is like 75 percent of university labor, and we're just waiting for the time when that labor overspills to transform the structure itself.*

---

12. Stefano Harney and Fred Moten, *The Undercommons: Fugitive Planning and Black Study* (Wivenhoe/New York/Port Watson: Minor Compositions, 2013), 42.

AP: In *The Undercommons*, Moten and Harney say, "The only possible relationship to the university today is a criminal one."[13] As artists, what should our relationship to powerful institutions like the university or the museum be? I think this is another part of our imagination that has been far too constrained.

I've been doing a lot of reading lately on institutional critique art, and Andrea Fraser, for example. In 2016 Fraser did a work called *Down the River* where she recorded ambient noise in Sing Sing prison and then played these recordings in the Whitney Museum, trying to make this connection between the institution of the prison and the museum. Fraser also did this big research project, *2016 in Museums, Money, and Politics*, which documents the reported political contributions made by trustees of more than 125 art museums representing every state in the 2016 election.[14] She argues that institutions are not just buildings or organizations like museums or universities, but internalized and performed social and economic relationships. So in these critiques, she seems to touch on the structural nature of institutional realities that needs to be challenged, but stops short of presenting an alternative vision other than to take on the project of reforming and rehabilitating it/ourselves ("it's not a question of being against the institution: we are the institution"[15]).

I do appreciate this kind of work, I think documentation is relevant and useful. I just don't understand what audiences are supposed to take from it in a museum context other than to feel bad or to feel guilty. Like somebody goes into the Whitney Museum—well, what kind of people visit the Whitney Museum? And then they hear this audio from Sing Sing and they read her wall text talking about the parallel growth of museums and prisons without really talking too much about the carceral state, but just that the growth of these things are happening at the same time and "we should make connections." Who is that work for? What is the viewer supposed to take away from that? Are they supposed to see that work and then go write their congressman

---

13. Harney and Moten, *The Undercommons*, 28.

14. Andrea Fraser, *2016 in Museums, Money, and Politics* (Cambridge, MA: MIT Press, 2018).

15. Andrea Fraser, "From the Critique of Institutions to an Institution of Critique," *Artforum* 44(1), September 2005: 278–283.

or be overwhelmed and just feel guilty? I'm not sure. I think if what your critique is doing is just leaving people with a sense of sadness or powerlessness, it doesn't go nearly far enough. What should I do with this bad, guilty feeling? I don't think that guilt is a good basis for political action. I want art that claims to be critical to go beyond this.

Compare Fraser's work to the campaigns at the Whitney by Decolonize This Place, for example, or The Illuminator's project *Where in Brooklyn Do Vultures Roost?*[16] on the Brooklyn Museum. Both directly tie gentrification to the actions and politics of these institutions. They bring in active community groups from the neighborhood, explicitly connect institutional decision-making to wider systems of oppression, and make specific demands of the museum. I would say that both Andrea Fraser's work and the work of these groups fall under "institutional critique," but while Fraser's work stops short at liberal calls for institutional reform and inclusion, the other projects prefigure other potential relationships to the institution. The difference is who they imagine their audience to be.

What I appreciate about Moten and Harney's framing is the unapologetic clarity of both the demand and the recognition that who *we* are matters very much.[17] Fraser writes that "every time we speak of the 'institution' as other than 'us' we disavow our role in the creation and perpetuation of its conditions.[18]" But who is the *we* she's addressing? We are not all equally powerful or influential in this conversation. Artists need to be explicit here.

BL: *I actually really liked the Sackler P.A.I.N. campaign that exposed the Sackler family. Nan Goldin organized artists to advocate*

---

16. "Where in Brooklyn Do Vultures Roost?," *The Illuminator*, March 6, 2016, http://theilluminator.org/vultures/.

17. On the institutional relationship between the university and prisons, for example: "The slogan on the Left, then, 'universities, not jails,' marks a choice that may not be possible. In other words, perhaps more universities promote more jails. Perhaps it is necessary finally to see that the university produces incarceration as the product of its negligence. Perhaps there is another relation between the University and the Prison—beyond simple opposition or family resemblance—that the undercommons reserves as the object and inhabitation of another abolitionism." [Harney and Moten, *The Undercommons*, 41.]

18. Andrea Fraser, *From the Critique of Institutions to an Institution of Critique.*

for refusal of Sackler family funds at art institutions—because of their profiteering on Oxycontin, with its associated addiction and death. It was amazing, because they made a strong demand, and they shamed and blamed and did it. Which is probably better than putting a bunch of pills on display in a museum.

AP: Exactly. I think something like that, that's the point. Then it's more like a campaign almost, right? Like you have a demand: why am I doing this? It's not just a catalogue of how all the trustees of these boards donated to Trump's campaign. Then here's the catalogue and we put it in the museum and everyone can read it. Maybe I just approach all of this from this very practical position, where I think if you're going to say you're making a critique, I want some kind of counterproposal, some kind of action or way into action about it. Don't just critique, but go further and propose something better, different, or a way forward for people to engage with it, don't just put this overwhelming document in front of them.

BL: *That brings us to the language of the "proposal" and this sense that there's a more interactive process to call people into. Political artists or social movement artists have to work against the assumption that in making a demand, your work is reduced to some kind of predetermined meaning and all there is in the reception of that work is to either accept or refuse the demand. But instead, you're saying that art is part of a process of negotiation towards social change that's more participatory. But it can't just be nothing. It can't just be, put the name in the museum—it really does actually have to make a proposal.*

AP: I think so. I like that a lot: "art is part of the process of negotiation towards social change that's more participatory." People have been working with "institutional critique" as a distinct genre since the 1970s, and I think we're a bit beyond the time when "pointing to" and "exposing" and "problematizing" in these esoteric spaces is enough. I'm frustrated. I want artists to be providing tools, I want us to be reshaping narratives, I want us to be helping people think differently, imagine differently, tell different stories, whatever. But not just point to issues that are bad. We're all already overwhelmed with how fucked up this world is.

BL: *If you put it in that kind of timeline, I think about neoliberalism as a response to the upheavals of the mid-late twentieth century, and of "critique" supplanting revolutionary proclamation. While "problema-tizing" holds potential as its own practice, it also allows for an end to more strident demands for more just outcomes.*

AP: I think this is really the trap and the poverty of liberalism, to be honest. There's a great piece in *Hyperallergic* by Betty Marín, Heather M. O'Brien, and Christina Sanchez Juarez called, "The Artist's Guide to Not Being Complicit With Gentrification."[19] In it, they talk about collectively "acting their way into thinking" through organizing as artists with tenants' movements, as opposed to relying on theory and only "pointing at problems." I think collaborations like this really show a way forward, outside of both the limits of the liberal imagination and capitalist recuperation.

The liberal trap is the belief that critique takes place in a marketplace of ideas, and then the public uses this new knowledge to make an informed decision that inspires them to buy into political action somewhere else: at the ballot box, voting with your dollars, whatever. So from a liberal perspective, the critical artistic gesture, the pointing out or problematizing is really all that's required, because politics is already located somewhere else. If, from a leftist or anarchist perspective, we understand politics as located in everyday social relations, we have to go further—the just outcome has to be built into the practice of the artist and therefore the work itself.

19. Heather M. O'Brien, Christina Sanchez Juarez, and Betty Marin, "An Artist's Guide to Not Being Complicit With Gentrification," *Hyperallergic*, June 19, 2017, https://hyperallergic.com/385176/an-artists-guide-to-not-being-complicit-with-gentrification/.

ABOUT THE CONTRIBUTORS

Jesus Barraza is an interdisciplinary artist and is pursuing an MFA in Social Practice and a Masters in Visual Critical Studies. He holds a BA in Raza Studies from San Francisco State University. He is a co-founder of Dignidad Rebelde a graphic arts collaboration that produces screen prints, political posters and multimedia projects and a member of JustSeeds Artists Cooperative a decentralized group of political artists based in Canada, the United States and Mexico.

Melanie Cervantes (Xicanx) has never lived far from the California Coast having been born in Harbor City, California and raised in a small city in the South Bay of Los Angeles. Now making her home in the San Francisco Bay Area she creates visual art that is inspired by the people around her and her communities' desire for radical change and social transformation. In 2007 she co-founded Dignidad Rebelde, a graphic arts collaboration that produces screen prints, political posters and multimedia projects that are grounded in Third World and indigenous movements that build people's power to transform the conditions of fragmentation, displacement and loss of culture that result from histories of colonialism, genocide, and exploitation. Dignidad Rebelde's purpose is to translate the stories of struggle and resistance into artwork that can be put back into the hands of the communities who inspire it.

Priti Gulati Cox is an interdisciplinary artist living in Salina, Kansas. Set against a global backdrop of perpetual war, exploitation, environmental catastrophe and our elites' tendency to channel concern and actions via selective sympathy, her continuing project titled "Caste, Capitalism, Climate" attempts to communicate the practice of the caste system in India, an institution that is thriving more than ever today under neoliberal economic fundamentalism and the Hindutva-friendly regime of the country's current government headed by prime minister Narendra Modi. Some of the places she has exhibited and performed include the 2010 US Social Forum Exhibition, Detroit, MI; the 2011 Women's Caucus for Art's Conference on Art and Social Justice, St Louis, MO; Unfinished Portrait: Iraq and Afghanistan, in collaboration with American Friends Service Committee, Kansas City, MO, 2012; Create This Revolution, Gallery 101, Ottawa, Canada, 2013; Exuberant Politics, Legion Arts Center, Cedar Rapids, IA, 2014. Her writings have been published by *AlterNet*, AlJazeera, *Countercurrents*, and *CounterPunch*.

Nick Estes is Kul Wicasa from the Lower Brule Sioux Tribe. He is assistant professor of American studies at the University of New Mexico; cofounder of *The Red Nation*, an organization dedicated to Indigenous liberation; and author of *Our History Is the Future: Standing Rock versus the Dakota Access Pipeline, and the Long Tradition of Indigenous Resistance.*

Stefanie Fock was born in 1982 in Hamburg (Germany). Since 2003 she lives in between Barcelona and Granada (Spain). Her education includes a BA in Sociology (focus on critical investigation of the histories of racism), practical and theoretical studies in different fields of photography, and the Master's degree in GEMMA-Women and Gender Studies. Currently she is active as an independent researcher, photographer, and visual educator. Since 2012 she is the head of the creative and educational project Gender as Collage, and in 2015 she co-founded Nómadas Visuales, a collective dedicated to the creation of Spaces of Collaborative Learning in Photography and Visual Investigation.

David Gilbert has been an activist since the early 1960s and a New York State political prisoner since 1981. David would love to hear your feedback. Feel free to write to him at:

David Gilbert 83–A–6158
Wende Correctional Facility
3040 Wende Road
Alden, New York 14004–1187

Joy James is a member of the Abolition collective and F.C. Oakley 3rd Century Professor at Williams College.

Katherine Freeman is a labor and community organizer. She is also a PhD Candidate in Gender and Women's Studies at the University of Arizona.

Kelly Sharron is a lecturer in the department of women's, gender, and sexuality studies at California State University, Long Beach. Sharron completed her PhD in gender and women's studies at the University of Arizona in 2019. Her current project, "The Caring State: The Politics of Contradiction in Ferguson, Missouri," considers the multiple state tactics at play in police brutality including the extension of a feminist ethic of care in producing violent effects.

Abraham Weil is an Assistant Professor of women's, gender, and sexuality studies at California State University, Long Beach.

MIKE KING is an Assistant Professor in the Criminal Justice department at Bridgewater State University. He received his Ph.D. in Sociology from the University of California – Santa Cruz in 2013. His research generally focuses on social movements, policing and race. His writing has recently been featured in the journals *Race & Class* and *Critical Criminology*, and he is also a regular contributor to the online magazine *Counterpunch*. He is currently working on a book which examines race, political affect and the rise of far-Right political movements.

BROOKE LOBER is a feminist teacher and scholar, currently researching and writing about late 20th century histories of Jewish anti-Zionism and anti-imperialist feminist activism in the Bay Area of California. She is a member of the Abolition Collective.

ROBERT NICHOLS is an Associate Professor of political theory in the Department of Political Science at the University of Minnesota–Twin Cities. He is the author of *Theft Is Property! Dispossession and Critical Theory*.

AMANDA PRIEBE is an artist and graduate student in Spatial Strategies at Weißensee Kunsthochschule Berlin. She is a collective member of Abolition: A Journal of Insurgent Politics and her work can be found in radical journals, books, magazines and, hopefully, on the streets near you. www.amandapriebe.com

PAUL RAEKSTAD works on the political theory of human emancipation. Their work focuses on concepts of freedom and democracy, future economic institutions, and how to achieve them - with a particular focus on prefigurative politics and proposals for a Green New Deal. Their recent co-written book titled *Prefigurative Politics: Building Tomorrow Today* is published by Polity.

SHANA L. REDMOND is the author of *Anthem: Social Movements and the Sound of Solidarity in the African Diaspora* (NYU Press, 2014) and associate professor of Musicology and African American Studies at UCLA. She is currently writing a book about Paul Robeson's afterlife.

DYLAN RODRÍGUEZ is a Professor in the Department of Media & Cultural Studies at the University of California, Riverside. He is the author of two books: *Forced Passages: Imprisoned Radical Intellectuals and the U.S. Prison Regime* (2006) and *Suspended Apocalypse: White Supremacy, Genocide, and the Filipino Condition* (2009). He is a founding member of Critical Resistance: Beyond the Prison Industrial Complex and the Critical Ethnic Studies Association, and has worked in or alongside various social movements and activist collectives.

STEVEN SALAITA is the author of eight books, most recently *Inter/Nationalism: Decolonizing Native America and Palestine*. He writes at stevesalaita.com

J SEBASTIAN is a graduate student in Ethnic Studies at the University of California, Riverside and holds a Juris Doctor from the City University of New York School of Law. As a white genderqueer scholar and activist, they seek to critically engage constructions of whiteness, power, and the law. J can be reached at jsebaoo1@ucr.edu.

ROBYN C. SPENCER is a historian who specializes in the history of the Black freedom movement. She has written widely about the Black Power movement and is the author of *The Revolution has Come: Black Power, Gender and the Black Panther Party in Oakland*.

MICHELLE VELASQUEZ-POTTS is an educator and writer living between Oakland, CA and Austin, TX. Presently, she is an Embrey Postdoctoral Fellow at UT Austin where she teaches in the Center for Women's and Gender Studies. Her work focuses on the relationship between medicine and punishment, and in particular the rise of force-feeding post-9/11. She has published essays in *Women and Performance, Public Culture, Captive Genders: Trans Embodiment and the Prison Industrial Complex* (AK Press 2011), and forthcoming in *Art Journal Open*.

KIM WILSON holds a Ph.D. in Urban Affairs and Public Policy from the University of Delaware. Her research and activism focus on the impact of mass incarceration on communities. You can follow her on twitter @phillyprofo3.

STEVIE WILSON is a Black queer abolitionist activist, writer, and organizer from Philly imprisoned at SCI-Smithfield. @agitateorganize on Twitter, and member of @studyabolition - abolitioniststudy.group. They can receive mail at:

Stephen Wilson LB8480
268 Bricker Road
Bellefonte, PA 16823

INDEX

A

Abolition Collective, 3, 5–6
Abu-Jamal, Mumia, 10–17, 19–22, 120, 120n9
Academia, 8–9, 202–207, 210–211
Africa, John, 22
Africa, Pam, 17, 22
Africa, Ramona, 17
Agamben, Giorgio, 56, 56n37
Alexander, Michelle, 15
Algonquin, 184, 186–190, 192–194
Anarchism, 64, 89, 100–101
Angus, Charlie, 189
Animas River 49, 53
Arvin, Maile, 177
Associated Press, 29
Azzellini, Dario, 92, 92n2, 112
Azoulay, Ariella, 231–236

B

Bakunin, Mikhail, 6, 93n5, 100–101
Baldwin, James, 152, 153n42
Begaye, Russell, 52–53
Black Elk, Nicholas, 182
Black Lives Matter, 15, 15n19, 17–18, 88, 93n4, 134
Black Panther Party, 2, 10, 16, 18, 120, 155n44, 207
Black Power, 14, 217
Biopolitics, 46n12, 55–56
Bookchin, Murray, 105n33, 106, 245, 245n9
Bourgeoisie, 77, 82, 84, 238n1
Bray, Mark, 103n31, 112
Brown, Mike, 134
Brown, Wendy, 148, 152
Bukhari, Safiya, 16–18
Butler, Judith, 152, 152n41

C

Cabral, Amilcar, 64, 64n1
Campaign to Bring Mumia Home (CBMH), 10, 16
Canada, 88, 191, 194–195, 242
capitalism ,1–2, 43, 46, 48, 48n14, 56, 65, 67–74, 82–89, 107, 110, 139, 163, 172, 177–181, 215, 242, 244; racial capitalism, 3, 5, 13, 178
Central Park 5, 120, 120n8

Césaire, Aimé, 46, 46n10, 46n11, 48
Civil Rights Movement, 66, 132, 135, 139
Clemente, Rosa, 152, 152n39
Clinton, Hillary, 18, 116, 118, 120–121, 125
colonialism,2, 6, 8, 54, 80, 161, 162n10, 163–164, 168–171, 178–181; neocolonialism, 18, 76, 161, 180
Coulthard, Glen Sean, 44, 44n7, 159n1, 243
CrimethInc, 101n29, 111
Critical Resistance, 15, 15n12, 229n54

D

Danner, Deborah, 115, 115n2, 117
Davis, Angela, 4–5, 4n4, 14, 14n10, 15, 71, 120, 215, 248
Dean, Jodi, 111, 111n44, 113
Declaration on the Rights of Indigenous Peoples (UN DRIP), 159
decolonization, 5, 76, 200, 207–208, 211, 243
democracy, 4–5, 9, 55n35, 59–62, 66, 78, 105–107, 116–122, 156
Diaz, Junot, 18
Diderot, Denis, 106
Diné (Navajo), 49, 51, 53
Driskill, Qwo-Li, 170, 170n46
Du Bois, W.E.B., 8
DuVernay, Ava, 120

E

Electoralism, 2, 101, 116–119, 121–122, 124–125, 133
Emergency Management Assistance Compact (EMAC), 191
Emergency Management Assistance Program (EMAP), 191
Engels, Friedrich, 66, 71, 88, 100, 103
EPA Spill, 2015, 47, 49–54
Estes, Nick, 183, 196, 196n2, 199n2
European Union (EU), 108

F

Fanon, Frantz, 5, 9, 18, 43, 45n8, 47, 47n13
Faulkner, Daniel, 12
Federici, Silvia, 71, 142n21, 172n50, 247
Ferguson, Missouri, 15, 134
Fernandez, Johanna, 10, 12n3, 17
Fisk University, 8
Floyd, George, 2, 43,

Foster, John Bellamy, 69, 83, 83n8
Foucault, Michel, 43, 43n4, 46n12,
Four Corners Region, 47, 49–54,
Free Mumia Coalition, 16

G

Gilens, Martin, 98, 98n19, 99n20
Gilmore, Ruth Wilson, 1n1, 15, 146n33
Global Justice Movement, 107
Global North, 72, 83
Global South, 65, 71–72, 75–78, 83, 88–89
Gold King Mine, 49, 52
Goldwater, Barry, 123
Graeber, David, 97n13, 98, 98n18, 100,
    100n27, 101, 105, 105n33, 112
Grantham, Nancy, 52
Gray, Freddie, 117, 191
Guattari, Félix, 62, 62n48
Guevara, Che, 78

H

Harney, Stefano, 5, 248, 250–251
heteropatriarchy, 6, 45–46, 48, 56, 159–162,
    167, 170–177, 179–182
Hopitu (Hopi), 49, 51, 53
hunger strikes, 15, 15n17, 212–229

I

imperialism, 13, 64, 69–70, 72, 74–76,
    77–81, 87, 199
INCITE!, 15, 15n14, 229n54
Ioanide, Paula, 13n1, 144–146
International Monetary Fund (IMF), 108
Israel, 199–200, 202–204, 208, 210

J

James, Selma, 71
James T. Vaughn Correctional Center
    (JTVCC), 29, 33, 35
Jericho Movement, 15, 15n13
Jim Crow, 7, 136, 138
Johnson, Walter, 71
Jones, Van, 120
Jonna, R. Jamil, 83, 83n8

K

Kaba, Mariame, 4, 4n5
Krasner, Larry, 21

L

Lenin, Vladimir, 64, 74, 79
liberalism, 142–143, 253
Lugones, Maria, 170
Luxemburg, Rosa, 74

M

Malcolm X Grassroots Organization, 15, 15n11
Mandela, Nelson, 14
Mangrove Association, 88
Manuel, Arthur, 195
mass incarceration, 10, 13, 16, 18, 31–32,
    119–121, 131
Martin, Trayvon, 15
Martínez Salazar, Elga, 48, 48n15, 48n16, 50
Marx, Karl, 64, 66–71, 73–74, 82–84,
    88–89, 96, 99–101, 102n30, 106, 112
Marxism, 64–68, 88–89, 100
Marxist-Leninist parties, 64, 77, 88
Massumi, Brian, 101
Mbembe, Achille, 55–58
Minneapolis Police Department, 2
Morgenson, Scott, 169–170
Morrill, Angie, 177
Moten, Fred, 5, 248–251
MOVE, 13, 13n5
Movement for Black Lives (M4BL), 15, 16n22
Movement of the Squares, 92, 93n4, 112

N

Ndeh (Apache), 49
necropolitics, 55–58
neoliberalism, 24, 55n35, 58n41, 59, 132,
    139, 141, 143, 253
New Democracy Movement, 92
New Left, 13–14
New Right, 135
Nichols, Nichelle, 18
Neihardt, John G., 183
Nixon, Richard, 119n7, 141

O

Obama, Barack, 117–118, 125, 131, 133, 159
Obergefell v. Hodges, 159, 160n3
Oikonomaki, Leonidas, 93, 93n3, 93n4
Olson, Joel, 9, 97, 143, 151
Omi, Michael, 132, 141,
Ortiz, Simon, 50, 53
Oyewùmi, Oyéronké, 160n6, 170

P

Page, Benjamin, 98, 98n19
Palestine, 77, 199, 200–202, 204, 207–209,
Pasternak, Shiri, 186–189, 192–193
Pennsylvania Department of Corrections, 24
Philadelphia, 12–13, 17
Podesta, John, 120
Poucachiche, Marylynn, 193
Priebe, Amanda, 3, 237
prison-industrial complex (PIC), 4, 14, 19, 24–25, 42, 59, 221n28, 229
Prison Litigation Reform Act, 1996, 19
Prison Policy Initiative, 15, 15n16

R

Rancière, Jacques, 61
Reagan, Ronald, 139–141
Revictimization Relief Act, 16
Rishi Valley, India, 88
Rojava Revolution, 88
Roos, Jerome, 93, 93n3, 93n4

S

San Juan River, 49, 51–52
Sanders, Bernie, 118, 120
Say Her Name, 15
SCI Mahanoy, 11–12, 15
Schuylkill County, 12
settler colonialism, 1–2, 160–161, 169, 177–178, 180, 190, 192, 196
sexuality, 8, 46, 55, 57–58, 68, 160, 169–171, 173, 175–176, 215
Shakur, Afeni, 18
Shakur, Assata, 120, 124n1
Shelby County v. Holder, 118
Simmons, Paul Z., 112
Simpson, Audra, 209
Sirvent, Roberto, 6
Sitrin, Marina, 92, 92n3, 110, 112
slavery, 5, 7–8, 57, 69, 71–73, 76, 97, 116, 119–122, 136, 163, 248–249
Snowden, Edward, 120
socialism, 67, 77–79, 82, 100, 106
sovereignty, 56, 58, 87–88, 110, 187, 194, 196, 209, 216
Spade, Dean, 175
Spinoza, Baruch, 96, 100n26, 106, 112
Standing Rock, 191, 196, 208, 245
Students for a Democratic Society (SDS), 68
Supreme Court, 44, 159, 185
surveillance, 13, 16, 32, 108, 218–219

T

Third World, 65–66
Tourmaline, 178–179
Trade in Services Agreement (TiSA), 108
Transatlantic Trade and Investment Partnership (TTIP), 108
transnational corporations (TNCs), 72
transphobia, 48n14, 65, 69, 86
Trump, Donald, 12, 18, 29, 55, 58–59, 116, 118–121, 125, 131–133, 141, 148, 252
Truth, Sojourner, 7
Tubman, Harriet, 7
Tuck, Eve, 177
Tung, Mao Tse, 64, 78
Tupac, 18
Turner, Nat, 7
Tutu, Desmond, 14

U

Unist'ot'en Indigenous encampment, 88
Ute, 51

V

Vaid-Menon, Alok, 174
Vesey, Denmark, 7
Via Campesina, 88
Vietnam, 66, 77–80,
de Vitoria, Francisco, 159–169, 171–172

W

Waters, Maxine, 18
white supremacy, 1–2, 8, 45, 48, 48n14, 56, 59, 69–70, 86, 116, 127, 131, 133–139, 142, 144–146, 151, 153–156, 160, 171, 177, 179–181; aggrieved whiteness, 131–135, 139, 143, 147–153
Williams, Ash, 18
Williams, Eric, 71
Williams Jr., Robert, 162
Winant, Howie, 132, 141
Wolfe, Patrick, 161
Wollstonecraft, Mary, 106

Y

Young, Kalaniopua, 176

Z

Zapatistas, 3, 248
Zionism, 199–203, 208–210
Zuni, 49

ABOUT COMMON NOTIONS

Common Notions is a publishing house and programming platform that advances new formulations of liberation and living autonomy. Our books provide timely reflections, clear critiques, and inspiring strategies that amplify movements for social justice.

By any media necessary, we seek to nourish the imagination and generalize common notions about the creation of other worlds beyond state and capital. Our publications trace a constellation of critical and visionary meditations on the organization of freedom. Inspired by various traditions of autonomism and liberation—in the United States and internationally, historically and emerging from contemporary movements—our publications provide resources for a collective reading of struggles past, present, and to come.

Common Notions regularly collaborates with editorial houses, political collectives, militant authors, and visionary designers around the world. Our political and aesthetic interventions are dreamt and realized in collaboration with Antumbra Designs.

commonnotions.org | info@commonnotions.org

BECOME A SUSTAINER

These are decisive times, ripe with challenges and possibility, heartache and beautiful inspiration. More than ever, we are in need of timely reflections, clear critiques, and inspiring strategies that can help movements for social justice grow and transform society. Help us amplify those necessary words, deeds, and dreams that our liberation movements and our worlds so need.

Movements are sustained by people like you, whose fugitive words, deeds, and dreams bend against the world of domination and exploitation.

For collective imagination, dedicated practices of love and study, and organized acts of freedom.

By any media necessary.
With your love and support.

Monthly sustainers start at $10 and $25.

At $10 monthly, we will mail you a copy of every new book hot off the press in heartfelt appreciation of your love and support.

At $25, we will mail you a copy of every new book hot off the press alongside special edition posters and 50% discounts on previous publications at our web store.

Join us at commonnotions.org/sustain.

MORE FROM COMMON NOTIONS

Abolishing Carceral Society
Abolition Collective

978-1-942173-08-3
$20.00
256 pages
20 Illustrations

Beyond border walls and prison cells—carceral society is every-where. *Abolishing Carceral Society* presents the bold and ruthlessly critical voices of today's revolutionary abolitionist movements.

This collection of essays, poems, artworks, and interventions are brought together to create an inciteful articulation & collaboration across communities, movements, and experiences embattled in liberatory struggle. In a time of mass incarceration, immigration detention and deportation, rising forms of racialized, gendered, and sexualized violence, and deep ecological and economic crises, abolitionists everywhere seek to understand and dismantle interlocking institutions of domination and create radical transformations.